Unafraid

Unafraid

365 DAYS WITHOUT FEAR

Gracie Malone

FaithWords

NEW YORK BOSTON NASHVILLE

Unless otherwise noted, all Scripture quotations are taken from the *New American Standard Bible*. Copyright © 1960, 1962, 1963, 1968, 1971, 1972, 1973, 1975, 1977, 1995 by The Lockman Foundation. Used by permission. (www.lockman.org)

Scripture quotations marked AMP are taken from *The Amplified Bible*. Copyright © 1954, 1958, 1962, 1964, 1965, 1987 by The Lockman Foundation. Used by permission. (www.lockman.org)

Scripture quotations marked ASV are taken from the American Standard Version of the Bible.

Scripture quotations marked ESV are from the ESV® Bible (*The Holy Bible*, English Standard Version®), copyright © 2001 by Crossway, a publishing ministry of Good News Publishers. Used by permission. All rights reserved.

Scripture quotations marked AV and KJV 1900 are taken from the King James Version of the Holy Bible.

Scripture quotations marked MSG are taken from *The Message*. Copyright © by Eugene H. Peterson 1993, 1994, 1995, 1996, 2000, 2001, 2002. Used by permission of NavPress Publishing Group.

Scripture quotations marked NIV and NIV84 are taken from the *Holy Bible*, New International Version. Copyright © 1973, 1978, 1984, 2011 by Biblica, Inc. Used by permission of Zondervan. All rights reserved worldwide. (www.zondervan.com)

Scripture quotations marked NKJV are taken from the *New King James Version*®. Copyright © 1982 by Thomas Nelson. Used by permission. All rights reserved.

Scripture quotations marked NLT are taken from the *Holy Bible*, New Living Translation. Copyright © 1996, 2004, 2007 by Tyndale House Foundation. Used by permission of Tyndale House Publishers, Inc., Carol Stream, Illinois 60188. All rights reserved.

Scripture quotations marked YLT are taken from the *Holy Bible*, Young's Literal Translation.

Scripture quotations marked PHILLIPS are taken from *The New Testament in Modern English*, 1962 edition, published by HarperCollins.

FaithWords
Hachette Book Group
1290 Avenue of the Americas, New York, NY 10104
www.faithwords.com

Printed in the United States of America

RRD-C

First Edition: October 2015

10 9 8 7 6 5 4 3 2 1

FaithWords is a division of Hachette Book Group, Inc.

The FaithWords name and logo are trademarks of Hachette Book Group, Inc.

The publisher is not responsible for websites (or their content) that are not owned by the publisher.

Library of Congress Cataloging-in-Publication Data

Malone, Gracie.
    Unafraid : 365 days without fear / Gracie Malone.—first [edition].
        pages cm
    Includes bibliographical references.
    ISBN 978-1-4555-8685-1 (hardcover)—ISBN 978-1-4555-8684-4 (ebook)   1. Fear—
Biblical teaching.   2. Fear—Religious aspects—Christianity—Meditations.   3. Devotional
calendars.   I. Title.
    BS680.F4M35 2015
    242'.2—dc23   2015024171

No Fear; No Guilt; Much Grace!

One Sunday, a preacher began his sermon by asking, "Do you know what is the most often repeated imperative in the Bible?" He paused, then interrupted our thoughts by saying, "Do not be afraid! I've heard it is repeated more than 365 times! If so, that would be one for each day of the year." He smiled and added, "I didn't count them." Most of us were surprised at the topic, and a ripple of contagious joy came from the congregation.

Throughout the week, I couldn't stop wondering if the preacher's claim was really true. So one morning, I went to the search engine on my Bible study program. I searched for the phrase "do not be afraid," then added several similar terms like "fear not," "do not fear," "do not be anxious," "do not be troubled," and "do not despair." After searching seven different translations, the program collected 426 verses on fear. Even after eliminating duplicates, there were still enough passages to write a devotional for every day of the year. Now I believed the pastor!

If repetition of a matter has anything to do with importance, this imperative could be the most important in the Word of God. I decided to call the words an "imperative" rather than a command or admonition because of the tone used by the writers. The words are spoken by God, angels, disciples, or other believers in a compelling, encouraging way, like a parent speaking to a fearful child.

To the grief-stricken widow and a heartbroken wife, God said, "Do not be afraid, my daughter." To the pregnant, unmarried, virgin Mary, the angel spoke tenderly: "Fear not!" At the birth of Jesus, he said to the shepherds, "Do not be afraid...I bring good tidings of great joy." To families in poverty, God spoke through Joseph, "Do not be afraid, I will provide for your little ones." To the guilty and those in prison, Jesus said, "Fear not, I am with you." To those moving or separated from family, the promise came: "Fear not, I go before you." When facing death or living in loneliness, God said, "Do not fear, I am with you always." When reproached, reviled, or misunderstood: "Do not be afraid of them, for I am with you." To the poor and deprived: "Do not fear, I am your treasure."

When dealing with His children who are afraid, even those feeling willful or defiant, Jesus promises, "Never will I leave you, never will I forsake you. So we may say with confidence, the Lord is my helper I will not be afraid. What can man do to me?"

Into these and many, many more situations of life, the Word of God gives us the imperative not to fear and brings us light. The more I thought about how much our Father loves His children, the more my heart filled and spilled over with love right back to Him. So I started to write. Each devotional begins with one of the imperatives from the Bible and closes with a biblical solution. In some of the devotionals you may find a touch of humor, a descriptive story, quotes, questions, or a simple prayer. I am certain that when you read *Unafraid: 365 Days Without Fear*, you will be able to say with confidence, "Whenever I am afraid, I will trust in You" (Psalm 56:3 NKJV).

WINTER

*Blessed is the man who trusts in the L*ORD*,*
whose confidence is in Him.
He will be like a tree planted by the water
that sends out its roots by the stream.
It does not fear when heat comes;
its leaves are always green.
It has no worries in a year of drought
and never fails to bear fruit.

JEREMIAH 17:7–8 NIV84

*I am afraid that . . . your minds will be led astray from the
simplicity and purity of devotion to Christ.*

2 CORINTHIANS 11:3

Between Eden's perfect beginning and the future day when all creation will become God's ideal, things have been far from perfect. Adam and Eve's disobedience brought the first taste of sin and introduced guilt, shame, painful insecurity, and torturous fear to our world. Everything God declared good was polluted; things beautiful became broken. As we live right now, we deal with issues that began in that fateful time. Thankfully, we have a Redeemer; through faith in Christ we find freedom and are led by the abiding Presence of the Holy Spirit. We also have the Word of God that we may know the truth.

Paul is transparent about his personal struggles with fear. Persecuted, tortured, imprisoned, betrayed, and taunted by the devil, he persevered, writing words of truth and grace to help us conquer fear and walk in faith. To the believers in Corinth he confided a different kind of fear—a love-filled fear that they would stray from the simplicity and purity of devotion to Christ to follow another gospel.

In this New Year, may we feel the deeply spiritual angst of Paul, guard our hearts, and vow not to stray from the simple, the pure, and the real. Jesus Christ is All Sufficient, and that means His arms are big enough to handle all our fear.

---

*The eternal God is a dwelling place, and underneath are the
everlasting arms.*   DEUTERONOMY 33:27

Fear not, Abram: I am thy shield, and thy exceeding great reward.

GENESIS 15:1 AV

God promised Abram a descendant and a land. He also pledged Himself—I AM your shield; I AM your very great reward. I AM made three things clear to His chosen leader. First, Abram must deal with his fear. The imperative—do not fear—had come to him in a vision. God had basically said, "Don't be afraid of this vision or of the future for I am in control."

Next, He claimed to be Abram's shield. It is a metaphor for salvation, protection, and victory. By calling Himself "shield," God assured deliverance, security, and rest. The third assurance was "I am your exceeding great reward." God was not talking about giving Abram a prize or pinning a medal on his robe; He was emphasizing that He Himself would be his reward. By expounding on His name, He revealed Himself—I AM both your Shield and Reward.

Knowing God is an achievement that spans a lifetime. At ninety, Abraham knew God as El Elyon, the Most High God; at almost one hundred, he knew Him as El Shaddai, the great I AM, the All-Sufficient One. When he needed God most, he learned that He was Shield and Reward. Do you know God as your I AM? Is He your All-Sufficient God?

The LORD is my rock, my fortress, and my savior . . . in whom I find protection. He is my shield, the power that saves me, and my place of safety.   PSALM 18:2 NLT

You must go to everyone I send you to and say whatever I
command you. Do not be afraid of them.

JEREMIAH 1:7–8 NIV

There's no man on earth like Jeremiah. Not then, not now, not ever. The same could be said about every one of us. We're all uniquely created for God's purpose. Still, there are times when another person seems so near-perfect that we wish we could be a clone. That's how I feel about Jeremiah. A writer par excellence with words still in print today!

He spoke only the words given by the Holy Spirit in his own uninhibited style using visual aids and costumes. Unashamed of emotion, he wept openly, unapologetically, and out of concern for others. Misunderstood, ridiculed, thrown into a pit, and jailed, he pressed on. But that's only part of the story. Jeremiah was real—sometimes weak, tired, depressed, and susceptible to one common human flaw—*fear*!

When commissioned by God, the first thing Jeremiah did was offer an excuse laced with fear. "Ah, Sovereign LORD," I said, "I do not know how to speak; I am only a child" (Jeremiah 1:6, NIV84).

Those words contradict themselves! For how can one acknowledge the LORD as "sovereign" and then say "I cannot"? Doesn't sovereignty mean having *all* power, *all* authority? Doesn't God's sovereignty provide for those He has called? No matter what our excuse, what fear we face, remember how God came to Jeremiah, dispensing large doses of truth and love.

Do not be afraid of them, for I am with you to deliver you.

JEREMIAH 1:8

Do not be afraid; for I know that you are looking for Jesus who has been crucified. He is not here, for He has risen, just as He said.

MATTHEW 28:5–6

Grief draped the shoulders of Mary and Mary Magdalene like a heavy shawl as they arrived at the tomb. The stone was pushed aside and an angel sat on top glistening white as snow. I'm thinking the women stopped dead in their tracks, dropped their ointment, and began looking for a place to hide. Even the guards shook. Another writer said they "quaked." The angel told the women not to fear. Hear the words reverberating off the rocks and hills: "He is not here, for He has risen just as He said" (Matthew 28:6). Now, why would a couple of women in a graveyard be afraid of that?

Fear made them forget what Jesus had previously revealed. Fear is thought-crippling! It rattles the most stable among us, short-circuits brain waves, sabotages good deeds, and separates us from God. That's when we need a voice of reason: "Go quickly and tell His disciples that He has risen from the dead; and behold, He is going ahead of you into Galilee." (Matthew 28:6–7). It took only a moment for the women to gather their skirts and run in the right direction, full speed, supercharged with mixed emotions: fear and joy.

When you are afraid, find Jesus. You won't have to run far, for He is always near. Just stop quaking and say his name.

Jesus, Jesus, Jesus. There really is something about that name.

*Don't be afraid. Go home and do as you have said. But first
make a small cake of bread for me from what you have and
bring it to me, and then make something for yourself and your
son . . . The jar of flour will not be used up and the jug of oil will
not run dry until the day the L*ORD* gives rain on the land. . . .*
1 KINGS 17:13–14 NIV84

Of all the fears that people in my neighborhood face, most *do not*
fear going hungry. In fact, most of the people I know are trying to
eat less! Still, as we sort through our refrigerators and set the table
for dinner, we know that in other parts of town, children go to bed
with gnawing stomachs. Around the globe millions of people are
starving. A worldwide reality, hunger is often mentioned in Scripture. Famine, drought, crop failures, and plagues punctuate the
story of God's people, as do blessings and prosperity. Remember
Elijah? His future was uncertain as famine and drought threatened
to cripple Israel. But before fear had time to grip him, he sought the
LORD, trusted His Word and knew exactly what to do. He would follow a plan that would require exceptional courage and fearless faith.

He packed his camping gear, laced on his boots, and walked with
God. Thirteen miles and three days later, he camped near a brook.
Before nightfall ravens dropped his first meal near his tent. Then
twice a day the birds delivered berries and grain and the stream
flowed freely. Such are the ways of God as He cares for you and me.

---

*I have been young and now I am old, yet I have not seen the
righteous forsaken or his descendants begging bread.*
PSALM 37:25

> *God's promise of entering his rest still stands, so we ought to*
> *tremble with fear that some of you might fail to experience it.*
>
> HEBREWS 4:1 NLT

Rest seems a simple imperative for us to follow—a promise appealing to both body and soul. But the second half of the verse adds mystery and a challenge. "We ought to tremble with fear" that some might miss it. A few sentences further into the chapter you will find one of the most descriptive verses about the Word of God. The two thoughts are connected, but how?

They describe a purpose—rest, followed by a divine road map so that we may arrive at our destination safely. The journey may include hearing, reading, studying, memorizing, and meditating upon truth—not as a discipline or to gather facts, but to know God and understand ourselves. "For the word of God is living and active and sharper than any two-edged sword, and piercing as far as the division of soul and spirit, of both joints and marrow, and able to judge the thoughts and intentions of the heart" (Hebrews 4:12). Being "alive" and "active" means having divine life, and being full of spiritual energy. Because it is living truth, it has a life-giving, life-changing effect on us.

Like standing under a shower allowing warm water to wash over us, being under the influence of truth cleanses the thoughts and intentions of our hearts. We begin to understand why we are afraid, why we want to control, why we can't let go of certain problems or people. We figure out why we function (and dysfunction) the way we do. We see areas where we need to grow. With this insight comes a great sense of peace...and rest.

> *He will come to us as the showers, as the spring rains that water*
> *the earth.*
>
> HOSEA 6:3 ESV

> *I am sending you to them who are stubborn and obstinate*
> *children . . . whether they listen or not . . . they will know that a*
> *prophet has been among them . . . Neither fear them nor fear*
> *their words.*
>
> EZEKIEL 2:4–6

Imagine knowing before you speak that the audience is "stubborn and obstinate." Suppose you'd heard they will not listen, much less take notes, and probably will not give your message one later thought. What if they had rejected God for generations? That's enough to strike fear in the heart of the most courageous speaker.

The Sovereign LORD knew Ezekiel would experience fear. Three times He told him not to be afraid. Not of his audience, not of their words, not of their facial expressions. Then He added, Do not be terrified! Oh, the angst Ezekiel must have felt as he packed his bag and prepared his message.

You may be thinking *I'm glad God wasn't speaking to me!* But doesn't the LORD send all of us out? Don't we all, at times, feel the Spirit leading us to speak to someone who doesn't really want to hear? Ezekiel obeyed, ignoring his fear. And we can too. The LORD always supplies just the right word when we need it, and He opens our ears to hear. What He asks you to do is doable because His unlimited power is infused into you.

> *I have strength for all things in Christ Who empowers me [I am*
> *ready for anything and equal to anything through Him Who*
> *infuses inner strength into me].*
>
> PHILIPPIANS 4:13 AMP

> *Now, my daughter, do not fear. I will do for you whatever you*
> *ask, for all my people in the city know that you are a woman of*
> *excellence.*   RUTH 3:11

Nobody really knows who first wrote the story of Ruth. (What a pity!) But we do know that behind the author's pen stood the Spirit of the living God breathing life into the words. The story is not fiction—no need for a writer's character development or outline. It is a true story of a young woman, living in a pagan culture, doing ordinary things, who became known as "a woman of excellence." It is a grace story, just as is your story or mine or that of any ordinary woman who has encountered God.

What was it that made Ruth an excellent woman? What changed a heathen girl into the wife of Boaz, her kinsman redeemer? How did she advance from a descendant of Lot into the lineage of our savior? How did she leave behind her broken life, wounded reputation, grief, and poverty to eventually become the great-grandmother of David? The same way that paupers become adopted children of Christ's family. By grace!

Ruth learned of God, perhaps through her first husband, and God never let her go. He healed the widow's broken heart, drew her into a pursuit of truth, and sustained her relationship with Naomi, her mother-in-law. He strengthened her—body and soul—in preparation for what would come later. He called her to Himself and she believed.

Someday, when our story is written, may it also read, *She was excellent because of grace.*

> *But now that their father was dead, Joseph's brothers became*
> *fearful. "Now Joseph will show his anger and pay us back for all*
> *the wrong we did to him," they said.*
>
> GENESIS 50:15 NLT

Joseph's brothers were afraid, and no wonder! They had tossed their youngest sibling into a deep well and told their daddy he was dead. They even poured sheep's blood on his coat of many colors and showed it to Jacob as proof that his son had been killed violently. They later sold Joseph into slavery. Through a course of events he ended up in the king's palace in Egypt living in a position of great power, capable of wiping out his entire clan.

Although Joseph had been treated badly by his brothers when he was younger, he did not hold a grudge; nor was he looking for ways to retaliate.

But the devious mind works differently! It can only process problems and evaluate people by what it knows. Apparently these brothers knew nothing of compassion, forgiveness, and grace. Joseph was different. His heart belonged to God, his character formed in relationship with Him. Convictions do not change in a sanctified heart even when the closest family ties tangle into knots. In your troubled times, may your heart be free and full of God's grace and love.

> *Blessed be . . . the Father of mercies and God of all comfort, who*
> *comforts us in all our affliction so that we will be able to comfort*
> *those who are in any affliction with the comfort with which we*
> *ourselves are comforted by God.*
>
> 2 CORINTHIANS 1:3–4

But even if you should suffer for what is right, you are blessed…
Do not fear.

1 PETER 3:14 NIV

Suffer for doing what's right? How puzzling! Yet that teaching runs throughout Scripture as a major theme. Each mention presents a conundrum—pain, trials, tests, mixed with joy; suffering alongside glory, perseverance, and faith worth more than gold. Suffering and blessing flow together in a river over rocks, becoming a life-giving stream.

The making of a saint doesn't occur in a laboratory but in the field of experience; we do not grow in spite of pain but *because* of it. Deny it, ignore it, or try to explain it away—pain is part and parcel of our lives on planet Earth. It may always confuse us, while at the same time it draws us into a more intimate walk with Christ. He knows all about suffering for doing what's right, even to the point of dying on our behalf—the just for the unjust.

While we may suffer unjustly, we realize that every single pain and problem has a purpose, perhaps one as simple and as important as knowing Jesus better, loving Him more, and trusting Him more completely. When trials happen, lean into Him. Resting in His embrace all our fear disappears and we are truly blessed.

———

These have come so that the proven genuineness of your faith—
of greater worth than gold, which perishes even though refined
by fire—may result in praise, glory and honor when Jesus
Christ is revealed.   1 PETER 1:7 NIV84

"Do not fear what they fear; do not be frightened." But in your hearts set apart Christ as Lord.

1 PETER 3:14–15 NIV84

After warning Christ-followers that suffering would come even when they did the right thing, Peter added a triple imperative about fear so they would know what to expect and how to respond. Peter mentions two kinds of fear—their fear and our fear—fear of the faithless; fear of the faithful. One overwhelmingly, entirely, unreasonably frightening. The other, intimidating or troubling, but with some good in it! Good fear wakes us up, stops us at the edge of a cliff, and, sensing danger, sends us running to God.

The good within fear moves us to speak truth in a society that desperately needs to hear it. Is the reason for your hope on the tip of your tongue? How can we always be ready? Study the Bible? Memorize Scripture? Pray for help? Seek an uncluttered mind? Yes, all of the above! But most important, does "your heart set apart Christ as Lord"?

Being ready is not so much a matter of cramming truth as it is knowing, loving, and yielding to the lordship of Christ. Basking in the presence of the One we love, the One who is the way, the truth, and the life, we are sanctified for His purposes. After that, truth comes naturally.

For out of the overflow of the heart the mouth speaks.

MATTHEW 12:34 NIV84

In this you greatly rejoice, even though now for a little while, if
necessary, you have been distressed by various trials.

1 PETER 1:6

Peter, who died on an upside-down cross out of respect for Jesus'
crucifixion, knew how fearful our trials would be. Even when our
suffering comes from problems of our own making, or from our
brokenness and tendency to sin, how we respond is important.
Peter used the word "distressed," a word with "stress" smack in the
middle of it, to describe this kind of fear. It means "to cause grief,
to throw into sorrow, to affect with sadness, to be fearful."

Our trials are of various kinds—variegated or multicolored.
Remember Joseph's coat of many colors? The writer of that story
used the Hebrew word for variegated to describe the coat. How variegated are the trials you face? Do they come in many colors, in all
sorts of ways, at unseemly times? Whether they occur because of
your misdeeds or because of someone else's sin, we all find ourselves in need of grace.

We can face trials by faithfully receiving "God's grace in its
various forms" (1 Peter 4:10 NIV). *Various!—various* trials, *various*
grace! For every color of trial, there are matching colors of grace.
For every sin, weakness, genetic flaw, dysfunctional behavior, or
unrealized dream, grace beams toward us from the full spectrum
of light with colors as beautiful and as dramatic as a rainbow.

Once we know the unconceivable, extravagant grace of God, we
will live fearlessly.

So don't be afraid; you are worth more than many sparrows.
                              MATTHEW 10:31 NIV84

In an assisted living facility, an elderly woman found joy watching birds eat from the feeder and splash in the birdbath outside her window. She loved seeing the different species, including the simple sparrows. She wouldn't allow even one disparaging word about them even though they traveled with flocks of friends, ate pounds of seed, and left a mess on the sidewalk. "Jesus knows every sparrow that falls," she said. "I like to feed them."

Most of her declining years, she celebrated the smallest of God's creatures—the humble sparrows, the playful squirrels that tried to steal the seed, even a rat that occasionally peered into the window. Her attitude exuded joy, and visitors often heard her singing "His eye is on the sparrow and I know He cares for me." Near the end of her life she said, "I have never known a lonely day!"

There is not enough room in a heart filled with joy for a load of complicated fears. As light dispels darkness, joy displaces fear and leaves in its place a holy reverence for things simple, lovely, divine. Spend part of today sitting still before the Gift Giver, being thankful. Take a walk and feed the birds! And do not be afraid.

———————

Even the sparrow has found a home, and the swallow a nest for herself, where she may have her young—a place near your altar, Lord Almighty, my King and my God.

                              PSALM 84:3 NIV84

They all saw him and were terrified. Immediately he spoke to
them and said, "Take courage! It is I. Don't be afraid."

MARK 6:50 NIV

The disciples set out with confidence following Jesus' simple
request—row to the other side of the lake and wait. Jesus climbed
the mountain for some time alone with His Father. For these men
accustomed to dropping their nets and hauling in hundreds of fish
at a time, waiting became boring. But things got scary when an
unexpected wind began to batter them and water threatened to
swamp the boat. Where was Jesus?

He had been gone all afternoon, and it was getting dark. Probably at least one disciple thought, *There is a time to pray and a time*
to row! Of course they were afraid! Then they saw something that
turned their fear into terror. Was it a ghost? They yelled and Jesus
answered. When they recognized the Lord's voice, their fear vanished like a vapor. Whew! He stepped into the boat and the wind
ceased.

What a difference the presence of Jesus makes in the midst of
turmoil. The men were amazed and beside themselves with wonder.
We can always count on Jesus. When winds threaten shipwreck or
deep waters wash over our heads, He is there. He sees every splash
or swift current. He walks atop your surging seas. His hands reach
deep into our troubled waters, and His grip will hold. He will not let
go until your feet are solidly on shore. His grip will hold.

The LORD is gracious and merciful; slow to anger and great in
lovingkindness.   PSALM 145:8

The LORD is for me; I will not fear; What can man do to me?

PSALM 118:6

According to a recent survey of people in the United States, their second greatest fear is speaking in public. (The first greatest is snakes.) One psychologist, who has trained thousands of speakers, claims most people have a greater fear of public speaking than of death. That's hard to believe! When I speak, I admit that sometimes my mouth goes dry and my heart beats too fast. But once I'm settled before the group, the juices start flowing, I remember my outline, ideas come, and stage fright vanishes like morning frost. When it comes to snakes? Let's just say *I would vanish*, and it might take days to find me.

It's comforting to know that even the greatest saints, even some of the world's notable speakers battle stage fright. Whether your fear is stage fright, snake fright, or some other fear, there's one solution that works every time: Relax, and then breathe. Most audiences are sympathetic and kind. They know you are one among a majority of people, including themselves, who deal with the same fear.

God may take you out of your comfort zone. But He will never intentionally embarrass you. He will provide opportunities for you to speak words of life to those you love. Do not be afraid.

My flesh and my heart may fail, but God is the strength of my heart and my portion forever.

PSALM 73:26

Do not fear those who kill the body but are unable to kill the
soul; but rather fear Him who is able to destroy both soul and
body in hell.

MATTHEW 10:28

One way to dilute the power of fear is by asking "What is the worst thing that can happen?" A little boy put his fear in the right perspective one day when he, his siblings, and his dad got the family SUV stuck in the mud. While the other kids giggled, this boy took the predicament seriously. In fact, he was gripped with fear. His dad, consoling him, asked, "Son, what's the worst thing that can happen?"

With a melancholy personality prone to seeing things on the dark side, he answered, "We could starve to death and die!"

"Why, we'll just get our feet muddy and walk home," the dad said as he placed the child on his shoulders, gathered the others, and began walking. What seemed a tragedy became an adventure. Soon they met a farmer working his field with his tractor. The farmer grinned and offered to pull the car onto solid ground. Today the kids still talk about the greatest Saturday ever, one complete with all the things they loved—mud, tractors, riding on Daddy's shoulders, and walking along country roads.

Muddy roads are always an opportunity. Whatever trouble, no matter how loud the cacophony of fear, it is a time to climb on our Father's back and hold on tight.

———————

The mind of man plans his way, but the Lord directs his steps.

PROVERBS 16:9

The LORD himself goes before you and will be with you . . . Do not
be afraid; do not be discouraged.

DEUTERONOMY 31:8 NIV84

Do you wish God would speak to you today, directly, face to face?
Do you long for His presence, the way He showed himself to the
patriarchs and disciples? While you may long for an epiphany, he is
nearer to us today—His words are more available.

Before she could read, a tiny girl sat on her porch swing, her legs
dangling as she held a Bible in her lap. Even though her parents
never attended church, she somehow knew that she was holding
something very special. She liked to leaf through the pages and
look at the pictures and maps. Before long, she learned that the
words printed in red were the words of Jesus. She felt close to Him
as she located passages in red letters and wished she could read
them.

Someone told her that G-O-D spelled God, so she looked for the
word, traced its letters with her finger. Little by little, day after day,
her longing to know God grew stronger, her legs longer. When she
became old enough to walk to the little country church nearby, she
found grace and love. There she learned about God and believed in
Jesus.

Did this child find Jesus or did He find her? Did the God-search
begin on that front porch, or did it begin within the portals of
heaven in eternity past, from the heart of Elohim?

———————

The Word was with God, and the Word was God.

JOHN 1:1

Do not fear, Abram, I am a shield to you; your reward shall be very great.

GENESIS 15:1

These words came from the mouth of the LORD to the ears of Abram as he waited for an heir. God said similar words to us: "Above all, taking the shield of faith, wherewith ye shall be able to quench all the fiery darts of the wicked" (Ephesians 6:16 AV). We all need a shield!

Think about the children of Abraham in battle with their enemies: swords flashing, arrows sailing, soldiers marching, horses stomping, chariots rattling. The army, immense in scope and power, points its weapons in the direction of God's people. They would retreat in fear, except for one fact: They have a Shield, not the clumsy full-metal kind but a living one. The very presence of Jehovah the Self-Existent One stands in front of every soldier, protecting each of them with omnipotent power and with a visual presence that strikes fear in the heart of the strongest enemy.

Now compare their wars with the spiritual battles against the forces of darkness that we experience frequently—the rulers, the powers, the world forces of this darkness, and the spiritual forces of wickedness (see Ephesians 6:12). When we step onto that battlefield, Jesus Himself stands in front of us, creating an impenetrable shield as we face the most fearsome of enemies.

Be strong in the Lord and in the strength of His might. Put on the full armor of God . . . stand firm against the schemes of the devil.   EPHESIANS 6:10–11

*Because you are precious in my eyes, and honored, and I love
you, I give men in return for you, peoples in exchange for your
life. Fear not, for I am with you.*

ISAIAH 43:4–5 ESV

Precious. Honored. Loved. How many people in this world feel
that way about you? Were you showered with love by your parents?
Did they tell you how special you are? Did they compliment and
encourage you, or criticize and complain? Were you disciplined
harshly, out of anger, in unsuitable ways? Did they speak about
your appearance more than your accomplishments?

Whether you received healthy doses of love, negative attention,
or no attention at all, the insecurities and fears that developed earlier in your life don't have to keep wounding you today. Your Father
loves you just as you are, with strengths and weaknesses, failures
and successes, no matter who you are. His love is unconditional
and consistent because you belong to Him.

When He said, "I will give people for your life," He meant something like this: My love will reproduce through your life many more
disciples. How wonderful it is to be loved so much by God that He
wants to reproduce your likeness in others! That can only happen
as we exchange our lives for His.

---

*No one can sum up all God is able to accomplish through one
solitary life, wholly yielded, adjusted and obedient to Him.*

ATTRIBUTED TO D. L. MOODY

Sarah was afraid, so she denied it, saying, "I didn't laugh." But the Lord said, "No, you did laugh."

GENESIS 18:15 NLT

Abraham spotted three visitors approaching his tent. He must have recognized it as a divine encounter, for he bowed to the ground and uttered, "Lord." After a meal while they were resting under the trees, Sarah overheard them say she would give birth to Abraham's promised son. She couldn't hold back laughter, thinking, *After all these years, now that we are too old to have children—no way!* It was actually the pre-incarnate Christ who heard her laugh. Ooops! When Abraham questioned her irreverence, she was filled with fear and denied it.

On this occasion Abraham was the godly man in charge of his family, but earlier he too had fallen on his face and laughed. *Will a child be born to a man one hundred years old?* (Genesis 17:17). Since both had laughed for the same reason, why was Sarah's lapse called a lack of faith but Abraham's was not? Was it a cultural issue? Were women judged by stricter standards? Or was Sarah's fear showing? Was God dealing with her fear as well as her faith? For there would be no room for fear in the heart of the mother of nations; no place for fear in her love for Yahweh.

Though some details are missing in the middle of the story, we know the ending. Abraham "believed in the Lord; and He reckoned it to him as righteousness" (Genesis 15:6). Sarah "considered Him faithful who had promised" (Hebrews 11:11).

Faith overcomes fear every time!

Do not be afraid of those who kill the body but cannot kill the soul.

MATTHEW 10:28 NIV84

Even though Matthew's words do not promise a life surrounded at all times by those who love us, they do provide great encouragement. Our souls cannot be touched by name-calling or any other mistreatment from antagonists. They may hurt our feelings, stir up trouble, try to defame us, erect roadblocks on our path, but our life is not theirs to take. There is a kind of insanity in fear that produces confusion about fear itself. That kind of fear is illogical, based on the unknown and the impossible.

Even in the midst of mental, emotional, or physical pain, knowing our Savior endured the same fills our hearts with comfort. It transports our soul and spirit into amazing grace where we discover sweet fellowship, deep intimacy, and the greatest joy possible this side of heaven. What an honor to complete the sufferings of Christ. In union with the One who knows us completely, who walks hand in hand with us, we are free from the fear of man. What can man do to me?

Since I, the master of the household, have been called the prince of demons, the members of my household will be called by even worse names.

MATTHEW 10:25 NLT

Tell fearful souls, "Courage! Take heart! God is here, right here, on his way to put things right and redress all wrongs. He's on his way! He'll save you!"

ISAIAH 35:4 MSG

Have you ever felt alone? Maybe even within a hubbub of activity, you feel lonely. It happens because we're human! What we really want and need is somebody who knows all about us and loves us anyway. A person we can connect with and talk to on a level deeper than news, weather, and sports. One who accepts us as we are and will never leave us alone.

Perhaps you have a deep-seated problem or a relationship tangled with knots hard to work out. We may have a dozen things going great, but the one thing that is not keeps us awake at night and afraid in the daytime. Why do we allow one relationship blunder to cast a shadow over all other blessings? Why do we mull it over until it becomes bigger than it has to be?

We want smooth-sailing, warmhearted relationships without storms. When we lose or fear losing that, the enemy attacks and turns our thoughts upside down. This is the time to welcome the Friend of Sinners. He is with you always, no matter what.

I will not in any way fail you, nor give you up nor leave you without support. [I will] not, [I will] not, [I will] not in any degree leave you helpless nor forsake nor let you down (relax My hold on you)! [Assuredly not!]

HEBREWS 13:5 AMP

Do not be afraid because of the words that you have heard.

ISAIAH 37:6 ESV

Words! It only takes one to make a person feel good—a simple compliment, a pleasant greeting, an expression of joy, a word from Scripture. It takes only one to make a person feel bad—a criticism however well meant, a thoughtless suggestion, unsolicited advice, an outburst of anger, a profane word.

If only a certain grandmother had thought more carefully before she said to her teenage granddaughter, "Honey, have you ever thought about losing weight?" Those words, meant to help, instead cut like a knife and still produce fear in the young woman who is obsessed with being physically fit.

Another young woman, obese since she was nine, attended church regularly hoping she would encounter the deacon who never failed to greet her with a smile and compliment her for carrying her Bible to church. Love-starved and needing attention, the girl cherished those moments of encouragement. From that day forth, she has cradled the Bible in her arms at every service of worship. She became a lover of God's Word, and later a teacher and a writer. How wise was this deacon who understood the impact of kind words spoken at the right time.

———

Watch the way you talk. Let nothing foul or dirty come out of your mouth. Say only what helps, each word a gift.

EPHESIANS 4:29 MSG

He who dwells in the secret place of the Most High Shall abide under the shadow of the Almighty. I will say of the LORD, "He is my refuge and my fortress; My God, in Him I will trust... You shall not be afraid."

PSALM 91:1–2, 5 NKJV

When it comes to knowing God, some are content with simply joining the ranks of those who believe. Others want more—more fellowship with Him, more knowing Him as He is, in the "secret place of the Most High." There He is known as El Elyon, the Most High. He is above all rulers, kings, monarchs, and angelic princes. Mere mortals who dare reach toward such lofty heights, who want to settle down and dwell there, are those who "abide under the shadow of the Almighty."

Like all journeys, your spiritual pursuit of El Elyon begins with one definitive step. You can begin by studying His Word and resting in its truth. Then step by step, day after day, continue on—making sure the distance between you is closer than a whisper. Moving to the rhythm established by the Most High, you proceed upward—from knowing, to dwelling, to abiding, to resting. God-seekers find contentment settling in His shadow, nestling close to the Protector's heart. There we find nourishment succored by the "Almighty—El Shaddai." He delights in his little ones, sustaining, empowering, and, best of all, holding us close in matchless love. In that sacred place, grace and love overcome fear.

Be exalted above the heavens, O God; let Your glory be above all the earth.   PSALM 57:5

> *Be at ease, do not be afraid. Your God and the God of your*
> *father has given you treasure in your sacks; I had your money.*
>
> GENESIS 43:23

Money—kids do chores for it, prepubescent tweens and teens think they're entitled to it, couples fight over it, dads and moms work hard for it, and governments take it. And while we gather, spend, and plan for more of it, God stands behind the curtain, watching the drama unfold and prompting us not to forget that the world and everything in it belongs to Him alone. The simple yet life-altering truth in this passage is this: God is in charge.

In the passage above, we see that He puts treasure away for us. He knows how many times the money has been taken out, put back in, and traded around. He cares because in divine sovereignty, your wealth was His first, and the way you manage it reveals something about your love for Him. Where is your heart when you think about money? It is an important question. For the love of money is the root of all evil. Not money itself, but the *love* of it. Guard your heart when it comes to what you possess. And listen carefully to His voice whenever you make a purchase or an investment or give a gift.

> *For the love of money is a root of all sorts of evil, and some by*
> *longing for it have wandered away from the faith and pierced*
> *themselves with many griefs.*
>
> 1 TIMOTHY 6:10

When she was in severe labor the midwife said to her, "Do not fear, for now you have another son."

GENESIS 35:17

As Jacob prayed at Bethel, God Almighty appeared and spoke to him face to face, changing his name from Jacob to Israel. To the third generation, with Israel as its head, the promise given to Abraham was reiterated to Isaac, including that he would be blessed with descendants, a nation and a company of nations, kings, and land. But the promises hung upon one thing: the birth of twelve sons who would eventually form the tribes of Israel, and Rachel's last pregnancy had ended in miscarriage. Now, with his wife in labor and both mother and child in jeopardy, Jacob was distraught.

Even in the direst of circumstances, God is still the giver of every good and perfect gift. On this occasion, El Shaddai holds in His Almighty hands the most precious of gifts, the gift of life. The atmosphere sparked with fear, Rachel was near death as the rigors of childbirth tore at her aging body. Almost simultaneously, God's perfect gift slipped into the world and her soul departed. The midwife comforted her, "Do not fear, for now you have another son."

The mother's last whisper was her newborn's name. The twelfth son of Jacob and Rachel, Benjamin, would know special favor from his father as the son of his right hand. This story is so very typical of human life. Pain making friends with joy, fear holding hands with delight.

For from Him and through Him and to Him are all things.

ROMANS 11:36

Do not be fainthearted. Do not be afraid, or panic, or tremble before them.

DEUTERONOMY 20:3

What an unusual word is "fainthearted"! It means tenderhearted to a fault, soft of heart, timid, or weak. God takes seriously all of our fear problems. He says, "Do not be fainthearted!" It sounds as if our heart, being overwhelmed, might shrivel and wither away. No one can overcome an enemy as potent as fear with methods that depict weakness, softness, or timidity. Victory takes courage, fortitude, and faith.

Four times in this one verse God warns His warriors against fear. The truth is sliced thin, the words stacked upon each other, unique by definition, but closely connected—fainthearted, afraid, panic stricken, then trembling in terror. Such care taken in the writing of it ensures that soldiers preparing for battle, and followers like you and me, will grasp the multifaceted truth the Almighty wishes to convey. As we contemplate the meaning of these harmful emotions, little by little we gain clarity, faith grows, and fear disappears.

Do you see fear's spiraling regression? There are downward steps from a *heart that faints*, to full-blown *fear*, developing into panic, then morphing into all-out terror. But at any place on the steps toward greater fear, we can stop, catch our breath, and turn around with the knowledge that God will protect us.

———————

The LORD is my strength and my shield; my heart trusts in Him, and I am helped; therefore my heart exults, and with my song I shall thank Him.   PSALM 28:7

*Give your entire attention to what God is doing right now,
and don't get worked up about what may or may not happen
tomorrow. God will help you deal with whatever hard things
come up when the time comes.*

MATTHEW 6:34 MSG

There is something terribly wrong with our fascination with the
future. We can barely handle one day at a time, but still we pile on
anxious care and needless fear by worrying about what's next. One
translation of the verse above reads: "Sufficient for the day is its
own trouble" (ESV). Another simply states, "Each day has enough
trouble of its own" (NIV). Still, the warning often fails to take hold
in our hearts. While it is good stewardship to manage our time
well, it's a little bit crazy when we attempt to manage the time we
don't yet have.

The next quote had been cut from a magazine and used as a
bookmark in my mother's Bible. The author is unknown. "This is
the Blessed Life—not anxious to see far in front, nor careful about
the next step, not eager to choose the path, not weighted with the
heavy responsibilities of the future, but quietly following behind
the Shepherd, one step at a time." Seems my mother had discovered the great solution for fear and one of the greatest secrets of life.

---

*Whom have I in heaven but You? And besides You, I desire
nothing on earth.*

PSALM 73:25

Do not be afraid. Stand firm and you will see the deliverance the LORD will bring you today.

EXODUS 14:13 NIV

Why do some problems continue a lifetime, while God removes others quickly? It may have to do with our wrong concept of time or our limited point of view. Our calendars are not synced with His—His eternal plan versus the data on our cell phone. He always delivers, in His time.

His name in the verse above is LORD. It means Jehovah, YHWH, the Self-Existent One, the Eternal God. It is his personal name first spoken in Genesis, identifying him to his covenant people. Adam knew God as Yahweh. Later He revealed himself to Abraham as Jehovah (Genesis 12:8), promising redemption. Jehovah defined His name when He said to Moses, "I AM Who I AM" (Exodus 3:14). These names, along with others, help us understand who God is, teach us His character, and reveal His love. When we know Him by name, and call Him by name, He seems to delight in living up to His name.

Being on a first-name basis with the LORD shows we are intimately connected to him as His beloved, His friends, and that kind of fellowship opens our hearts to His will, and His heart to our needs. Seek to know Him by name, call upon His name, and deliverance is sure to follow—in His time and in sync with who He is.

There is none like You, O LORD; You are great, and great is Your name in might.

JEREMIAH 10:6

I am the God of your father Abraham; do not fear, for I am with
you. I will bless you, and multiply your descendants, for the sake
of My servant Abraham.

GENESIS 26:24

Abraham was the father of Isaac, grandfather of Jacob, great-grandfather of his twelve sons who became leaders of the tribes of Israel, patriarch of fourth and fifth generations, and, spiritually speaking, the Father of us all. His descendants knew the blessings of Yahweh, to fulfill God's promise. As his growing family added one generation after another, I wonder how often Abraham thought about that night God said, "Now look toward the heavens, and count the stars, if you are able to count them...So shall your descendants be" (Genesis 15:5).

While the family line was important, the New Testament reveals that Abraham was really chosen because of his faith. It was by grace—the same way that everyone who believes comes into God's family. We respond to the truth imparted and God's relentless love conveyed from generation to generation of believers.

Faith also sprouts in unexpected places, like blades of grass through cracks in a sidewalk—a stubborn, persistent faith rooted deeply in the grace and mercy of a sovereign God who seeks and finds His own. As this day winds down, look up and give thanks for the bountiful blessings given to you. Do not fear. By grace and faith, you too are numbered among the stars of heaven.

For God is with the righteous generation.

PSALM 14:5

For they shall graze and lie down, and none shall make them afraid.

ZEPHANIAH 3:13 ESV

The greatest invitation in the Bible is a simple verb of one syllable—*come*. Of all the invitations received, it is simplest in design, grandest in content, most personal, and from the Greatest Dignitary. Jehovah, the Self-Existent God, Yahweh Himself issued it. How honored we are! The Bible speaks the word enough to make it a major theme. And we are glad that Jesus said, "No one can come to Me unless the Father who sent Me draws him" (John 6:44). Every person who knows Jesus first received His invitation.

Jehovah invited Noah, "Come in, thou and all thy house, unto the ark" (Genesis 7:1 YLT). Inside, they would fear no evil; there they would be safe from the flood. God invited the animals to come. As clouds darkened and drops of rain pelted the roof, some came two by two and others seven by seven. Compelled by instinct? Possibly. Stirred by an ominous feeling in the air? Maybe. Still, it was God Who issued the call, and they came, finding food, shelter, and safety. The final invitation will be issued from the Holy Spirit in the last days. "The Spirit and the bride say, 'Come.' And let the one who hears say, 'Come.' " (Revelation 22:17).

Today, between the first and last invitation, countless more invitations are being sent, including this one from Jesus: "Come to me...and I will give you rest" (Matthew 11:28).

Come into His Ark!

Do not fear, for God has come to test you, that the fear of Him may be before you, that you may not sin.

EXODUS 20:20 ESV

Whatever trial you are facing today has already passed through the fingers of our Heavenly Father. Even if it originated in the mind of some sinister spirit, an evil enemy, or the devil himself, God is in control of it and can quash it anytime He pleases. Before the test reaches you, God has allowed it, sanctified it, cleansed it, and turned it around so that it is actually good for you. For one thing, tests help rid our hearts of destructive fear and help us grow in the only beneficial fear there is—the fear of God! If we develop a strong, healthy fear of Him, it guards our hearts from any departure from Him. Fear loses its grip in the presence of the Almighty.

Paul wrote the book of Philippians during one of his most difficult trials. From a dark, cold prison he penned words full of joy, reminding all of us to rejoice, always. In the quiet place of solitary confinement he discovered something that you and I need to know. We do not have to be a prisoner of circumstances, no matter how difficult or confining. We can rise above them by learning to rejoice in the Lord.

I count all things to be loss in view of the surpassing value of knowing Christ Jesus my Lord.

PHILIPPIANS 3:8

Do not fear the people of the land, for they are bread for us.
Their protection is removed from them, and the LORD is with us;
do not fear them.

NUMBERS 14:9 ESV

Knowing the LORD is with us and trusting Him to never leave us satisfies the deepest longing of the Christian's heart. The better we know Him, the less we fear other people. Think about the following blessings we have in Him. All of these are from Ephesians 1.

- Spiritual blessings: *Every spiritual blessing in the heavenly places in Christ.*
- Security: *He chose us in Him before the foundation of the world.*
- Grace: *The glory of His grace, which He freely bestowed on us in the Beloved.*
- Redemption: *Redemption through His blood, the forgiveness of our trespasses.*
- Purpose: *Having been predestined according to His purpose who works all things after the counsel of His will.*
- A future: *In all wisdom and insight He made known to us the mystery of His will.*
- Adoption: *In love He predestined us to adoption as sons through Jesus Christ to Himself, according to the kind intention of His will.*
- An inheritance: *In Him also we have obtained an inheritance.*
- Hope: *We who were the first to hope in Christ would be to the praise of His glory.*
- Eternal salvation: *After listening to the message of truth, the gospel of your salvation—having also believed, you were sealed in Him with the Holy Spirit of promise.*

Do not fear him, for I have given him into your hand; and you
shall do to him as you did to Sihon, king of the Amorites.

NUMBERS 21:34

What is your greatest enemy in life? Now picture that problem, that
unreasonable person, the system that holds you down, that flaw of
character you can't seem to mend in the hollow of your upturned
hand. It is yours. It is not bigger than you, for it sits in your palm;
it is not stronger than you, for you could easily close your fist
around it. It is not fastened to your hand but resting there, so you
can throw it away.

It is possible for you to do the very thing done by the people of
God throughout history—obey! Camped nearby in the wilderness,
Moses and his people sought permission to pass through the enemies' land, vowing to stay on the King's Highway and walk straight
through, border to border.

King Sihon, ungodly tyrant that he was, said no! Then he gathered an army and set out to slaughter God's people before they
even got close. But he failed to consider one thing—*these were*
God's people!

The battle was over before the flash of one sword, because Yahweh had given the king into the hands of His people. What is in
your hand? Toss it aside, grab hold of what God offers, then with
clean hands and a fearless heart, start walking. And as you go, go
singing joyfully.

"I am walking in the King's Highway!"

*You shall not be partial in judgment. You shall hear the small
and the great alike. You shall not be intimidated by anyone, for
the judgment is God's.*

DEUTERONOMY 1:17 ESV

Writing to the church in Rome, Paul reminded New Covenant
believers not to judge others. We are all servants of God responsible to the One we serve, not to those who make judgments and
criticize. "Who are you to judge the servant of another?" (Romans
14:4). This is one of the most important concepts in Scripture.
Christ-followers can become so opinionated that we forget to be
Christ-like. Since we think our way is right, our mission becomes
one of trying to change the minds of others. I wonder, while we are
busy doing that, what is the Holy Spirit doing?

In matters of conscience, stand like an oak; in matters of pref-
erence, bend like a willow. Let us hold fast to the truth about the
essentials of our faith, but yield to others about issues nonessential.
The moment we believe, every Christian launches into a spiritual
journey, continually making progress, discovering new insights,
learning new truths. Don't take from others their joy of discovery,
or impose your beliefs upon them before they're ready. Give them
time to learn from the Master.

Author A. W. Tozer captured the spirit of Romans 14 in one
sentence: "Always it is more important that we retain a right spirit
toward others than that we bring them to our way of thinking, even
if our way is right."[1]

See, the LORD your God has set the land before you. Go up, take
possession, as the Lord, the God of your fathers, has told you.
Do not fear or be dismayed.

DEUTERONOMY 1:21 ESV

When God gives, we have the pleasure of receiving His gift, whatever it is—a talent, an aptitude, ability, or something we need or
want. It all comes from the "Father of lights, with whom is no vari-
ation or shifting shadow" (James 1:17). A gift is free for the taking,
but before it is ours we must accept it, possess it, cherish it, and use
it. Fear and the dismay that fear causes are often healed by some
spiritual gift from God entrusted to another believer, then passed
on to someone who needs it. Have you ever conquered a certain
fear through the help of an older or wiser Christian? The grace of
giving is made complete by the grace of receiving!

If God has blessed you with the ability to make money, share
it. If you radiate self-confidence, encourage the depressed. If you
write, never cease writing the message. If you have survived great
difficulties or losses in life, tell the story. Don't waste any sorrow
by keeping it to yourself. Sow your experiences like seed in the
fertile fields that Jehovah Elohim has set before you. Rest unafraid
until the seed sprouts, sends down roots, and grows a crop of
righteousness.

How lovely is your dwelling place, O LORD of Hosts! My soul
longs, yes, faints for the courts of the LORD; my heart and flesh
sing for joy to the living God.

PSALM 84:1–2 ESV

Do not be shocked, nor fear them.

DEUTERONOMY 1:29

Don't be shocked? As a society, we have almost reached that place! Nothing much shocks the most pious Christian as we walk among our neighbors and friends. We read books, our eyes trying to overlook jarring words of profanity. We attend movies, backyard parties, and socialize around the coffeepot at work, failing to notice words that used to make us blush. Disrespect, discrimination, and gossip saturate the air until someone dismisses it with a chuckle or a shrug or by simply walking away. We are losing our ability to be shocked! And few are willing to confront the issue.

If we look hard, we may find there is some good in being "unshockable." We are becoming stronger, more resilient, more stable, more experienced. More suitable for today's societal changes and spiritual battles and better prepared for the future. While we may not be in the midst of a literal war, we are all engaged in an invisible war against our souls. It is the most fearful war of all. The enemies that assail us do not ride upon horses or chariots, wearing armor and brandishing swords. They ride upon the wind, invisible, incomprehensible! We dare not be naïve. We must not give in to fear. Instead, we must stand strong and secure, clad in the whole armor of God.

Therefore take up the whole armor of God, that you may be able to withstand in the evil day, and having done all, to stand firm.

EPHESIANS 6:13 ESV

Do not fear him, for I have delivered him and all his people and
his land into your hand.

DEUTERONOMY 3:2

When God gives something into your hand, you hold the sway over
what happens next. When the Almighty delegates a certain part
of work to you, you assume the responsibility of its management.
On this occasion, God put a wicked king, the king's people, and
all his land into the hands of Israel. Quite a gift! What an opportunity! Decidedly a huge responsibility. A task of such magnitude
is enough to cause fear in the most accomplished servant. But he
equips us for the work He calls us to do.

We are not to hear God's Word and remain unaffected, nor to
simply hear and attempt to understand the Word. But we are to
hear, understand, and then actively obey! As for the scope of your
ministry, you may follow this advice, attributed to Mother Teresa:
"I never look at the masses as my responsibility, I look only at the
individual. I can love only one person at a time. I can feed only one
person at a time. Just one, one, one."

If you are energized rather than exhausted by your work, blessed
instead of burdened, and if fear turns to joy, you have found your
place. Pick up your divine work orders and do it.

Let the message about Christ, in all its richness, fill your lives.
Teach and counsel each other with all the wisdom he gives.

COLOSSIANS 3:16 NLT

Do not fear them, for the LORD your God is the one fighting for you.

DEUTERONOMY 3:22

David, the least of his family, was a young shepherd with few warrior skills. But he did know how to use a slingshot; he had used one to guard his lambs from wild animals. See him preparing for a fight he was too small to win. Imagine him testing the laces of his simple leather weapon, pocketing a few smooth stones, trying on armor that was much too big for his frame, deciding it more a hindrance than a protection, then stepping forward to confront the enemy without so much as a shield.

What was the lad thinking as he stepped toward the giant? Was he afraid? What did he say? "You come to me with a sword, a spear, and a javelin, but I come to you in the name of the LORD of hosts, the God of the armies of Israel, whom you have taunted" (1 Samuel 17:45). David may have been small in stature, but his faith stood tall and strong.

Are you facing a giant? Will you stand strong? David faced more than one giant in his lifetime, and you will, too. But God is greater than gigantic fears.

The LORD is my rock and my fortress and my deliverer, my God, my rock in whom I take refuge, my shield, and the horn of my salvation, my stronghold and my refuge, my savior; you save me from violence.

2 SAMUEL 22:2–3 ESV

You shall not be afraid of them but you shall remember what the
Lord your God did to Pharaoh and to all Egypt.

DEUTERONOMY 7:18 ESV

God is a God of second chances—and third chances, fourth
chances, and more. How many opportunities did He give Pharaoh? After years of rebellion and refusal to let God's people go, the
Lord God initiated ten plagues upon Egypt, ten chances for him to
change his mind, ten strong motivations to do life God's way. But
with every plague, Pharaoh's heart grew harder, his will more stubborn, his choices more senseless, and his attitude more belligerent.

"What doesn't kill you makes you stronger!" I've heard. After
considering Pharaoh, I'm wondering if that statement has been
around as long as the book of Exodus. Pharaoh would not relent
until he was visited by the angel of death. Only after the loss of his
firstborn son did he consider a change of heart. How sad for him,
but how life-changing it is for the captives who witnessed it, and
how crucial for Christians today to understand! Fear diminishes
when we obey God's directive—you need to remember what the
Lord did to Pharaoh. Yahweh Elohim is full of amazing grace and
infinite mercy! But He is a God of justice too.

The great trials that your eyes saw, the signs, the wonders, the
mighty hand, and the outstretched arm, by which the Lord your
God brought you out. So will the Lord your God do to all the
peoples of whom you are afraid.

DEUTERONOMY 7:19 ESV

Do not be terrified by them, for the LORD *your God, who is*
among you, is a great and awesome God.

DEUTERONOMY 7:21 NIV84

Speaker Louie Giglio said, "God opened His mouth and a ball of
fire burst forth traveling at a speed of 186,000 miles a second,
and with His words, *Let there be light*, billions of stars were created
including more than 100 billion in our own galaxy, the Milky Way.
In that galaxy our one star, our sun, circles the earth. At its core the
sun is 27,000,000 degrees."[2]

Since I don't do numbers well, it is hard for me to envision a
billion of anything. And there's no way I can comprehend twenty-
seven million degrees. The hottest hot I know about is living
through Texas summers, and that is hot enough! Still, I am thankful to Mr. Giglio for revealing this mystery of God's creation; it helps
me understand the words of Isaiah: "Who has measured the waters
in the hollow of His hand, And marked off the heavens by the span,
And calculated the dust of the earth by the measure, And weighed
the mountains in a balance And the hills in a pair of scales? . . . Who
stretches out the heavens like a curtain, And spreads them out like
a tent to dwell in?" (Isaiah 40:12–13, 22).

When you focus upon the greatness of our God, your problems, sin, worries, and fear drift away like debris into outer space.
Release it and it floats into the vast unknown.

> *When a prophet speaks in the name of the LORD, if the word does
> not come to pass or come true, that is a word that the LORD has
> not spoken; the prophet has spoken it presumptuously. You need
> not be afraid of him.*
>
> DEUTERONOMY 18:22 ESV

Why are some of us so obsessively preoccupied with the unknown?
Isn't it clear that we're to live one day at a time? If you are worried
about some calamity you might face, "Sufficient for the day is its
own trouble" (Matthew 6:34 ESV). When you are trying to change
some bad habit, addiction, or crippling thought pattern, "The LORD
directs the steps of the godly. He delights in every detail of their
lives" (Psalm 37:23 NLT). If you fret about the spiritual growth of
someone you love, be confident that "He who began a good work
in you will carry it on to completion until the day of Christ Jesus"
(Philippians 1:6 NIV). These blessed assurances are yours for the
taking, read the words often, memorize them, and say them aloud
every day.

More than one-fourth of the Bible is prophecy—more than eigh-
teen hundred verses in both the Old and New Testament. And not
one word of His prophecy has ever failed.

> *For the word of God is living and active and sharper than any
> two-edged sword, and piercing as far as the division of soul and
> spirit, of both joints and marrow, and able to judge the thoughts
> and intentions of the heart.*
>
> HEBREWS 4:12

*When you go out to battle against your enemies and see horses
and chariots and people more numerous than you, do not be
afraid of them; for the LORD your God, who brought you up from
the land of Egypt, is with you.*

DEUTERONOMY 20:1

Being sent to the front lines again and again to battle the fiercest of
enemies was enough to cause Israel's finest and best to be terrified.
Many times the enemy had larger armies, faster chariots, stronger
horses, but still the LORD said, "Do not be afraid of them!" How is it
possible to face an army like that and not be terrified?

By having a faith that pays little attention to rattling chariots,
rumbling hoofs, and clanging swords; by possessing a faith that
looks up, a faith that knows that Jehovah Elohim, the One who
brought His people out of Egypt is still with His own, ready to
rescue.

For Christ-followers today, Egypt symbolizes the world devoid
of godliness, sold out to pleasure, fascinated by riches, worshipping idols. Most of us do not fear lapsing into that exact lifestyle,
but we may fear being tempted by worldliness, affluence, position,
a certain passion outside the will of God. That is an honest fear
but not an unconquerable one. We sail upon an ocean called faith,
clinging to what God has said and what He has done for us.

---

*Now thanks be to God who always leads us in triumph in
Christ, and through us diffuses the fragrance of His knowledge
in every place.*

2 CORINTHIANS 2:14 NKJV

You will not be afraid of the terror by night, or of the arrow that flies by day.

PSALM 91:5

My husband and I had not been married long before we took up a sport that we could enjoy together: archery. He bought a magnificent bow made of dark wood, highly polished, tightly strung, with metal stabilizers mounted strategically on the front. A powerful piece of equipment, that bow! I remember the twang of the string as he released the arrow, the zing as it split the air, the thud when it hit the bull's-eye with fifty pounds of pressure. It was enough to make me cringe! My bow was cute. Made from light blond wood with a turquoise fiberglass strip between the layers. I even bought a matching outfit to wear for target practice.

Surprisingly, I became a good archer—good enough to leave six arrows in a circle about the size of a paper plate—an extra-large paper plate. I know how arrows fly and the force with which they hit their target. No wonder arrows are used as a symbol in the Bible to represent power, calamity, and injury, and, more than once, to illustrate words launched from an uncontrolled tongue. Think about it—when words fly with a certain force behind them, they penetrate, cut deep, and cause injury hard to heal.

Let us consider how we may spur one another on toward love and good deeds. Let us encourage one another—and all the more as you see the Day approaching.

HEBREWS 10:24–25 NIV84

No need to panic over alarms or surprises, or predictions that
doomsday's just around the corner.

PROVERBS 3:25 MSG

Seven million people in the United States have panic disorders,
and about one-third of them develop agoraphobia—fear of having
a panic attack in a place where they might not be able to escape or
find help. That is like being afraid of being afraid. How sad! Many
others struggle with apprehension and social unease. Feelings
that strangle joy, complicate family life, reduce productivity, and
become a snare in developing healthy relationships. Surely there is
a way to deal with the complexities of our lives without giving way
to panic.

Doctors may prescribe medication. Psychologists may help you
cope. But there is one solution that professionals and pastors agree
upon, one that is available to every person: Breathe! Relax and let
go. Some say you should confront the panic, head into it. But do
not face it alone. Instead of avoiding situations that might cause
panic, take it directly to the LORD in prayer. Breathe out stale air;
breathe in the Holy Spirit.

Delight in the LORD! Not in His gifts, not in His answers to
prayer, not in His provision, but in Him alone. And He will give
you the desires of your heart—lavish, lovely, life-altering gifts that
you may not even know you need will come your way.

————————

One thing I have asked from the LORD, that I shall seek: That I
may dwell in the house of the LORD all the days of my life.

PSALM 27:4

Be strong and courageous, do not be afraid or tremble at them,
for the LORD your God is the one who goes with you. He will not
fail you or forsake you.

DEUTERONOMY 31:6

Forsaken! A dreadful word! Nobody wants to be abandoned, deserted, or left alone, but many fear the possibility. "He will not fail you or forsake you." The promise is written again and again in the Bible. He simply *will not*! You are safe. Have you read this? "Blessed be the LORD the God of my master Abraham, who has not forsaken His lovingkindness and His truth toward my master... the LORD has guided me in the way" (Genesis 24:27).

The promise is based upon two unalterable characteristics of Jehovah—lovingkindness and truth. He will not forsake you because He would have to alter His nature to do so. He is truth! He is lovingkindness! It is a beautiful compound word that couples God's steadfast love with His great kindness, the manner in which love is given. Some theologians say the word is the Old Testament equivalent of grace. You may rest without fear, knowing you are secure in the love and kindness of our LORD.

Those of us who have watched the Olympic Games know that a victory may be won or lost by one one-hundredth of a second. Do not waste even one millisecond fearing that you might lose Him. Instead, may your heart race toward the finish line while celebrating endless grace and truth.

For the LORD will not abandon His people, nor will He forsake
His inheritance.   PSALM 94:14

It is the Lord who goes before you. He will be with you; he will not leave you or forsake you. Do not fear or be dismayed.

DEUTERONOMY 31:8 ESV

The verse begins with a fourfold promise: He goes before you, He is with you, He will not leave you, and He will not forsake you. Once we grasp this reality, there is simply no room for fear. It is truth we may need to hear again and again! Memorize it, soak in it, believe it, and the fear of losing your faith will disappear. When you do not have the strength to hold on, He is holding on to you. Paul wrote a comprehensive list of things that will not separate us from God: "neither death, nor life, nor angels, nor principalities, nor things present, nor things to come, nor powers, nor height, nor depth, nor any other created thing, will be able to separate us from the love of God, which is in Christ Jesus our Lord" (Romans 8:38–39).

A double imperative follows the promise from Deuteronomy. "Do not fear, do not be dismayed." The word "dismayed" takes us deeper into the effects of unresolved fear. It means "broken into pieces" or "broken down." It is frightening that a person who knows the Lord could become beaten down by fear. But it does happen. It will not happen to you because "it is the Lord who goes before you."

Be at rest once more, O my soul, for the Lord has been good to you.

PSALM 116:7 NIV84

You drew near when I called on You; You said, "Do not fear!"
                                            LAMENTATIONS 3:57

Most of us at one time or another are hit broadside by an unexplainable event. Bizarre circumstances, a distressing situation, or some perplexing problem leaves us wondering if the omniscient Father has blinked or turned His back on the children He loves. Our first reaction is to ask why. We want to figure it out, solve the problem, or find closure. Yet some things remain unresolved. You may ask questions. But don't be surprised if you fail to get an explanation.

A woman and her husband were near retirement, looking forward to celebrating the Golden Years, when they decided he would work one more year, and save for a special need. Before that year came to a close, he was killed in a bizarre accident at work. Of course the family asked questions. Why did they delay retirement? Why did he have to die, in such an inexplicable manner? Was God punishing them? The family faced doubt and confusion. But they got through the maze of thoughts and emotions by faith one day at a time.

You are not the only one who has questioned God's love, doubted His plan, or wondered about the veracity of His Word. There are some things we can't comprehend by human logic, but we can understand by faith.

Faith is the assurance of things *hoped for, the conviction of* *things not seen.*   HEBREWS 11:1

This day is sacred to our Lord. Do not grieve, for the joy of the
Lord is your strength.   NEHEMIAH 8:10 NIV84

God's people were secure within rebuilt walls and gates. Life in the square had taken on a new normal. Children played in the streets as their parents meandered along the walkways. Huddled in the doorway of the bakery, some hoped to purchase matzo or spices. Others sat on stone benches. The crowd swelled to more than thirty thousand before Ezra the Scribe stepped to the podium. In his hand was the book of the Law of Moses.

When he opened the book, everybody stood. Ezra began by blessing the name of Yahweh, the Great Elohim. With hands lifted, the crowd began shouting praises, but when Ezra began to read, a sacred silence enveloped them. From morning's first light until noonday, he read the Scriptures and the people listened. Thirteen priests walked among the crowd to explain the words and meet spiritual needs. "They bowed low and worshipped the Lord with *their* faces to the ground" (Nehemiah 8:6). Many of them wept! Then Nehemiah, the governor, spoke words that are well-known even today: "Do not be grieved, for the joy of the Lord is your strength" (Nehemiah 8:10).

On this first day of the Feast of Trumpets, those present received multiple blessings—hearing God's Word, feeling Yahweh's presence, finding renewed strength, and relief from grief and fear. When the joy of the Lord fills us, it is powerful, passionate, and liberating.

Open my eyes, that I may behold Wonderful things from Your
law.   PSALM 119:18

Go and enjoy choice food and sweet drinks, and send some to
those who have nothing prepared. This day is sacred to our
Lord. Do not grieve...

NEHEMIAH 8:10 NIV84

One morning a girl of nine gave her life to Christ, then cried most of the afternoon. She would gain control, talk about the experience, and cry again. She had encountered Eternal Love and Grace, and she was overwhelmed. The tears finally stopped when her mother quietly served her sandwiches and sweet iced tea.

This was only one of many times good food and tea were shared at that oak table in their kitchen. It was an altar of sorts, a place where children would speak freely, where problems were solved, decisions were made, and love was expressed. And on that table there was food—"choice food and sweet drinks." Sometimes the best thing one Christian can do for another is offer food. It meets our most basic need, calms fear, comforts grief, and soothes troubled hearts.

All through His earthly ministry, Jesus is called Bread—He satisfies the soul of every living thing, He is the bread of life, This is the true bread out of heaven, The Bread of God gives life to the world, This is my body broken for you. Throughout the story of redemption, bread has been broken, dispersed among crowds, served at tables, distributed on trays, and placed upon tongues. And every time Bread is served, it deepens our concept of Him and gives us reason to celebrate.

Then they said to Him, "Lord, always give us this bread."

JOHN 6:34

And you, son of man, neither fear them nor fear their words...
But you shall speak My words to them whether they listen or
not, for they are rebellious.

EZEKIEL 2:6–7

While we live among people with strong preferences, bold ideals, and unwavering opinions, it is refreshing to meet a person who is willing to yield. A willingness to give in, to be lenient and kind is the most Christ-like of all traits. He who dined with sinners, attended secular events, made wine for a wedding, and spent the majority of his years on Earth hanging out with carpenters, fishermen, and tax collectors is the example for us. He did not exclude anyone from his circle of friends. His pattern was to fear neither people nor their words.

As a child He yielded to the discipline of His parents, as a preteen He yielded to the teachers in the temple, as a young adult He submitted to the courts, as a man He submitted to the abuse of cruel soldiers, and as our Savior He yielded up his spirit. Someday He will be enthroned as King of kings and Lord of lords and receive the majesty and praise He deserves. Praise to the King who has invited you and me to the coronation and to the banquet that follows. In the meantime, let us always remember His kindness and grace when dealing with others.

Worthy is the Lamb that was slain to receive power and riches
and wisdom and might and honor and glory and blessing.

REVELATION 5:12

Do not be afraid to go down to Egypt, for I will make you a great nation there.

GENESIS 46:3

What kind of hard decisions are you facing today? Do you fear putting yourself in jeopardy? Do you suspect an ambiguous outcome? If so, you know something of the quandary Jacob faced as he processed his decision. He longed to spend some time with his youngest son, Joseph. But to see him, he had to visit the land of Pharaoh and do some time in enemy territory. Imagine the pull on the old gentleman's heart as he struggled with the decision. Thankfully he waited upon God before he made his choice. One night he heard a voice: "Jacob, Jacob" and he answered, "Here I am."

Scripture records what happened next. "I am God, the God of your father; do not be afraid to go down to Egypt, for I will make you a great nation there. I will go down with you to Egypt, and I will also surely bring you up again" (Genesis 46:3–4).

God spoke as if He had a first and last name, "I am God the God..."—literally, "I am *El* the *Elohim*, I am El singular, the One True God; I am the plural, three-in-one Elohim." Hearing His name removed all Jacob's fear.

Don't you love the sound of His name? He delights in knowing yours—"Jacob, Jacob" or the name of your child, "Joseph, Joseph." What joy to fellowship with God on a first-name basis. It clarifies every decision and thrills our human soul.

For he will be like a tree planted by the water . . . its leaves will be green, And it will not be anxious in a year of drought nor cease to yield fruit.

JEREMIAH 17:8

As I write on a spring afternoon in Texas, the television in the other room is predicting a tornado. We are familiar with those circular winds that dip down and wreak havoc on our lives. Trees and buildings splinter, buses overturn, cars flip. People we love may be seriously injured, sometimes killed. You may have never witnessed a tornado and its aftereffects, but you know about hurricanes, tidal waves, or floods. Sometimes the weather is downright fearsome!

We fear the weather because we can't control it! But how we have tried! Seeding clouds, and bombarding them with laser beams, and creating sonic booms. We have been at it since the 1940s. Today we are more sophisticated. We try to control the atmosphere that might produce storms—by controlling fires, reducing emissions, managing the fuels we burn. Sigh! While we take timorous steps, some of God's people are full of fear and anxious about the future of the whole wide world. Why can't we fix the weather? With all the ambiguity, maybe it's time to whittle our fears down to bite-sized pieces we can handle and trust the One who created the atmosphere in the first place.

Let us cling to the promise God made in the Garden.

While the earth remains, seedtime and harvest, and cold and heat, and summer and winter, and day and night shall not cease.

GENESIS 8:22

The LORD *said to him, "Peace to you, do not fear."*

JUDGES 6:23

Peace to you! At Jesus' birth the angels shouted it, later Psalmists sang of it, Isaiah proclaimed it, John explained it, and Jesus fulfilled it. His name is Prince of Peace. When you believe in Him and receive Him, you receive Perfect Peace.

In the 1800s, a Presbyterian pastor lost everything he owned in the Great Chicago Fire. In an effort to lift the hearts of his wife and children, he planned a family vacation. They boarded the SS *Ville du Harve* one morning filled with happiness, knowing their husband and father would join them later.

But midway in the Atlantic, the ship hit another vessel. Despite the heroic efforts of the captain, the craft sank before help arrived. All four daughters were among the 226 who drowned. Their mother was miraculously saved. When he heard the news the husband and father was deeply troubled, as one would expect. Later as he sailed toward Wales to meet his grieving wife, the ship's captain announced that they neared the place where the *Ville du Harve* had gone down. As the man stood at the rail, looking into the deep blue water, unexpected peace and comfort flooded his soul, enabling him to write what has become a well-known, deeply loved hymn. It begins with these words: "When sorrows like sea billows roll...it is well with my soul." Such is the hope and faith we have in Jesus.

God is our refuge and strength, a very present help in trouble.

PSALM 46:1

Do not let your heart be troubled . . . I go to prepare a place for you.

JOHN 14:1–3

All that we need to know about heaven is revealed in the Bible. It is the dwelling place of God, and a place of no more tears. We will reunite with the people we love along with those we've been waiting to meet. And we will know Jesus, be able to touch him, speak to him, and worship him. I know that I will have a new body, that I will not obsess about having a better one, that I will be busy, and that I will reign with Jesus. We may sit and strum harps, but only if we want to, for most of the time, we will have important work to do.

Will heaven be beautiful? Of course! The Earth is beautiful. Will it be colorful? Yes—the Designer inserted a wide spectrum of colors into its light including hues in light waves beyond our ability to see with Earth-eyes. Will there be music? As we have never heard with deeper tones and higher notes than human ears can now hear. But most important, we will rest in the divine presence of God for eternity. Sometimes when I think about our Creator unleashed, our planet untarnished by sin, I want to go to heaven today!

"What no eye has seen, nor ear heard, nor the heart of man imagined, what God has prepared for those who love him"— these things God has revealed to us through the Spirit. For the Spirit searches everything, even the depths of God.

1 CORINTHIANS 2:9–10 ESV

Take care and be calm, have no fear and do not be fainthearted
because of these two stubs of smoldering firebrands.

ISAIAH 7:4

Message T-shirts are a big fad today. A recently popular one reads: "Keep Calm and Carry On." After that shirt hit the market, spin-offs flooded stores with assorted messages, one for every man, woman, and child! *Keep Calm and Dance On, Keep Calm and Play Soccer.* Christian bookstores got in on the trend with *Keep Calm and Pray On.* One day while looking for the right T-shirt for a grandchild facing finals, I spotted one that said *Freak Out and Run About.* Perfect! This is the way of fads. They burst on the scene as a good idea and quickly grow and grow until they end up downright ridiculous!

Today's fad may be rooted in "Take Care and Be Calm" from the pen of Isaiah. Why, the idea has been around longer than we've been alive! It may stay around too, because hundreds of "smoldering firebrands" scorch the terrain, and we must keep calm so we can carry on—with or without the shirt!

No amount of angst or anxiety can put out a fire. But calm steady steps, one at a time, in step with the Holy Spirit will get you through hot spots of fear, around the parched ground of anxiety, and into green pastures.

———

Now may the Lord of peace Himself continually grant you peace
in every circumstance.

2 THESSALONIANS 3:16

You are not to say, "It is a conspiracy!" ... And you are not to
fear what they fear or be in dread of it.

ISAIAH 8:12

It's not my fault! It's a conspiracy! What lengths we go to in order to
blame somebody else. Assuming responsibility for our own mistakes requires character that we may not have acquired. Admitting
we have sinned takes maturity we may not have reached. So we
fear what others fear and we dread what they dread. We sometimes
believe we are no different from them. But we can be! And we must
be! For one fear keeps another fear alive. And while blame keeps
the wound open, forgiveness heals.

The LORD had promised to be with His people, but many
refused to believe Him. Isaiah was faithful. He warned the people of Judah they should not be afraid of Israel's alliance with the
enemy or fear their threats looming on the horizon. Instead they
should have been afraid of the LORD. He is the one they should fear
and dread. The LORD is a sanctuary, a place of safety for those who
believe in Him, but for those who do not, He will be the means of
destruction—a stone, a rock, a trap, and a fearsome snare.

O for the grace to believe, the grace to wait upon God, the grace
that comes in Jesus.

For of His fullness we have all received, and grace upon grace.
For the Law was given through Moses; grace and truth were
realized through Jesus Christ.

JOHN 1:16–17

Do not fear or be dismayed; tomorrow go out to face them, for the Lord *is with you.*

2 CHRONICLES 20:17

The king of Judah was afraid, but he knew what to do. He began to seek the Lord and proclaimed a fast throughout Judah. People gathered in the house of the Lord and the king began to pray. What a prayer it was! He reverently appealed to Yahweh the God of our Fathers and proclaimed Him the triune God. He showed honor and submission to Him by calling Him Ruler over all the Kingdoms of Earth. He declared that no one could stand against Him. He praised Him for the things He had done for His people and pledged allegiance to Him. He expressed his faith by saying, "Your people Israel...cry to You in our distress, and You will hear and deliver us" (2 Chronicles 20:7–9).

Then, only then, did he ask for anything. All Judah was standing before the Lord when the king asked: "We are powerless before this great multitude who are coming against us; nor do we know what to do, but our eyes are on You" (2 Chronicles 20:12).

After his prayer, the fight was unnecessary. God told them to stand still and see the salvation of the Lord.

Today, we have made prayer difficult. It is not a guilt-producing discipline but a fear-relieving practice.

The Lord *will give strength to His people; the* Lord *will bless His people with peace.*

PSALM 29:11

*If a ruler loses his temper against you, don't panic; a calm
disposition quiets intemperate rage.*

ECCLESIASTES 10:4 MSG

Let's pray today for a calm disposition. Not that we might learn
to squelch our anger or control our temper, but that our angry
temperament might be changed. That takes grace! Grace is not a
product of discipline, certainly not a result of mind manipulation
or willpower. You cannot set a reminder on your phone, as I do
for appointments or prayer requests. We need much more than a
reminder. We need an extreme makeover that comes from above.
Let us pray like David: "Create in me a clean heart, O God, And
renew a steadfast spirit within me" (Psalm 51:10).

When our reactions are showing, we can't fix it by dealing
with the reaction itself. That would be like spilling coffee on your
shirt and trying to clean up the mess by getting a new cup! What
really matters is what exactly is inside the cup. If there is coffee in
your cup, and someone bumps your elbow, coffee spills out—not
green tea or chocolate milk or strawberry soda. Whatever fills your
cup spills over the top, and when your life is bumped, whatever
is in your heart overflows, touching everybody within splashing
distance.

God specializes in bringing order out of chaos and He always
works from the inside out.

For I am confident of this very thing, that He who began a good
work in you will perfect it until the day of Christ Jesus.

PHILIPPIANS 1:6

Thus says the LORD to you, "Do not be afraid and do not be dismayed at this great horde, for the battle is not yours but God's."   2 CHRONICLES 20:15 ESV

The Spirit of God spoke to Judah's king, revealing the plans for battle. The enemy would ascend the mountain through a pass from the Dead Sea to the wilderness of Judah. There they would face the king's army following God's eternal plan. They were to station themselves, stand and watch to see what the LORD would do on their behalf.

Imagine an army so disciplined they would stand still and watch, trusting God to work! Judah would obey. The next morning, the king appointed a praise team to accompany his troops. They lined up and began singing praises about the LORD's faithful love that endures forever: As the first word passed their lips, the enemy topped the hill, saw the army, heard the singing, and became so confused they started killing each other. They didn't stop until every man on the battlefield was dead. Afterward, for four days, the king's men gathered the plunder from the Valley of Blessing.

When your battle is the LORD's, don't expect Him to follow a standardized plan of action. The path to triumph will be different every time. Purposefully so! For the LORD wants your undivided attention and step-by-step cooperation. Only one thing is always the same: Prayer and praise are the most powerful weapons in the Christian's arsenal.

———

This is the victory that has overcome the world—our faith.
                                                    1 JOHN 5:4

My soul is cast down within me... Deep calls to deep at the roar
of your waterfalls; all your breakers and your waves have gone
over me.

PSALM 42:6–7 ESV

Going deeper with God may be an adventure that could include
the roar of waterfalls, with breakers and waves going over you.
There may be times you are afraid, but O what blessings you will
know!

Recently scientists focused the Hubble telescope on a dark place
in deep space—a place of complete blackness. As the telescope
stayed in place with an open lens for seven full days, multitudes of
stars became visible that had never been seen before. "Deep space"
is not a new concept. Long before scientists used the term, while
the earth was void and without form, darkness covered the face of
the deep, and the Spirit of God hovered over the waters. The Holy
Trinity then began moving, speaking, creating, in deep space.

Today the Hubble telescope is finding stars that God formed
then. His crowning achievement had not yet begun. From the dust
of the earth, God created man and breathed into him the breath of
life, then man became a living soul. In the human soul there is a
"deep space," a hidden place, an emptiness or void that can only be
filled by the presence of God. Today, as the Spirit hovers over our
personal deep, He is completing the work He began in us before the
foundation of the world.

Oh, the depth of the riches both of the wisdom and
knowledge of God!   ROMANS 11:33

The LORD said to him, "Peace be to you. Do not fear."

JUDGES 6:23 ESV

When the LORD called Gideon to deliver his people from Midian, he was afraid. Especially after he heard Him say, The LORD is with you. He knew that no man could see Him and live. Gideon managed to utter two questions. "If the LORD is with us, why then has all this happened to us? And where are all His miracles which our fathers told us about?" (Judges 6:13).

Then the warrior offered an excuse. His family was the smallest tribe, and he was the least in his father's house. God was not worried about the size of the tribe or the height of the man. There was no doubt that the Sovereign One had chosen the right man for the task. As the story goes, the Valiant Warrior yielded. Good choice! He bowed before God and placed an offering on the altar. The LORD stretched forth His staff, the offering burst into flames, and He vanished from sight. Gideon built an altar and the LORD Himself named it Yahweh Shalom—The LORD Is Peace.

We are all like Gideon in many ways. We ask, "Why this? Where are the miracles?" We make excuses, feel inept, and are afraid. But when God shows up, victory is on the way. Today He does not appear then disappear. He comes in the person of the Holy Spirit, and He does not just stop by. He abides forever, filling our lives with power, love, joy, and good fruit.

For to me, to live is Christ and to die is gain.

PHILIPPIANS 1:21

*Oh that they had such a heart in them, that they would fear Me
and keep My commandments always, that it may be well with
them and with their sons forever!*

DEUTERONOMY 5:29

One year, as my mother's birthday passed, I became lonely. The pain of losing her has diminished, but I do still miss her—especially on certain occasions. Then I relive the past, the precious moments, her rock-solid wisdom, her great recipes, and the funny episodes. Today I'm feeling a bit nostalgic.

Mother and I had gone to visit her mama, my grandmother. Standing at the foot of the bed, I felt overwhelmed by her aged frame barely making a lump beneath the sheets. *Mama's lived entirely too long*, I thought, *why doesn't she give up? Why doesn't God take her on home?*

My mother warmed a cloth and began to wash her face. She brushed her hair and applied lotion to her gnarled hands. I overheard her saying, "Everything's okay, Mama, I'm here, I love you." My heart melted as I thought about my rich heritage from these two women and suddenly my grandmother's 103 years were not enough.

Later, my fear of the future faded as I prayed, thanking God for the accumulated years of health and well-being the women in my family had received. I thought of the bright future we would have together in heaven, sitting in the shadow of the Most High. And my heart filled with joy and peace.

Faithful is He who calls you, and He also will bring it to pass.

1 THESSALONIANS 5:24

Peace I leave with you; my peace I give to you. Not as the world gives do I give to you. Let not your hearts be troubled, neither let them be afraid.

JOHN 14:27 ESV

One Sunday morning our pastor said something that should remove all fear and provide perfect peace to those bemoaning the aging process, or facing a precarious situation, or fearing leaving planet earth. "I know that my days are predetermined by God." He grinned and added, "Until He is finished with me, I am indestructible. When it's time for me to go, it's indisputable." Then he pushed his hands into his pockets, shrugged, and added, "That's why I ride motorcycles."

I laughed along with the rest of the congregation, but those words have stayed with me, reminding me that God is totally in charge of life. And He is especially close in those sacred moments near the end. Do not let your heart be troubled or afraid; as you settle into God's plan, you are indestructible! We cannot do anything to override His Sovereignty. Be courageous Adventurous Seekers of truth, you are totally safe in the hands of our all-powerful, sovereign God, and He is not finished with you yet.

All the days ordained for me were written in your book before one of them came to be.

PSALM 139:16 NIV84

Do not fear or be dismayed because of this great multitude, for the battle is not yours but God's.

2 CHRONICLES 20:15

How fearless would your heart be while living among masses with a different belief system? Could you live out your faith and follow Christian beliefs in an atmosphere of indifference? When there is oppression? When in danger of losing your family? When you fear persecution or even death?

Today we can no longer assume that the Bible is revered and respected in the world, that it is believed by most, or acknowledged as true. Even in the United States, a nation that from its inception has been called "Christian," many question the Bible's place as the basis of our system of laws and the foundation of our society. How do these changes touch your ministry, your family, or your own life?

What can we do? We can teach the truth to our children and to others who trust us. We can reach out in love to the seeking, the hurt, and the wounded. We can do the things that touch a human heart. After all, that is where Jesus dwells today, and that is where love makes a difference. Do not fear, even if you are in the minority, because the Lord is with you *and the battle is God's.*

"I will vindicate the holiness of My great name which has been profaned among the nations . . . Then the nations will know that I am the Lord," declares the Lord God, "when I prove Myself holy among you in their sight."

EZEKIEL 36:23

"I am the LORD your God; you shall not fear the gods of the Amorites in whose land you dwell." But you have not obeyed my voice.

JUDGES 6:10 ESV

As a young woman married with children, I attended a Bible study class taught by a teacher I adored. Permanently attached to the wall behind her chair was a poster declaring: "There is One God; You are not Him." It made me smile, as it was meant to do. The absurdity of it was laughable. But in reality, dysfunctional beings that we are, we try to usurp His role without really thinking what we are doing. We might never assert it aloud; we might not build an idol or openly deny our faith. But in our self-centeredness, we may simply choose another god, one that pleases ourselves. We can be subtle idolaters—forgetting to ask before making a decision, failing to seek God's face, allowing the pressures of life to direct our path.

Do not take this type of idolatry lightly. Don't laugh it off or think it funny. And do not be afraid to admit or confront it. Instead, talk to the LORD your God. Run into His arms and rest upon Him. He always accepts you just as you are. And He changes a person's soul from inside out, upside down, and in response to repentance and humility.

I am the way, and the truth, and the life. No one comes to the Father except through me.

JOHN 14:6 ESV

Do not let your heart be troubled; believe in God, believe
also in Me.

JOHN 14:1–2

Jesus is God! "I am in the Father, and the Father is in Me" (John 14:10). Jesus is in the Father. The Father is in Jesus. They are so completely one that even the words Jesus spoke were considered words of the Father.

Jesus is Creator. We often think about Jesus and God as separate beings, but in the writings of John, their union as One God becomes clear. "In the beginning was the Word, and the Word was with God, and the Word was God. He was in the beginning with God. All things came into being through Him, and apart from Him nothing came into being that has come into being" (John 1:1–3). During creation, the Trinity—God the Father, God the Son, God the Holy Spirit—were One as they put the earth together from its state of being without form and void.

Jesus is Life and the Life is the Light of all men (see John 1:4). Jesus brought light into our spiritual darkness, atoned for our sins through His death, and revealed the promise of redemption through His resurrection. He said that seeing Him was equivalent to seeing the Father (see John 14:9). Seeing is about more than visual recognition. We see with the mind, become acquainted by experience, and perceive in the heart. The more we see Jesus, the less we know fear.

I am in My Father, and you in Me, and I in you.

JOHN 14:20.

Even though I walk through the valley of the shadow of death, I fear no evil.

PSALM 23:4

The metaphor of the shepherd came easily to an author like David, for he spent his teen years taking care of his father's sheep. What he learned in green pastures is revealed to us in one of the best-loved, most often memorized poems in the Bible. In the heart of the psalm, he gives two reasons why he is fearless: I fear no evil, for you are with me; I fear no evil because your rod and staff comfort me. Today in life's darkest circumstances, fear is washed in light as He leads us. On days when we stumble, His rod and staff guide us one timorous step at a time.

The shepherd's rod and staff were not instruments of punishment; rather the rod was but a simple walking stick and the staff was a smooth shepherd's crook used to guide the sheep when they wandered from the flock, to stop them from walking too close to a cliff, or to lift them when a foot became stuck in a crevice.

We are promised not only protection but green pastures, quiet waters, secure places to rest, and knowledge that the shepherd would lead us safely home. Do not be afraid, His lambs. You are perfectly safe in the arms of the Great Shepherd of the Sheep.

He tends his flock like a shepherd: He gathers the lambs in his arms and carries them close to his heart; he gently leads those that have young.

ISAIAH 40:11 NIV84

O My people who dwell in Zion, do not fear the Assyrian who strikes you with the rod and lifts up his staff against you.

ISAIAH 10:24

The same instruments that brought comfort to David's sheep brought fear to God's people when clutched in the hands of an enemy. How significant! For it is always so. It's not the rod itself, not the staff, not a rock, or a knife or a sword that wounds the Christian soldier. Those are inanimate objects. It is the person with a sinful heart that must be changed. The Assyrians were the most fearsome of Israel's enemies. Their reputation for brutality and savagery was known throughout the land. Thankfully, after God used them to accomplish His purpose among His own people, His anger turned toward Assyria. God in fairness was merciful to the people of Zion.

Let us pray for hearts that see beneath surface problems and into the soul of human need. May we love others for who they may become in Christ. May we befriend the friendless, love the sinner, and accept those with different points of view. And as we walk in today's world, may we represent the Christ well.

Lord, I am often overwhelmed by the needs of the world around me. Thank you that you are responsible for the world and that I am not. Help me see the individual today—the one, the one, the one—that the words and actions that flow from my life might reflect your life.

PETER SCAZZERO[3]

When the disciples saw Him walking on the sea, they were terrified.

MATTHEW 14:26

The disciples could barely see land from where they had drifted, waves battered their small boat, and the wind was fearsome. I think I understand, even though I am not even close to a lake. We celebrated Mother's Day recently and I thought about my children. I am the mother of three adult men. One now dwells far from the land he calls home, literally halfway around the globe in a country I know little about. Another, battered by waves of trouble, had not called. Yet another is flattened by the strong winds of adversity and chronic illness. I felt weak, afraid, and lonely.

As I waited before the Lord, a picture came to mind of Jesus walking on the water, and beneath his feet were all the things that troubled me, including my three sons bobbing in the sea. My heart soared as I remembered something I'd heard once at a conference. "What is over your head is under His feet." Jesus was there with those children of mine! He was also here with me!

Before long, my cell phone rang and I talked with International Son. Then I made plans with Eldest Son for dinner; and later, just as I headed off to bed, Mischievous Son called to say, "I just wanted to be *last* to wish you Happy Mother's Day." As we laughed together, what had been over my head disappeared under the Master's feet. While He walked on water, I slept peacefully.

"What is over your head is under His feet."

Do not be afraid of them. Remember the Lord, who is great and awesome.

NEHEMIAH 4:14 ESV

The word "awesome" has been used so frequently and haphazardly that it has lost its true meaning. It means much more than being "cool." It defines an emotion of absolute astonishment and awe, describes a person or thing so exceptional or so holy that it inspires reverence. Really, there are only a few things in this world that are truly awesome. Our Lord may be the only Person worthy of being so called!

He is awesome in His very nature: Almighty, all-powerful, always present, ever aware, in control of all things. He is love, the fullness of grace, and the embodiment of truth. When you hear the word, used or misused, may it remind you to praise the only One who is "totally awesome."

The Lord is also great! He is great because of what He has done, because of what He is doing, and because of what He is capable of doing. He is the creator, sustainer of life, the author of salvation, our redeemer, our Father, our Husband, our Friend. He is good, and wise, and all sufficient. May His praise be forever in my mouth!

I will praise the Lord at all times. I will constantly speak his praises. I will boast only in the Lord; let all who are helpless take heart. Come, let us tell of the Lord's greatness; let us exalt his name together.

PSALM 34:1–3 NLT

*Don't be afraid of the enemy! Remember the Lord, who is
great and glorious, and fight for your brothers, your sons, your
daughters, your wives, and your homes!*

NEHEMIAH 4:14 NLT

God's people were rebuilding the walls of Jerusalem. Divine work
orders had been issued. Laborers were committed to the work and
were making progress. Then they became entangled in an unlikely
battle with some bystanders—psychological warfare, complete
with taunting, heckling, and wrong accusations. The builders
became discouraged; the bullying had been effective. The real truth
of the matter was quite evident—the walls were halfway built, the
gaps were filled in; they just needed to build upward and finish.
The enemy was afraid of them and their success.

Why is it, when you reach the halfway point in a God-given
project, the enemy drops by clanging spoons on dishpans, throw-
ing rocks over walls, or sending e-mails to slow you down? The
war is fought on the battlefield of your mind, where words become
more powerful than arrows! If you think you can, you can. If you
think you cannot, well...you crumple, defeated from inside out.
The wall-builders sought God and received a plan. Half the people,
including families, stood guard while the other half stacked stones.
A similar plan works well for us today. Rally together, and do not
quit!

---

*Wait for the LORD; be strong and let your heart take courage;
yes, wait for the LORD.*

PSALM 27:14

*You will be hidden from the scourge of the tongue, and you will
not be afraid of violence when it comes.*

JOB 5:21

Job, critically ill with a disease that was destroying his skin, experienced excruciating pain. But that was not his only concern. He
had lost his health, his fortune, his wife, and ten children. Still,
fear is seldom mentioned in Job's story. When it was, it involved
"the scourge of the tongue." Not the fear of infected skin, not fear
of divorce, not even fearing the death of his children, but of someone's tongue! It was a fear that proved seemly!

News of Job's trouble traveled fast. Mike Mason, author of *The
Gospel According to Job*, wrote, "What a blessing it would be to have
just one friend who would drop everything at a moment's notice,
travel any distance and stick by one's bedside night and day for
an entire week!"[4] Job had three. For seven days they sat with him
and mourned silently. Unfortunately, still bodies do not mean
quiet minds! They decided that Job must have sinned. Then they
felt led to share! They should have remained silent, for they got
it all wrong. God's ways are always totally incomprehensible and
unexplainable—apart from faith!

---

*You have heard of the steadfastness of Job, and you have seen
the purpose of the Lord, how the Lord is compassionate and
merciful.*

JAMES 5:11 ESV

Do not be afraid when a man becomes rich, when the glory of his house is increased.

PSALM 49:16

It is a problem that has been around from wealthy Abraham, to the poor man begging at the temple gate, and includes throngs of people today. Whether gathering, spending, or working to acquire more, wealth causes fear in the hearts of us all. The poor are intimidated by the rich. The rich are frightened by the poor. And the in-betweens fear both.

What counts is not *how much* wealth you possess but how you handle what you have! It is *the love of money*, not money itself, that is the root of all evil. Wealth is a blessing from the owner of everything—the cattle on a thousand hills along with the earth and all it contains. If you love money, if your security is all wrapped up in it, if you hoard it and shut your ear to the cries of the poor, then incorporate this quote into your financial strategy: "If riches increase, do not set *your* heart *upon them*" (Psalm 62:10).

Every single one of us needs grace to handle our possessions in righteous ways. We need grace to give and grace to receive. Whatever your financial state, no matter how you invest or save, do not fear. It is "In God we trust"! His name is Jehovah-Jireh, the God Who Provides.

God is able to make all grace abound to you, so that having all sufficiency in all things at all times, you may abound in every good work.

2 CORINTHIANS 9:8 ESV

The LORD is my light and my salvation; whom shall I fear? The
LORD is the stronghold of my life; of whom shall I be afraid?

PSALM 27:1 ESV

The LORD does not *give* us light; He *is* our Light. Light within us,
light surrounding us, light reflected through us, light revealed to
us. He illumines the darkness of our spiritual condition, reveals
the light of His truth, and He abides with us always becoming the
lamp for our feet and the light for our path. When we believe and
receive Him, He doesn't simply grant us salvation; He *becomes* our
salvation. Delivered from sin and freed from temptation, we find
daily grace to live a blessed life and future grace to know eternal
security. The LORD is our stronghold and our defense. We dwell in a
strong, fortified place where nothing can harm.

With these provisions in Him, *"of whom shall I be afraid?"* The
answer is nothing and nobody—not darkness, not the fear of man,
not calamity, not fear of being lost, not fear of being separated from
God. We are altogether perfectly confident, and we assert it boldly
as David did.

Confidence in Him assures complete confidence. Our fearlessness rests upon a rock-solid foundation—the supreme power of
the Omnipotent, Great, I AM.

For it is you who light my lamp; the LORD my God lightens my
darkness. For by you I can run against a troop, and by my God I
can leap over a wall.

PSALM 18:28–29 ESV

Though a host encamp against me, My heart will not fear;
though war arise against me, in spite of this I shall be confident.

PSALM 27:3

David is confident even though an army may pitch their tents and set up camp to hinder his forward movement; even if a great host of spiritual enemies attempts to stop all advancement. Even in the midst of battle, when enemies flash their swords or prepare to lob firebombs in his direction, David says, "I will not fear...I shall be confident." There is no hesitancy in his declaration of fearlessness, no timidity in asserting his confident state of mind. Why? Because he is not talking about *self-confidence* but *God-confidence*.

When God is the source of your confidence, to proclaim it shows no pride. It reveals the opposite, the very essence of humility. *He is what I am not and I bow before Him.* What is your confidence level? What is your source of confidence?

The LORD is exalted when His people put their confidence in Him. So He waits. He waits to extend grace; He waits to show mercy; He waits for you to place yourself and your confidence in Him. Then He invites you to wait for Him. Both giver and receiver must wait! And His timing is always perfect.

Therefore will Jehovah wait, that he may be gracious unto you;
and therefore will he be exalted, that he may have mercy upon
you: for Jehovah is a God of justice; blessed are all they that wait
for him.

ISAIAH 30:18 ASV

*He will not fear evil tidings; his heart is steadfast, trusting in
the LORD.*

PSALM 112:7

"Praise the LORD. How blessed is the man who fears the LORD"
(Psalm 112:1). The Psalm begins with praise and continues by
describing the blessings that come to a person who fears the Lord.
"Fear" in this instance means "to stand in awe" of Him, to "revere"
and "respect" Him. The world cannot see into a person's heart; it
only sees on-the-surface appearance. But people will find comfort
and joy in the blessings that sprout and grow in the tender soil
of a heart that is consecrated. Compassion pops through the soil
like crocuses in spring, and graciousness flowers day after day like
morning glories. Those who fear the Lord cultivate righteousness,
handle matters with justice, delight in His commandments, and
will never be shaken.

"*Praise the Lord*" cannot be repeated too much. We need to be
reminded. He is always deserving of praise, and we who love Him
should constantly offer it. His majesty, supremacy, and infinite
knowledge beg us to bow before Him in reverent fear. His endless
love, grace, and mercy lift our hearts, lift up our heads, and fuel
abundant praise.

―――――――

*I will praise the LORD at all times. I will constantly speak his
praises. I will boast only in the LORD; let all who are helpless take
heart. Come, let us tell of the LORD's greatness; let us exalt his
name together.*

PSALM 34:1–3 NLT

He was afraid and said, "How awesome is this place! This is none other than the house of God, and this is the gate of heaven."

GENESIS 28:17

Jacob received a blessing from his father, Isaac, and left his homeland to settle in the land of Abraham. On the way, he stopped to spend a night beneath the moon and stars. Choosing a stone for a pillow, he fell fast asleep. In a dream, he saw a ladder stretching up to the heavens with angels ascending and descending on its rungs. At the top stood Yahweh.

Jacob was afraid! And no wonder! But his fear was ungrounded. The LORD had come bearing good news! Promising to exalt him, to establish him, to bless him. Yahweh's presence had surrounded and sanctified this mountaintop place, so Jacob set his stone pillow as a marker, anointed it with oil, and called the place Bethel—the house of God and the gate of heaven.

An experience exactly like Jacob's will never happen to you or me! But we can know Him. We have the complete, divinely inspired, and carefully translated Word of God. It is authentic, efficacious, and easily understood. Whatever your need, however deep your fear, however broken your heart, the answer is found at Bethel—go back to the House of God and rediscover His truth.

Behold, I am with you and will keep you wherever you go, and will bring you back to this land; for I will not leave you until I have done what I have promised you.

GENESIS 28:15

The LORD is for me; I will not fear; what can man do to me?

PSALM 118:6

Before you ask, "What can man do to me?" remember "the LORD is for me." Because the psalmist knew His name was LORD, he could say without a moment's hesitation, "I will not fear." What is it about the name that wipes out fear? When you see it written in capital letters, it means Yahweh (in Hebrew) or Jehovah (in English). It's the proper name of the one true God. Literally it means "being," "essence," or "life." So when you read "LORD" in the Bible, think of Jehovah as the only Being who needs no other source, because He is life; He is the One Who in Himself possesses essential life and permanent existence.

In *LORD, I Want to Know You*, Kay Arthur wrote, "Jehovah is the self-existent One—'I AM WHO I AM.' He is the eternal I AM, the Alpha and the Omega, the same yesterday, today, and forever. All of life is contained in Him. Why do we look elsewhere? Why do we not rest in His unchangeableness? He has never failed yet. Would He begin with me or you? Of course not! He cannot; He is Jehovah, the self-existent covenant-keeping God."[5]

What can man do to you when you live in continual union with Him? You too can declare with confidence and unshakeable faith "I will not fear!"

The LORD is my strength and my song; he has become my salvation.

PSALM 118:14 ESV

Do not fear, for I am with you . . . Surely I will uphold you with
My righteous right hand.

ISAIAH 41:10

Hands! They offer affection, show deference, validate friendship, give security, reveal tenderness, express love. But when God's *right* hand is extended to us, it's a display of honor, power, and conquering strength. In God's hands we are favored; in His right hand we are fearless. Two reasons are given why we do not fear. First, because God always promises "I am with you"—and that would be quite enough! Knowing we are never alone—God looking over us, Jesus beside us, the Holy Spirit within us. But He also promises "to uphold us with His righteous right hand."

Hands are mentioned over a thousand times in the Bible in at least twenty different ways, representing many different attitudes and actions. Hands speak of power, including God's power to deliver us. They represent service. When washed, hands speak of innocence; when kissed, they mean well loved; when extended, they indicate trust and friendship. When lifted up, they may mean dependence, submission to God, or worship. When the right hand is mentioned, it shows honor and favor or security and peace.

Today Jesus sits at the right hand of God where He intercedes for us. Someday we will sit at the right hand of Jesus. There we will reign with Him forever. Forever unafraid!

I have set the LORD always before me; because he is at my right
hand, I shall not be shaken.   PSALM 16:8 ESV

Lift up your voice mightily, O Jerusalem, bearer of good news;
lift it up, do not fear. Say to the cities of Judah, "Here is your
God!"

ISAIAH 40:9

One day a woman in our Bible study group showed me a glass containing about four ounces of water. She asked, "What do you see?" I knew the answer she wanted—a glass half full or half empty. Then she could figure out whether I was a pessimist or an optimist. I playfully eluded the question, saying, "Hmmm, all I see is a glass with some water in it." We both laughed and then I answered, "Today, the glass is about half full. Tomorrow, well . . . it might be half empty!" She walked away smiling!

It's not a question that can always be answered the same way. On a good day, the glass might overflow. But on a terrible, horrible, no good, very bad day, it may be almost empty. For most of us, the difference between being full or empty depends upon circumstances.

But our moods do not have to be a reflection of our circumstances. We have the opportunity of changing the direction of today by changing our focus. "Lift your voice mightily" and say, "Here is your God." You will find your heart brimming and running over with joy as you look up and proclaim the good news to those who need to hear. *"Lift it up; do not fear. Say to the cities 'Here is your God!'"*

———————

May your unfailing love rest upon us, O Lord, even as we put
our hope in you.   PSALM 33:22 NIV84

Thus says the LORD, "Do not ... be terrified by the signs of the
heavens although the nations are terrified by them."

JEREMIAH 10:2

From the Tower of Babel built to worship the stars, to ancient
astronomers seeking to find God at the end of a telescope, to present stargazers and fortune-tellers trying to make a living, people
have been fascinated and terrified "by the signs of the heavens."
How easily our minds and hearts can become distracted from
the majestic beauty and celestial light of our universe, to the
underbelly of the world, to a place where witchcraft and demonic
activity flourish and chaos and fear develop like mold in dark
corners. Rather than delighting in the grandeur of creation, we
have perverted it, turning beauty into ashes.

If you distort creation by placing confidence in fortune-tellers,
card-readers, or mediums, you may find yourself facing fear, anxiety, depression, and spiritual confusion. Thankfully, you can begin
to reverse the consequences by placing your affections for the fir-
mament in its God-designed place and setting your faith in God
alone.

When I consider Your heavens, the work of Your fingers, the
moon and the stars, which You have ordained; what is man that
You take thought of him ... You have made him a little lower
than God, and You crown him with glory and majesty! ... O
LORD, our Lord, how majestic is Your name in all the earth!

PSALM 8:3–5, 9

*Do not fear, O land, rejoice and be glad, for the L*ORD *has done great things.*

JOEL 2:21

Everything on our planet suffers the effects of the fall. Before sin contaminated the Garden of Eden, the trees bloomed, produced fruit, and stood tall. Berry vines, fig trees, and all manner of plant life flourished in the rich soil. Afterward, the ground produced briars, weeds, thorns, and soil that needed to be fertilized and tended. There is still a curse on the land that farmers, gardeners, flower lovers, and arborists must deal with today. Imagine the joy of having that curse lifted!

A land rich in natural resources, abundant produce, beautiful flowers, and fruit-bearing trees awaits us. A land without boundary disputes, unfenced, unrestricted, clean, and free. Jesus will be the King. His subjects may bask in His glory and bathe in the sun's warmth. There we will dwell for a thousand years and then throughout an incomprehensible eternity.

---

*Great is the L*ORD *and greatly to be praised in the city of our God! His holy mountain, beautiful in elevation, is the joy of all the earth, Mount Zion, in the far north, the city of the great King.*

PSALM 48:1–2 ESV

Do not fear, beasts of the field, for the pastures of the wilderness have turned green, for the tree has borne its fruit, the fig tree and the vine have yielded in full.

JOEL 2:22

When our son asked our pastor if his dog had gone to heaven, I was captivated by his answer. He bent low, holding his Bible in his hand, then knelt on one leg to reach eye level with our four-year-old. Resting his large hand around my child's tiny shoulders, he gently told him that, although the Bible doesn't say whether there will be dogs in heaven, all of God's creations are good and He never wastes anything. Because dogs are special to us, God loves them too. He will do what is right for them.

The child answered with a simple "Thank you" as the fear and worry faded from his wrinkled forehead. The pastor's kindness, his tone of voice, and his words of simple wisdom had soothed the troubled heart of our son and blessed mine as well.

Still, I didn't know how much God cares for animals until I read from the verse above. "Don't be afraid, you animals of the field" (Joel 2:22 NLT). Even animals live under the earth's curse. But someday they will live freely without fear. All of His creations thrive by His bounty.

When you open your hand, you satisfy the hunger and thirst of every living thing.

PSALM 145:16 NLT

I will save you that you may become a blessing. Do not fear; let your hands be strong.

ZECHARIAH 8:13

As the people were rebuilding the temple, the LORD offered encouragement. His intention was to save them from fear and help them "become a blessing." On another occasion, He spoke similarly to Zerubbabel: "Take courage...and work; for I am with you...The latter glory of this house will be greater than the former" (Haggai 2:4, 9). The assurance of being a future blessing always encourages the present task. Everybody needs encouragement. Without it we forget that we are valuable in God's kingdom.

But your words have the power to actually give courage and hope to others. That's what "en-courage" literally means! Ken Sutterfield wrote, "When we realize the value of mutual encouragement, consider the power unleashed, and what could be accomplished, it is exciting to think that God has challenged us to encourage one another. The power of your encouraging words, whether spoken or written can make the difference in the outcome of a single event or even one's life."[6]

Really? Then we need to speak up. You do not have to be a teacher, preacher, or saint; you don't need a degree or the gift of wisdom. Just open up your heart...and your mouth.

Let us consider how to stir up one another to love and good works...encouraging one another, and all the more as you see the Day drawing near.   HEBREWS 10:24–25 ESV

So I have again purposed in these days to do good to Jerusalem and to the house of Judah. Do not fear!

ZECHARIAH 8:15

"God is Great; God is Good; Let us thank Him for our food." A prayer simple in its wording, but deep in content. For God is both Great *and* Good. Do you need to be reminded? He is great in power, great in love, great in grace. He is good when giving. Good when protecting. Good when leading. Good when He allows tests. Good to permit pain. In everything and in all ways "God is Great, God is Good." With our focus upon these two attributes, irrational fear diminishes and fades quietly away.

In the words of Stephen Charnock: "The goodness of God comprehends all his attributes. All the acts of God are nothing else but the manifestations of his goodness. When Moses longed to see his glory, God tells him... 'I will make all *my goodness* pass before thee.' What is this but the train of all his lovely perfections springing from his goodness; the whole catalogue of mercy, grace, long-suffering, abundance of truth summed up in this word. All are streams from this fountain; he could be none of this were he not first good."[7]

Do not fear; God has purposed good for you.

The Lord is gracious and compassionate, slow to anger and rich in love. The Lord is good to all; he has compassion on all he has made.

PSALM 145:8–9 NIV84

"As for the promise which I made you when you came out of Egypt, My Spirit is abiding in your midst; do not fear!"

HAGGAI 2:5

When the Holy Spirit abides in our midst, all our fear is hidden in Him. The Holy Spirit fills our hearts to overflowing, infuses His love, grace, wisdom, kindness, patience, joy, and peace, so there is simply no room for an opposing attitude. Jesus explained it beautifully to His disciples like this when He gathered them on the shores of Galilee before his ascension.

He promised to pray for them because He was going away temporarily. He would ask the Father to send another comforter that would never leave them. This was a spiritual reality that the world could not possibly understand. But the disciples did, because they knew Him well. Jesus called the other comforter the "Spirit of Truth." "You know him," Jesus concluded, "for he abides with you and will be in you . . . In that day you will know that I am in my Father, and you in me, and I in you" (John 14:17, 14:20).

How incredibly close is the relationship between you and God! How safe! How unafraid we become! When the Holy Spirit, the Helper, and the Spirit of Truth abide in a person's heart, and that person abides in Jesus, and Jesus is in union with the Father, there is no room left for fear.

———

And they shall not teach . . . saying, "Know the Lord," for they shall all know me, from the least of them to the greatest.

HEBREWS 8:11 ESV

The LORD has taken away His judgments against you, He has cleared away your enemies. The King of Israel, the LORD, is in your midst; you will fear disaster no more.

ZEPHANIAH 3:15

You will not be judged, because the LORD has taken all judgment upon Himself. Your enemies have been removed. You will fear disaster no more! You are living under the rule of the King of Israel who is the Christ. There is no need to fear disaster. You are completely safe. What kind of day is the writer describing? A day when God's people will live without judgment, no enemy, no disaster, and no fear, under the rule of King Jesus? It must be "that day"! The great "Day of the LORD."[8]

And what a day it will be! God's Holy Hill will be inhabited by people who trust the LORD, who are good and kind, holy and fair. Jerusalem will resound with joyful voices of praise, and there will be no sorrow or tears. The former things will have passed away and all things will be new. This is the time when lions will lay down with the lambs and a child can safely play beside snakes and asps. Perfection. Holiness. Peace. Worship. Praise. Endless joy—perhaps with our favorite pets. And there will be no more fear! Maranatha! Come quickly, Lord Jesus!

Blessed be the name of the LORD from this time forth and forevermore! From the rising of the sun to its setting, the name of the LORD is to be praised!

PSALM 113:2–3 ESV

Fear not, O Zion... The LORD your God is in your midst, a
mighty one who will save; he will rejoice over you with gladness;
he will quiet you by his love; he will exult over you with loud
singing.

ZEPHANIAH 3:16–17 ESV

What is it that moves your heart to praise the LORD your God? Is it when you feel lonely and suddenly remember that He is always "in your midst"? When your heart is overcome with the reality that He is Omnipresent? Does praise surprise you sometimes when you are thanking Him for delivering you from sin and taking care of you every day? In unexpected moments of reality, in the discovery of some new truth, in times of intercession, does your heart erupt into praise? Of course!

But in the verse above, you are not praising Him; the LORD is praising you. Can you, broken and imperfect being that you are now, even imagine that there will be a day of receiving Yahweh's expressions of love and adoration and words of praise? Imagine perfect praise being directed toward you. Inexpressible, inconceivable. To say that the redeemed are not worthy would be to reject His love, so you yield, allowing Him to adore you, and He "quiets you by his love." And from the mouth that spoke the universe into existence, He begins to sing with notes clearer and purer than any heard before. It is the King singing to His rose of Sharon.

Then those who sing as well as those who play the flutes shall
say, "All my springs of joy are in you."

PSALM 87:7

I will not be afraid, for you are close beside me. Your rod and your staff protect and comfort me.

PSALM 23:4 NLT

Like two preachers talking theology, Jesus and Simon Peter had analyzed, scrutinized, and confirmed their relationship. Jesus asked three times if Peter loved Him. Peter had answered yes, but with words different from the Agape standard Jesus had set. Along with the questions and ambiguous answers, Jesus introduced another topic also three times—an addendum that put feet to their weighty discussion about love. See John 21:15–17, where Jesus told Peter, "Tend My lambs...Shepherd My sheep...Tend My sheep."

The word "tend" shows the duty of a pastor/shepherd "to promote in every way the spiritual welfare of the members of the church." To "shepherd" means to "rule, govern, furnish pasture, serve the body of Christ, and supply the requisites for the soul's need."

Jesus had a plan for Peter's life—to shepherd the church. A rugged fisherman, a man who had failed repeatedly, would preach to the crowd gathered in Jerusalem and over three thousand people would believe. The man whose name means "little stone" would become a mighty rock. Jesus was saying, *Peter, I know you are not perfect. You are weak in many ways. You don't even love Me the way you should, but you are usable. You are valuable to Me.*

God delights in using less-than-perfect, flawed individuals so it is obvious to all that everything praiseworthy comes from elsewhere.

———————

The LORD lives, and blessed be my rock; and exalted be the God of my salvation.   PSALM 18:46

SPRING

For behold, the winter is past;
the rain is over and gone;
The flowers appear on the earth,
the time of the singing of birds is come,
and the voice of the turtle dove
is heard in our land.
The fig tree ripens its figs,
and the vines are in blossom;
they give a good fragrance.
Arise my love, my beautiful one,
and come away.

SONG OF SOLOMON 2:11–13 ESV

On that day it shall be said to Jerusalem: "Fear not, O Zion; let
not your hands grow weak. The LORD your God is in your midst,
a mighty one who will save."

ZEPHANIAH 3:16–17 ESV

Another translation of the verse above reads "Do not let your hands
fall limp," which pictures a state worse than fear—that of despair.
What the LORD desires are hands lifted in faith, not hanging limp
in hopelessness. Hands of strength, hands of victory, hands of
triumph—a perfect display of adoration to the LORD. Someday He
will not only dwell in our midst, but He will rejoice over you with
gladness!

An elderly friend once said, "I didn't give my hands permission
to grow weak; they went there by themselves in spite of exercise,
good nutrition, and a few supplements. They are aging hands that
feel the pain of twisted, inflamed joints. Hands that want to help,
but I can't stop the weakness." After years of difficulty, the people of Jerusalem had grown tired and allowed their hands to grow
weak, their hearts heavy with fear.

Our hands, whether youthful and strong or aging and losing
their grip, need to be lifted up to Jehovah Elohim, the Mighty One
who is willing to save. Put your hands into His and rejoice in His
Almighty power.

Therefore lift your drooping hands and strengthen your weak
knees, and make straight paths for your feet, so that what is
lame may not be put out of joint but rather be healed.

HEBREWS 12:12–13 ESV

The fear of the LORD is the beginning of wisdom.

PSALM 111:10

If you seek wisdom, begin with a worthwhile, honorable, holy fear of God. For all who fear the Lord—have a heart that honors, reveres, respects, and adores Him—will gain wisdom, grow in wisdom, and communicate wisdom. The fear of the LORD comes first for that is the "beginning of wisdom."

One way to develop a healthy fear of the LORD is to search for wisdom in the book of Proverbs. Written by Solomon, the wisest man of his day, you will find 3,000 proverbs, 1,005 songs, and other collected bits of wisdom that he compiled. "In addition to being a wise man, the Preacher also taught the people knowledge; and he pondered, searched out and arranged many proverbs" (Ecclesiastes 12:9).

It becomes clear as you read Proverbs that wisdom has a deeply significant meaning. Try substituting "Christ" in the place of the word "wisdom," for He is the personification of wisdom. Paul affirmed this truth, writing "In whom lie hidden all the treasures of wisdom" (Colossians 2:3). Knowing Him is tantamount to knowing wisdom—wisdom for life, wisdom in relationship, wisdom for business, wisdom of conduct, wisdom in righteousness.

I ask him that with both feet planted firmly on love, you'll be able to take in with all followers of Jesus the extravagant dimensions of Christ's love. Reach out and experience the breadth! Test its length! Plumb the depths! Rise to the heights! Live full lives, full in the fullness of God.   EPHESIANS 3:15–19 MSG

> *"Do not fear, you worm Jacob, you men of Israel; I will help*
> *you," declares the LORD, "and your Redeemer is the Holy One of*
> *Israel."*
>
> ISAIAH 41:14

Worm Jacob! Why a description like that? Perhaps because you just can't get to a lower place than the dirty trails that worms follow! After years of struggle, depression, and homelessness, Israel's only hope of recovery and success as a nation came because the Israelites were God's people. They knew they could always count on Him, and He stood ready to help.

Have you ever felt like a worm? Hymn writer Isaac Watts did. Remember these words from his hymn "At Calvary." "Alas! And did my Saviour bleed. And did my Sovereign die? Would he devote that sacred head for such a worm as I"? One year when the hymnals were reprinted, the word "worm" had been changed to "sinners." Later in a continuing effort to make nice, "sinners such as I" was upgraded to "such a one as I." An unauthorized compulsion to toy with the editor's changes tempted me to mark out "one" and put "worm" back in. And that is exactly what one pastor did!

I take no joy in thinking of myself as a worm, but it does me good to remember from whence I came. And it causes me to jump up and down with joy that the LORD, my Redeemer, the Holy One of Israel, changed me from "Worm" to "Beloved" at Calvary.

> *Oh, magnify the LORD with me, and let us exalt his name*
> *together!*   PSALM 34:3 ESV

They will have no fear of bad news . . . trusting in the LORD.

PSALM 112:7 NIV84

A young, insecure mother raised her three daughters while in constant fear of bad news. Even after the girls entered college and later married, she still expected the worst things to happen. A random news report of an accident, abduction, or the discovery of some new virus would send her into a tailspin until she could talk to her daughters and make sure they were safe. At the sound of their voices by cell phone or words of assurance by text, her craft flew back on course and life would continue right-side up—until the next news cycle. Her children, who did not share her concerns, felt imprisoned. One daughter called her a helicopter mother—an apt description since she was always hovering.

The woman may have needed regular counseling, but more than anything else, she needed to take a large dose of faith and land her drone on the heliport. To let go sounds like a simple act—just open your clenched hand and let it fly—but for some it is hard to do. Faith develops as we know Christ better. "Faith comes from hearing, and hearing through the word of Christ" (Romans 10:17 ESV). Practically speaking, there is one way to make sure your faith replaces your fear. Spend time daily hearing, reading, and thinking upon the truth of the word of Christ, and in prayer take your needs to the LORD and leave them there.

Faith is a refusal to panic.

D. MARTYN LLOYD-JONES[9]

What I feared has come upon me; what I dreaded has happened to me.

JOB 3:25 NIV84

When you focus on the fear itself, if you continually ponder, worry, fret, and dread what might happen, you set yourself up to be overcome by the reality of the thing you fear. It becomes a self-fulfilling prophecy. "For as he thinks in his heart, so is he" (Proverbs 23:7 NKJV). In the words of Franklin D. Roosevelt, "The only thing we have to fear is fear itself."[10]

On the other hand, if you set your affections on things above, lift your eyes to the hills, consider yourself seated with Christ in heavenly places, you will not fear, you will not dread what might happen. For this too becomes real by faith. We learn, like author Philip Yancey, "that faith means trusting in advance what will only make sense in reverse."[11] Your heart, set upon things above, will soar like an eagle—up and over the mountains of difficulty, away from and above everything that is troubling you.

Bless the LORD, O my soul, And all that is within me, bless His holy name . . . Who redeems your life from the pit, Who crowns you with lovingkindness and compassion; Who satisfies your years with good things, So that your youth is renewed like the eagle.

PSALM 103:1, 4–5

*Do not anxiously look about you, for I am your God. I will
strengthen you, surely I will help you.*

ISAIAH 41:10

Some of us are easily distracted. It may be anxiety that makes our
eyes glance about. It might also be fear, lack of interest, stress, or
some mind-numbing situation that preoccupies your thoughts.
Your eyes can't stay focused, because your mind is a scrambled
mess. Distraction shows up in your eyes. When your heart is established your eyes are straightforward, bright, and clear. "Anxiously
looking about" happens in an unsettled heart. It is not enough to
calm yourself or make a determined effort to stay focused. The
problem is solved when we, like flowers in their beds, stay where
we've been planted and turn our faces toward the light.

The window to the soul is wonderfully complex! Perhaps one
day man might be able to create a prosthetic eye that can actually
see, maybe receive light and discern colors, but only God can create an eye that can reveal emotion and make a connection with
another person. Eyes reveal if we are well or sick, happy or not,
rested or tired, stressed or blessed. And much of what they express
is based upon whether they spend time looking anxiously about or
contentedly looking up.

---

*The eye is the lamp of the body; so then if your eye is clear, your
whole body will be full of light.*

MATTHEW 6:22

> *I sought the* Lord, *and he answered me and delivered me from all my fears.*
>
> PSALM 34:4 ESV

Parenting three sons challenged my skills, caused me to read dozens of books, and became a strong motivation to pray. Once a friend told me that when one of her daughters was out with friends, she sat in the hall outside their bedroom and prayed for them. I thought, *Well, that explains it!* I needed to sit in the hall to pray! I fell asleep on the floor only once before I decided it was not posture or passion that made the difference, but faith without fear.

How can you rid your mind of fear? What can you do to eradicate it? Discipline your mind? Set goals? Memorize Scripture? Pray harder? Or release the matter and place it into the hands of Yahweh—the Almighty God. Ask the Lord to deliver you! There is nothing too hard for Him. There is no work for you to do, no steps to observe, no plan of action required, no puzzle to solve. Pray for your children anywhere, anytime, according to His Word and His will and trust Him.

Faith is the direct opposite of fear. Faith supplants it, deposes it, overthrows it, and replaces it. Every single time we choose to trust God openly in any tight situation, we are free to find faith. In the words of Martin Luther, "All who call on God in true faith, earnestly from the heart, will certainly be heard, and will receive what they have asked and desired." Whatever seems impossible to you is more than possible by faith.

We can confidently say, "The Lord is my helper; I will not fear; what can man do to me?"

HEBREWS 13:6 ESV

The Lord is my helper. This is life's most relevant truth. We are never alone. Always safe. Forever attended. Daily delivered. Step by step supported. All accomplished by His grace through faith and made precious by His divine presence. He does more than walk beside and model behavior or hand out instructions; He abides within. He not only protects us with an impenetrable shield but infuses inner strength, alerts our soul to danger, and reminds us of spiritual truth. He brings to our heart peace, love, joy, and an indefinable sense of completeness. We are not robots but willing companions in a love relationship that surpasses all human ties. His is the Helper.

When we trust Him and call upon His holy name, we are blessed in Him, rest in His steadfast love, and find hope in Him. When Jesus came, He came as our Help, to free us from the bondage of sin, and when He went away, He sent another Helper, the Holy Spirit of truth Who will abide with us forever, reminding us of Jesus and directing us into good and righteous ways. He is always near and will always help because that is Who He is.

Our soul waits for the LORD; he is our help and our shield.

PSALM 33:20 ESV

If you do not carefully follow all the words of this law, which
are written in this book, and do not revere this glorious and
awesome name—the LORD your God—the LORD will send
fearful plagues . . . harsh and prolonged disasters, and severe and
lingering illnesses.

DEUTERONOMY 28:58–59 NIV84

It is possible to avoid many of life's fearful plagues and other fears
by following God's Word and honoring His name. His character is
revealed to us through His names. When we know Him by name,
we live in freedom and fellowship because we know Him better. In
this verse His name is written "the LORD your God, the LORD"—a
long name that literally means Jehovah Elohim, Yahweh. It really
is a "glorious and awesome" name.

We are exposed to supergerms, plagues, and unknown viruses
today more than ever, probably because international travel is easy
and important to our expanding culture. Sometimes we go places
where vaccines and proper health care are less important than
finding enough to eat. While it is proper to treat every health threat
seriously, we can relax knowing that every situation is within the
scope of God's knowledge and care. Today look to Yahweh, put
your fear into His everlasting arms, and "revere His glorious and
awesome name."

Bless the LORD, O my soul, and forget not all His benefits:
Who forgives all your iniquities, Who heals all your diseases,
Who redeems your life from destruction, Who crowns you with
lovingkindness and tender mercies.   PSALM 103:2–4 NKJV

Among those nations you will find no repose, no resting place . . .
The LORD will give you an anxious mind, eyes weary with
longing, and a despairing heart.

DEUTERONOMY 28:65 NIV84

As God's people dispersed, Moses provided them a long list of rules including curses and blessings. Reading through the curses should make us glad we live in New Covenant days. Who doesn't long for grace, especially when you have tried to live up to the demands of the law? God's people had tried and failed repeatedly. Now they were facing the last curse mentioned—being scattered and exiled. Their future would be spent living in fear's grip, having "eyes weary with longing" and "a despairing heart."

Even though we don't follow the letter of the law today, the principles apply to our daily lives. We will never outgrow the need to obey God. And, He blesses obedient children. Blessings abound—in the country or in the city, upon your basket and your bread bowl, in your barn and the offspring of your beasts, upon your children and your work. The LORD promised to open His storehouse for you, and "all the peoples on earth will see that you are called by the name of the LORD" (Deuteronomy 28:10 NIV). What grace we will know when we are established as a Holy People to Himself.

The LORD your God will set you high above all the nations of the
earth. All these blessings will come upon you and overtake you if
you obey the LORD your God.

DEUTERONOMY 28:1–2

I have known that ye are not yet afraid of the face of Jehovah God.

EXODUS 9:30 YLT

One morning, I opened my electronic notepad and was greeted by a two-second video of my son who is on a business assignment in Indonesia. He made a face and grinned, and I laughed out loud. LOL! Along with the picture came a message from our daughter-in-law: "I am going to see that face in nine days." Yep, we're all looking forward to some face-to-face with the guy we love. In his absence we have Skyped, e-mailed, iMessaged, texted, phoned, and FaceTimed. Wonderful ways to connect, but poor substitutes for the real thing! I want to see that face and lean into a mother/cub bear hug!

Those thoughts came as I considered being "afraid of the face of God." We know that He is too holy to be looked upon, but the truth is, most of us wish we could see Him. Moses begged, "Show me Your glory!" But God answered, "I will make My goodness pass before you; for no man can see Me and live!" (see Exodus 33:18–19 NIV). The LORD offered only a glimpse. He placed Moses in the cleft of the rock as His glory passed by, allowing him to see His back.

Today we live by faith, longing to see His face but content to see His goodness. We can talk to Him in prayer, know Him through His Word, experience Him as we fellowship with His people, knowing that someday soon we will see Him face to face.

My Presence will go with you, and I will give you rest.

EXODUS 33:14 NIV

Don't be afraid of me. Am I God, that I can punish you? You
intended to harm me, but God intended it all for good.

GENESIS 50:19 NLT

"You meant evil against me; but God meant it for good!" (Genesis
50:20). Joseph's words have been called the Romans 8:28 of the
Old Testament. There are no second causes in the life of God's
child. Do not fear, whatever happens, even if it was intended to hurt
you; from God's perspective, it is all good! What had happened to
Joseph was part of God's sovereign plan to deliver Judah from the
famine and bring about future blessings for his family.

Have you heard about the Romans 8:28 Pie? Being a Texas
woman, I think it is Southern Pecan. As you whip the eggs, add
sugar and syrup and other ingredients, it quickly turns into a
sticky mess. It could remind you of one of your relationship problems before you even top it off with nuts. But stirred gently and
baked correctly, that pie will be delicious beyond belief.

So it is with life. Ingredients handpicked by God, added to
our experience, blended well, baked at a preset temperature, for
a predetermined time, will change your messy characteristics into
excellent character. Do not be afraid, but pause to thank God for
the recipe He is following and for the special ingredient He is adding to your life today.

O taste and see that the LORD is good; how blessed is the man
who takes refuge in Him! O fear the LORD, you His saints; for to
those who fear Him there is no want.

PSALM 34:8–9

"No, don't be afraid. I will continue to take care of you and your
children." So he reassured them by speaking kindly to them.

GENESIS 50:21 NLT

Joseph spoke kindly to them! What a striking picture of Jesus, this
young ruler in Egypt! He didn't respond in self-defense, issued no
arguments, no accusations, no payback for evil done to him, no
withholding of love, no claiming of his rights, no discussion of his
position, no incitement to fear. Instead he spoke with kindness, listened intently, offered forgiveness, and promised to provide everything they and their children might need. The kindness of Joseph
reveals the story of grace—the providential, overruling grace of God.

Seems to me in the United States today we have a famine of kindness. Is the word archaic and without meaning? Have you known
kinder days? What can we do to make a difference? The fruit of
the Spirit is "kindness." According to the 1952 version of *Webster's
Dictionary* which I recently inherited, the word "kind" is defined
like this: "Disposed to do good to others, and to make them happy
by granting their requests, supplying their wants, assisting them
in distress, having tenderness or goodness of nature, benevolent,
benignant. 'Be ye kind to one another. Ephesians 4:32.'"

Yes, the verse of Scripture is included in the definition. Can
there be a better definition than that? Especially when considering
the entire verse:

————————

Be kind to one another, tender-hearted, forgiving each other,
just as God in Christ also has forgiven you.

EPHESIANS 4:32

As for those of you who are left, I will make their hearts
so fearful in the lands of their enemies that the sound of a
windblown leaf will put them to flight. They will run as though
fleeing from the sword, and they will fall, even though no one is
pursuing them.

LEVITICUS 26:36 NIV84

As a teen at youth camp, I mounted a horse that proved to be skittish. On our brief and well-chaperoned ride around the campgrounds, that horse balked and tossed his head at the slightest rustle in the trees or crunch of a leaf. I would have preferred a little more stability! Skittish horse; nervous teen! When the trail ended, I vowed to never ride another thing unless it had a steering wheel and a brake!

Those left in the land of their enemies during the days of the Levites were like a skittish horse without a barn. Their emotions whipped them like a crop. Shying at the sound of a windblown leaf, running with no one chasing. Imaginations stampeding wildly! They were afflicted with posttraumatic stress after four hundred years of oppression and slavery.

If you know the terror of being alone in a dark place, if you have wanted to run but didn't know which direction, take heart. God will provide a way.

————————

God is faithful; he will not let you be tempted beyond what you
can bear. But when you are tempted, he will also provide a way
out so that you can stand up under it.

1 CORINTHIANS 10:13 NIV84

This Book of the Law shall not depart from your mouth, but you shall meditate on it day and night, so that you may be careful to do according to all that is written in it. For then you will make your way prosperous, and then you will have good success. Have I not commanded you? Be strong and courageous. Do not be frightened, and do not be dismayed, for the Lord your God is with you wherever you go.

JOSHUA 1:8–9 ESV

The solution is given before the problem is revealed in these verses. Solution: If the "Book of the Law" is your meditation, if you think on its truth day and night, if you are careful to obey, you will become strong and courageous. You will not be frightened or dismayed. When His Word is your constant companion, "the Lord your God is with you wherever you go."

Meditate! Not meditating upon nothing, but pondering the words of Scripture, "O how I love Your law! It is my meditation all the day" (Psalm 119:97). Not emptying your mind, but filling it with truth, "From Your precepts I get understanding" (Psalm 119:104). Not trying to avoid logical conclusions as some religions teach, but growing in wisdom. Godly wisdom leads to righteous conclusions.

Your commandments make me wiser than my enemies...I have more insight than all my teachers, for Your testimonies are my meditation.

PSALM 119:99

Do not fear or be dismayed. Take all the people of war with you and arise, go up to Ai; see, I have given into your hand the king of Ai, his people, his city, and his land.

JOSHUA 8:1

After crossing the Jordan by a miraculous parting of the waters, and experiencing a supernatural victory over Jericho, Joshua's army was unexpectedly defeated at Ai. With confidence brimming, they had apparently underestimated the enemy. Because of the failure, doom and gloom permeated the troops and sent a chill into Joshua's heart as well. But then God spoke! When Joshua heard God's Word, his heart leapt, for they were familiar words—"Do not fear or be dismayed"—words spoken effusively by God whenever Joshua felt overwhelmed.

"Arise and go up to Ai," the LORD said, and He promised to turn the place of defeat into a place of victory. What is God's truth to you today in your place of defeat? Do you need to revisit a place of failure? Is there a relationship problem you need to reexamine? Where is your Ai? What is He saying to you?

To Nehemiah He said, "Arise and build" (2:18), to the paralytic He commanded, "Arise, and walk" (Matthew 9:5 ASV), to Jairus' daughter who had just slipped into the darkness of death He said, "Child, arise!" (Luke 8:54). Listen carefully as you study His Word; you may hear Him speaking to you.

Arise, shine, for your light has come, and the glory of the LORD rises upon you.

ISAIAH 60:1 NIV84

The LORD said to Joshua, "Do not fear them, for I have given them into your hands; not one of them shall stand before you."

JOSHUA 10:8

Joshua fought fearlessly against the enemies of God in absolute compliance with divine instructions. He had been told to completely destroy five Amorite kings and to conscript their wealth, animals, and land, leaving nothing behind. And he did! It had been a long day—the day that the earth stood still. "There was no day like that before it or after it, when the LORD listened to the voice of a man; for the LORD fought for Israel" (Joshua 10:14).

I don't know how that day was extended adding the extra hours the warrior needed, just that God handled the clock and Joshua did as he had been told, completing everything that God had commanded in the time preordained.

When the day ended, Joshua heard from God again. He would not have even one day to rest before he would face a massive coalition from the North, greater in size and power than those he'd conquered in the South. But he was equal to the task because he had faith and no fear.

The Lord did not promise us an easy time while serving Him; in fact, He said quite the opposite: His promise is for a life victorious.

These things I have spoken to you, so that in Me you may have peace. In the world you have tribulation, but take courage; I have overcome the world.

JOHN 16:33

*Do not fear or be dismayed! Be strong and courageous, for thus
the LORD will do to all your enemies with whom you fight.*

JOSHUA 10:25

Joshua won the victory at Makkedah. Then he took his chief soldiers to a cave to kill the five kings who had been captured and
held there. Joshua revealed to the commanders of his army a certain outcome—"thus the LORD will do to all your enemies with
whom you fight." The battle was brutal. The forces of God defeated
the enemy, putting them to death and then hanging them on five
trees. They hung there in plain view until evening. As ghastly as the
scene may be to our tender sensibilities, it encouraged the avengers
of God. If there was a celebration, it was to applaud the faithfulness
of Yahweh.

Perhaps you are thinking, *I could never be that brutal or cruel.* But
could you if you were dealing with the forces of evil, the embodiment of the devil—the archenemy of our souls? Could you if Jesus
said it was the only way to be free? As Joshua's soldiers stood with
their feet on the necks of their wicked enemies, Joshua spoke the
words of comfort you read above.

When facing evil today, victory is promised. Jehovah, the
Essence of Life, will fight our battle. But we must know our enemy,
be courageous, stand strong, and obey.

———————

*Be of sober spirit, be on the alert. Your adversary, the devil,
prowls around like a roaring lion, seeking someone to devour.*

1 PETER 5:8

Stand fast in one spirit, with one mind, striving together for
the faith of the gospel, and not in any way terrified by your
adversaries.

PHILIPPIANS 1:27–28 NKJV

In the last days, our enemies will be neutralized. The saints will
witness the demise of Satan as he is thrown into the "lake of fire"
that has been prepared for him and his demonic angels. From that
day throughout all eternity, sin will be no more. All fear will vanish, warfare will cease, and no one will be terrified of their adversaries. The last book of the Bible tells us how the victory will be
accomplished. "They overcame him because of the blood of the
Lamb and because of the word of their testimony, and they did not
love their life even when faced with death" (Revelation 12:11). Triumph comes to us today by the exact same strategic defense.

"By the blood of the Lamb"—Satan was defeated at the cross when
Jesus died for sin. Satan no longer has power over you. Because
of *"the word of their testimony"*—the deceiver will cower and slink
away when he hears truth expressed. Speak the Word of God. As
you confess the truth, the Lord will rebuke him. Because *"they did*
not love their life even when faced with death." They were not crippled
by the fear of martyrdom. Life and death are not within the limited
powers of the devil. We are safe in the sovereign power of God!

Hold me up, that I may be safe and have regard for your statutes
continually!

PSALM 119:117 ESV

I also sent to find out about your faith, for fear that the tempter
might have tempted you, and our labor would be in vain.

1 THESSALONIANS 3:5

Jesus knows the power and the fear of being tempted by basic human needs. Three times the devil approached and tempted Him to do something contrary to the Word of God. But He had no trouble recognizing the tempter of man and the twister of truth. He answered him by quoting Scripture, the verses that the Holy Spirit brought to His mind, those that suited the dangerous situation. He faced the enemy with the same and only offensive weapon available to believers in Him—the defense that always prevails: the sword of the Spirit, the Word of Truth!

Satan appealed to Jesus' deepest needs and desires—extreme hunger, the salvation of Jerusalem, and the fulfillment of His earthly kingdom. But Jesus fought back: "Man shall not live on bread alone" (Matthew 4:4). "You shall not put the Lord your God to the test" (Matthew 4:7). "You shalt worship the Lord your God, and serve him only" (Matthew 4:10). As the temptation came to an end, the devil disappeared and angels ministered to Jesus.

We will be tempted, our human needs will cry for attention, but when we counter with words of truth, the devil will flee. The temptations were genuine for Jesus. But instead of acting independently of the Father, He chose to worship and wait upon Him. That is the example for believers today.

Oh, guard my soul, and deliver me! . . . for I take refuge in you.

PSALM 25:20 ESV

*Don't hold back. Don't be timid. Be strong! Be confident! This is
what GOD will do to all your enemies when you fight them.*

JOSHUA 10:25 MSG

We can never win the battle with our enemy unless we know who
he is and what he is capable of doing. Thankfully the Lord has
exposed our greatest adversary. Do not be afraid.

He is the prince of this world with limited power over certain
things on earth: see John 12:31.

He is prince of the air, allowed to control demonic forces: see
Ephesians 2:2.

He is an angel of light and can deceive Christians: see 2 Corinthians 11:14.

He is the god of this world and keeps us from truth: see 2 Corinthians 4:4.

He is the tempter who tempts us to sin: see Matthew 4:3.

He is the wicked one who removes the Word of God: see Matthew 13:19.

He is Satan who twists the Truth: see Luke 4:10–11.

He is the father of lies and instigates lies and all things false: see
John 8:44.

He is Lucifer who weakens the nations: see Isaiah 14:12.

He is the accuser of the brethren who accuses us before God:
see Revelation 12:10.

God is in control of him, but we still must do our part.

———————

I long for Your salvation, O LORD, and Your law is my delight.

PSALM 119:174

Because he was too afraid of his father's household and the men
of the city to do it by day, he did it by night.

JUDGES 6:27

Gideon, the "valiant warrior," the one who had needed a sign before
he would believe, the one who became afraid when he saw the Lord,
had finally been granted peace. But soon, into that peaceful place
of surrender, God showed up again telling him specifically to tear
down the altar of Baal which his father had erected and to cut
down the Asherah pole that stood beside it. He was so afraid to
remove the idols that his heart beat fast and his stomach tied into
knots! Fear ousted his recently discovered peace.

Until a plan came to mind: He would do it after dark! Even with
his emotions flip-flopping, he would obey! Under cover of darkness, he could avoid the anger of his father's household. Perhaps it
was a decision born of wisdom as well as fear. That night, he tore
down the gods, built an altar, and sacrificed a seven-year-old ox to
Yahweh. And when the men of the city awoke, they refused to fight
for Baal. "If [Baal] is a god, let him contend for himself" (Judges
6:31). Gideon's accomplishment in the dark prepared the way for
him to lead his father's army to great victories in the light. When
fear comes, do not retreat from God-given battles!

[I pray] that He would grant you, according to the riches of His
glory, to be strengthened with power through His Spirit in the
inner man.

EPHESIANS 3:16

*Whoever is afraid and trembling, let him return and depart
from Mount Gilead.*

JUDGES 7:2–3

When is an army too large? When it thinks, *My own power has delivered me!*

That's the time when Wisdom sends some soldiers back home.
God told Gideon that his army was too big to win. He simply
had too many men for Yahweh to get the glory and the army to
resist the pride. The small-is-sometimes-greater-than-big concept
is hard to accept for those of us who live in our bigger-is-always-
better society. If a few can handle the job, dozens can do it better;
if dozens are better, give me thousands. But what if the Omniscient
God knew that having too many soldiers would hinder their faith
in Him? Yahweh knew! The army of twenty-two thousand was
reduced to ten thousand by asking one question: "Are you afraid?"
I suppose a warrior is worthless when he's afraid. But he is more
worthless when he is proud.

How does this story relate to your life? Do you trust God more
when you have all the resources needed? When well planned, prepared, and practiced? Or do you trust Him more when you have
a headache, or lost your notes, or stumbled on your way to the
podium? It is in the weak moments, the tired times, when enemies
surround, and friends are too busy. That is the time we run into the
arms of the Almighty. O that we would run to Him first!

———————

*O my Strength, I will sing praises to you, for you, O God, are my
fortress, the God who shows me steadfast love.*   PSALM 59:17 ESV

Why should I fear in days of adversity, when the iniquity of my foes surrounds me?

PSALM 49:5

If the devil could talk to you, he would say, "My name is fear." He is the embodiment of fear; he superimposes fear upon the gentle souls of children and bombards the greatest Christians with fear-filled grenades. He not only embodies but dispenses fear from his wicked arsenal of weapons. He has enough power in this world to cause adversity and pain as well as fear. We should have no trouble believing that fear is his name because all fear has its roots in unbelief.

Faith is the cure we need for whatever fear we face. Faith is defined in almost the exact words by three different writers in both Old and New Testaments. It is a major theme of God's Word: Habakkuk said, "Behold the proud, His soul is not upright in him; but the just shall live by his faith" (Habakkuk 2:4 NKJV). The Apostle Paul said, "That no one is justified by the law in the sight of God is evident, for 'the just shall live by faith'" (Galatians 3:11 NKJV). The author of Hebrews said, "Now the just shall live by faith; but if *anyone* draws back, my soul has no pleasure in him" (Hebrews 10:38). With those verses in mind, we want to cry out as the disciples did.

The apostles said to the Lord, "Increase our faith."

LUKE 17:5

I am young in years, and you are aged; therefore I was timid and
afraid to declare my opinion to you . . . But it is the spirit in man,
the breath of the Almighty, that makes him understand. It is not
the old who are wise, nor the aged who understand what is right.

JOB 32:6–9 ESV

Just because a person has lived many years, attends church, and
has even read the Bible does not always mean that he or she has
become sweeter, kinder, more amiable, or wise. Unfortunately,
sometimes people get set in their ways, resist new ideas, develop
strong opinions, and lose all inhibitions when it comes to sharing
their opinions.

Then along comes a Timothy. He's young, inexperienced, the
new man on the church staff, and just a bit timid. But, like Timothy-
the-original, what a spirit he reveals! Faithful to follow closely, great
love for the truth, deep love for the Lord Jesus, submissive to leadership. Like some of the new converts that you and I have met, he was
willing to sweep floors, set up tables, and polish pews so he could
be at church, gather with the saints, or talk with someone he trusts.

Let us pray for the church, for groups that include all ages, who
gather regularly, love each other fiercely, ignore differences, accept
each other's faults, and focus on the development of true wisdom
found only in Jesus.

Let no one despise you for your youth, but set the believers an
example in speech, in conduct, in love, in faith, in purity.

1 TIMOTHY 4:12 ESV

Have no fear of sudden disaster or of the ruin that overtakes the wicked.

PROVERBS 3:25 NIV84

Sudden disaster! In Texas, a family bought the house of their dreams. It was close to the water, sitting high on a cliff of limestone. The mansion bustled with activity on weekends and vacations. Its breathtaking view, gentle breezes, and sky-blue waters made the mansion a perfect place to relax and play, rest, and retreat. But there was one major problem. The house had been built on an unknown geographical fault.

One day the owners noticed a large fracture in the ground near the veranda; a few days later the fissure opened wider; before long the house was condemned and vacated. Consultants came, a decision was reached. The house would be removed by a controlled burn. I watched on TV as bales of hay soaked with diesel were pushed inside and lighted torches were tossed in to start the fire. The flames reached upward in a gigantic red-orange cone, as planks, brick, and tile fell into a blazing heap near the water seventy feet below. In forty-five minutes the home was rubble.

The experience is a parable of sorts. No matter how beautiful and enjoyable life is, it can fall apart quickly. Only when you build your life upon Christ, the solid Rock, will you be safe from the fear of disaster.

The LORD is my rock and my fortress and my deliverer; my God is my rock, in whom I take refuge, my shield and the horn of my salvation, my stronghold.   PSALM 18:2 ESV

Therefore thus says the Lord GOD of hosts: "O my people, who dwell in Zion, be not afraid of the Assyrians."

ISAIAH 10:24 ESV

One of my friends has two master's degrees in counseling. And since becoming my spiritual "daughter," she has needed both. Like the day she told me, "You will not be liked by everybody!" My mouth twisted sideways as she explained, "Most of us have a lot of acquaintances, a few loyal friends, one or two who might want you to be their 'mama,' and at least one enemy." Of course, she carefully explained that this was not my fault but just a human idiosyncrasy. Her words have proved to be true.

Thankfully, through the years some of my people-pleaser traits have diminished. Still, it seems most of us have what has been called an "irregular" person to balance our perspective and provide differences of opinion. And some of us have a radical person who could be described as an enemy.

For God's people dwelling in Zion, it was the Assyrians. But the Lord GOD of hosts told them not to be afraid. As dissimilar as their enemy was to ours, the way of escape God provided is helpful in both situations. Letting your fearful imagination run wild will destroy you before the battle even begins.

No matter the terror you face, there are spiritual resources, hosts of the strongest beings in heaven and earth who will deliver you. The Lord GOD fights for His own!

The name of the LORD is a strong tower; the righteous man runs into it and is safe.   PROVERBS 18:10 ESV

Say to those who have an anxious heart, "Be strong; fear not! Behold, your God will come with vengeance, with the recompense of God. He will come and save you."

ISAIAH 35:4 ESV

The verse describes a day that Israel has longed for since God called Abraham. If it sounds a lot like a New Testament prophecy of the Millennium, don't be surprised. As Isaiah wrote about a current situation, he was also describing a future event. Though the coming utopia will not take place until some distant time, he knew all about it and revealed it first in the Old Testament book that bears his name.

Someday God will gather believing Israel and the true church—the body and the bride of Christ—and He will establish an earthly kingdom. There will be no more sin, no more pain, no fear, and no brokenness of body, soul, or spirit. Indescribable beauty, rich productive land, perfect climate, clean air, crystal clear water, and abundant food will abound in the kingdom. And best of all, we will know the King. He will live among the people and let His glory be seen.

Today, there is much in life that is not fair, many things that need to be made right. Have you ever thought that? If so, do not be afraid. Step back and allow God to handle all offenses. He loves you more than you can know.

For the Lord with vindicate His people, and will have compassion on His servants when He sees that their strength is gone.

DEUTERONOMY 32:36

*Fear not, for you will not be ashamed... For your Maker is your husband, the L*ORD *of hosts is his name; and the Holy One of Israel is your Redeemer, the God of the whole earth he is called.*

ISAIAH 54:4–5 ESV

The LORD will bring His people back to Himself, the way a compassionate man would take back an unfaithful but repentant wife. What an amazing, life-altering truth! When we are forgiven, we can put away any fear of retribution. Forgiveness is complete and completely free. When God finds us, He forgives and removes all shame, confusion, and disgrace. Our reputation is restored. Because His love is loyal and consistent, there will be no payback. Israel is clean, redeemed, and safe. And so are we. The LORD reinforces this by reminding us of who He is.

Your Maker is your husband—the one who loves you perfectly, eternally, with total commitment. He is the LORD of Hosts—meaning that He is LORD of all people, and all spiritual beings, and the LORD Almighty—meaning that He is the victor. He is the Holy One of Israel and the God of all the earth, its Creator and Sustainer. But most important of all, He is the Redeemer—the One Who has the ultimate power of forgiveness no matter how great our sin.

He brought me to the banqueting house, and his banner over me was love.

SONG OF SOLOMON 2:4 ESV

*Is not your fear of God your confidence, and the integrity of your
ways your hope?*

JOB 4:6 ESV

Is our confidence based upon what God does for us or upon what
we do for Him? Are we saved by grace alone, or by our good works?
To trust in our own goodness, our virtuous ways, or our ability to
do good may reveal an attitude laced with pride: *"I've got this thing;
I can do this!"* Confidence never comes by having faith in our faith.
That *is not* where Job had placed his confidence! His faith was in
God alone. His only fear was the fear of God.

Faith always yields good works, but the believer is not to focus
on the work itself. Our focus should be upon the Faithful One who
actually does the work through us. The vine does not produce grapes
by self-effort—no sweat, no grunting or heavy lifting required—it
rests, rooted in the soil, its tendrils stretching gracefully upward to
taste the rain as the grapes grow and ripen in the sun.

Faith is trusting in the faithfulness of God; it is a divine virtue
imparted to those who will empty themselves and allow it to flow
unrestricted into and throughout their lives. My faith is the result
of God's faith planted deeply in me, not the other way around, "It is
the Father, living in me, who is doing His work" (John 14:10 NIV84).

---

*If fear is cultivated it will become stronger, if faith is cultivated it
will achieve mastery.*

ATTRIBUTED TO JOHN PAUL JONES

Listen to Me, you who know righteousness, a people in whose heart is My law; do not fear the reproach of man, nor be dismayed at their revilings.

ISAIAH 51:7

Only a remnant of devoted people remained in Zion. These were the righteous ones, those with a heart for God's Word, those who refused to find refuge in other nations. Sometimes they were afraid, but they stayed in the land holding fast to truth. Living within the small circle of light, fear, anxiety, loneliness, and even moments of despair became part of their daily experience. And, atop their distress, the faithless heaped reproach and revilings.

These words describe behavior worse than criticism or intimidation. They cut deep into the souls of men and women causing them to question their worth. These people felt abused, maligned, and belittled. The verbal onslaught proved to be an effective weapon. But the remnant still had Isaiah, a man who would speak comfort and hope. As he spoke of their future—a utopia that would follow these dark days—fear faded and the circle of light increased. We too still have Isaiah! As you read his words today, let them remind you of another day—a millennium of righteousness with Jesus as our King—and be comforted.

Indeed, the LORD will comfort Zion; He will comfort all her waste places. And her wilderness He will make like Eden, and her desert like the garden of the LORD; joy and gladness will be found in her, thanksgiving and sound of a melody.

ISAIAH 51:3

Thus says the LORD who made you and formed you from the womb, who will help you, "Do not fear... For I will pour out water on the thirsty land and streams on the dry ground; I will pour out My Spirit on your offspring and My blessing on your descendants."

ISAIAH 44:2–3

The passage begins with a precious reminder that we were designed in our mother's womb by the Creator and throughout life we are sustained by the Helper. In the mind of the Triune God we were preconceived, by the hand of the Almighty created, through Jesus redeemed, and in the Holy Spirit forever helped! How beautifully His love is expressed. See the Father pouring out His spirit upon us, like bucketing water onto thirsty land enough to create streams in dry ground.

Not until you admit dryness, acknowledge thirst, reveal parched lips and weak knees will His Spirit be poured out upon you. But how Living Water satisfies when we confess our need and our desires. He lifts a jug and begins to pour until water washes over our body and soul and overflows until it wets the ground beneath our feet. Still He pours! A trickle begins to course downhill, creating a stream that feeds a river. Crystal clear water blesses everybody we know including our children, grandchildren, and future descendants we've yet to meet.

O God, you are my God; I earnestly search for you. My soul thirsts for you; my whole body longs for you in this parched and weary land where there is no water.

PSALM 63:1 NLT

Do not tremble and do not be afraid . . . Is there any God besides Me, or is there any other Rock? I know of none.

ISAIAH 44:8

The Rock is Christ! How appropriate the name. He is the hiding place in the storm, a shelter from the winds of adversity, a refuge from the enemy, the resting place in a tempest. And the only place to run when facing fear. There is nothing stronger, no person safer, no place more secure than our Rock. He is the Foundation of our life, the Cornerstone of our faith. He never moves, never changes and is all-powerful.

Water pours from the Rock. It is pure, refreshing, life-giving, cleansing, and overflowing in abundance. The symbolism here is rich—both water and honey have been used to describe the Word of God. Paul wrote that God would sanctify the church "having cleansed her by the washing of water with the word" (Ephesians 5:26). And David declared that the Scriptures were "sweeter also than honey and the drippings of the honeycomb" (Psalm 19:10). Like water and honey, grace and mercy flow endlessly. "Is there any *other* Rock? I know of none."

He brought me up out of the pit of destruction, out of the miry clay, and He set my feet upon a rock making my footsteps firm.

PSALM 40:2

We will not fear, though the earth should change and though the
mountains slip into the heart of the sea; though its waters roar
and foam, though the mountains quake at its swelling pride.

PSALM 46:2–3

How is it possible to watch such annihilation of everything we count stable and secure and remain fearless? Because "God is our refuge and strength, A very present help in trouble" (Psalm 46:1). Knowing the truth about who He is (our refuge), what He provides (strength), where He is (present), and what He does (help) makes all the difference in whether or not we buckle under the load of fear or skip and dance in victory. There is no fear that is not common to all, and He is the solution to every single one.

In the morning, the sun peeks over my fence and casts its warm glow upon the shrubs and trees. Soon it will shine through my windows and bless my day, as it does every day of my life. As long as earth remains it will be so. It is indeed possible to rest in His blessings unafraid. If the earth should shift on its axis, the mountains slip into the sea, the waters foam, and we are swept away by the tsunami it produces, God is awake and in control. He is in charge of the universe, the nations, and the circumstances of my day.

Even though I walk through the valley of the shadow of death, I
fear no evil, for You are with me.

PSALM 23:4

*I will save you from afar and your offspring from the land of
their captivity. And Jacob will return and will be quiet and at
ease, and no one will make him afraid.*

JEREMIAH 30:10

A day is coming when Christ will appear and establish His kingdom. Jacob will once again serve the Lord and submit to the
authority of a new king named David. Some people think this new
King is Christ, who is from the line of David. Others believe the
historic David will be resurrected and take his place on the throne
once again to govern the restored, united Israel. If so, it wouldn't
be the first time someone came back to life and revisited our land.

Whether the King is David himself or the Christ, he will usher
in a period of tranquility, quietness, ease, and rest. God's chosen
people will be healed of all wounds, cleansed from all guilt, their
fortunes will be restored, and there will be no more fear! With
renewed spiritual health and a measure of wealth, the city of Jerusalem and the king's palace will be rebuilt. Israelites will not be the
only residents of the New Jerusalem. Believers in Jesus will join
them there where we will all serve God and enjoy fellowship and
rest together. Ahhh, sweet rest!

---

*They shall come and sing in the height of Zion, streaming to the
goodness of the LORD ... Their souls shall be like a well-watered
garden, and they shall sorrow no more at all.*

JEREMIAH 31:11–12 NKJV

> *But I will establish my covenant with Isaac, whom Sarah shall*
> *bear to you at this time next year . . . Sarah denied it, saying, "I*
> *did not laugh," for she was afraid.*
>
> GENESIS 17:21; 18:15 ESV

Sarah and Abraham wanted a baby, and God had promised! Not
only a child, but children, generations, multitudes of descendants,
many nations, kings, along with the whole land of Canaan, and
more! He had entered into a covenant with Abraham—an irrevers-
ible, unchangeable, nonnegotiable covenant that required only
faith from the recipient. So they waited, and waited, and waited.
Eleven years lapsed, and they were both in their nineties, which
seemed to them a bit late to start a family. Sarah not only lost hope;
she was overcome with fear.

Have you ever known a woman hoping for a baby? You watched
her struggle with fertility treatments, witnessed her disappointment, saw her face her greatest fear—*I will never become a mother!*
Maybe you are that woman. Maybe you long for some other kind
of birth—a marriage, a career, a book, or dream. You've waited for
an answer to your prayers with the same intensity and complexity.
You may be filled with fear. Take heart: If it is a God-given desire,
it will be satisfied.

God is never in a hurry. In His appointed time, not one promise
fails. Do not give up on anything El Shaddai has promised. Long
after Sarah's hot flashes ended and the way of women ceased, she
gave birth to Isaac, the child of promise.

Is anything too difficult for the Lord?   GENESIS 18:14

Fear not, for I am with you; I will bring your descendants from the east, and gather you from the west.

ISAIAH 43:5 NKJV

Disciples of Jesus are scattered all over the world. You can find them in tiny villages, across the broadest waters, in deep jungles, and in isolated places. They are in teeming cities, clattering townships, and on the farm. They are scattered! Much like the people of God were scattered from Eden, to Canaan, to Babel, and to the uttermost parts of the earth. In the United States, we have grown accustomed to our families being separated from each other—from one coast to another, from southern borders to northern Alaska and beyond. Occasionally we gather for a holiday or reunion, but even the best family get-together is nothing compared to the final gathering of saints!

God will bring them from the East and the West, from distant shores, and many nations to gather at home. Already, plans have been made, invitations selected, and the names are being engraved. A scribe is addressing the envelopes. How many more names are on the list? How many letters still to be written?

Is your name there? If you are uncertain, God does not want you to fear; instead He is calling you to come to Him and be included. Soon the list will be complete. The scribe will dip his pen one last time and declare it finished.

―――――――――

But to all who did receive him, who believed in his name, he gave the right to become children of God.

JOHN 1:12 ESV

I am the LORD your God, who upholds your right hand, who says to you, "Do not fear, I will help you."

ISAIAH 41:13

Occasionally most of us need a bit of help. Paul had no difficulty admitting it. In fact, he presented a list of problems to his friends in the Corinthian Church. He was being insulted, having to endure hardships, facing persecution, and laboring under great difficulties. Yikes! That brought the church to their knees! But what I noticed more than his struggles was the attitude he revealed at the time. He had no complaint about it—as if these sufferings were a common thing, maybe even essential for him to bear.

He was not only content but found joy in the midst of them: "For Christ's sake, I delight in weaknesses, in insults, in hardships, in persecutions, in difficulties. For when I am weak, then I am strong" (2 Corinthians 12:10 NIV). How is it possible to find delight in the midst of pain? Maybe Paul could because he had learned something that all of us need to know. "When I am weak, then I am strong."

Into every human weakness, need, and fear, Jesus comes extending his right hand and speaking comforting words: *Do not fear, I will help you.* When life gets hard, we have the strong current of Jesus' supernatural strength flowing through us, and our lives are supercharged with grace, just like Paul.

If I must boast, I will boast of the things that show my weakness.

2 CORINTHIANS 11:30 NIV84

*Be strong and courageous! Do not tremble or be dismayed, for
the LORD your God is with you wherever you go.*

JOSHUA 1:9

Joshua led God's people into Canaan, carrying on without hesitation exactly where Moses left off. Throughout their journey he
wrote of overcoming the enemy and occupying the Promised Land.
Joshua's writing supplies more courage and inspiration for fellow
crusaders than any other in the Old Testament. His theme? *It is
God's to give; it is ours to possess.*

Joshua, the leader who followed Moses, represents Christ in
many obvious ways. Moses could not go into the land, just as the
law does not bring about salvation. It takes a Joshua to lead them
into their inheritance, just as Christ alone brings us into all that He
purchased on the cross. When it comes to deliverance from sin—
our land of bondage—freedom in Christ is our land of promise.
Joshua's theme remains: "It is God's to give; it is ours to possess."

Do not fear what is happening in our nation, tremble when you
think about the future, or be dismayed when there is a lack of leadership, for the Lord God is with us. Jesus is our Joshua leading us
into the land—one that is filled with milk and honey.

---

*Behold, I stand at the door and knock; if anyone hears My voice
and opens the door, I will come in to him and will dine with him,
and he with Me.*

REVELATION 3:20

> *Thus says the LORD, your Creator, O Jacob, and He who formed you, O Israel, "Do not fear, for I have redeemed you; I have called you by name; you are Mine!"*
>
> ISAIAH 43:1

A boy's favorite toy was a sailboat that his father had helped him build. He handled it carefully as they sailed it in the waters of the cove. But one day the little craft was unattended for just a few minutes. It drifted away. The child and his father searched and inquired of mariners and fishermen, but it was lost. Even after the boy grew up and his father had passed away, he still thought about that toy craft and shook his head over its loss.

One day he walked past an antiques store in the village. In the window sat his sailboat with a For Sale sign attached. He pushed the door open and purchased his own boat! He displayed it in his office like a trophy, for now it was totally his—his in the first place by creation and in the second by redemption.

What a perfect picture! We belonged to God because He made us; when we drifted away Jesus redeemed us by paying the price for our sin. He saw us dirty, broken, useless, lost. And He bought us back because of His unstoppable love. I imagine Him calling us by name and saying, *You are twice mine. I created you, and I paid the price for you. You are my trophy!*

We are afflicted in every way, but not crushed; perplexed, but not despairing; persecuted, but not forsaken; struck down, but not destroyed.

2 CORINTHIANS 4:8–9

Afflicted, perplexed, persecuted, and struck down! Have you, like Paul, ever faced problems on all sides? In front there is a wall of affliction, on the left you are persecuted, on the right you're perplexed, and behind you there's a place to fall when you are struck down. "Do not be surprised...as though some strange thing were happening" (1 Peter 4:12). "To you it has been granted for Christ's sake, not only to believe in Him, but also to suffer for his sake" (Philippians 1:29).

That sounds pretty grim! Until you look at the things which *will not* happen. "We may be afflicted, but we *will not* be crushed! We will be perplexed, but *not despairing*! We will be persecuted, but *never forsaken*! We will be struck down, but *not destroyed*!" That makes me want to shout! Why? Because we are carrying about in our body *the life of Jesus*! He is being manifested—revealed, exposed, and openly publicized in our lives. He allows us to know Him and to represent Him day after day. If we will face our fears instead of denying them, if we yield to His authority, we can triumph in every situation—even with trouble on every side.

But thanks be to God, who always leads us in triumph in Christ, and manifests through us the sweet aroma of the knowledge of Him in every place.

2 CORINTHIANS 2:14

You have not received a spirit of slavery leading to fear again,
but you have received a spirit of adoption as sons by which we
cry out, "Abba! Father!"

ROMANS 8:15

My great-niece is adopted. That simply means she developed in her mother's heart instead of her womb. She doesn't have the same genetic code or blood type of her parents, nor of her grandparents, nor of me, her favorite great-aunt. While being bound together by blood is important, being tied together by spirit is more important. How precious she is to all of us. She was chosen before her birth, placed into the arms of her father moments after, tenderly cared for by her mother, and to this day doted upon by everybody in the family.

When I believed in God and trusted Jesus to forgive my sin, I did not become Hebrew, but I became part of the family of Abraham. I was adopted! "And if you belong to Christ, then you are Abraham's descendants, heirs according to promise" (Galatians 3:29 ESV). If you have believed in Him, your identity is certain and you need not fear being unaccepted or lost. As a part of the family of God, you are included in His covenant and as an heir to His promises.

Where are you today in your relationship with Jesus? Be thankful that there is nothing that can separate you from the love of God. God's promise is for all who believe "who were born, not of blood, nor of the will of the flesh, nor of the will of man, but of God" (John 1:12 ASV).

You said, "Do not fear!" O LORD, You have pleaded my soul's
cause; You have redeemed my life.

LAMENTATIONS 3:57–58

Jeremiah was no stranger to the darkness of depression, but he was
a shining example of how to deal with it. On one occasion, he was
turned over to the Babylonian officials because of his message and
thrown into an empty cistern where he became helplessly stuck in
the mud that had settled in the bottom. One might say Jeremiah
was "in the pit"—both figuratively and literally. He became hungry, thirsty, and desperate, and was near death before he was rescued. Thankfully, he lived to tell the story. "I called on Your name,
O LORD, out of the lowest pit. You have heard my voice" (Lamentations 3:55–56).

Hopefully you've never had an enemy so fierce that they wished
you were dead. But if your war is with the forces of evil, they would
like nothing more! No matter what kind of pit you face, God is
aware of the fix you are in. He sees and hears when you call out
to Him.

When you are afraid, facing an opponent, or tangled in a frightening spiritual conflict, call on the name of Yahweh, the Great I
AM. He will intervene and plead your soul's cause.

———————

When you pass through the waters, I will be with you; and
through the rivers, they will not overflow you. When you walk
through the fire, you will not be scorched, nor will the flame
burn you.

ISAIAH 43:2

> *And He said to them, "Where is your faith?" They were fearful and amazed, saying to one another, "Who then is this, that He commands even the winds and the water, and they obey Him?"*
>
> LUKE 8:25

Some of the disciples had jumped in the boat with Jesus to sail to the other side of the lake. Exhausted, Jesus fell asleep. Meanwhile a storm arose, the winds tossed the boat like a toy, and it began to take on water. Jesus slept on, while the disciples bailed. Finally they woke Him: "Master, Master, we are perishing!" Can you imagine just a tinge of irritation—*Do you mind giving us a hand here?* Jesus calmly stood and charged the wind to cease blowing. He rebuked the wind. Or was He rebuking an evil force behind the wind? With one word, Jesus changed the near disaster into a teachable moment.

"Where is your faith?" As soon as the storm ceased and the water stopped rolling, their troubled minds settled, and their faith began to grow. *"Who is this, that even the winds and the water obey Him?"* Today Jesus is asking you and me, *"Where is your faith?"* The answer is this: It is growing! Faith grows slowly when seas are tranquil; it grows faster in storms and squalls. With Jesus in our boat, we can rest beside Him knowing even the winds and water obey Him.

> *For I am confident of this very thing, that He who began a good work in you will perfect it until the day of Christ Jesus.*
>
> PHILIPPIANS 1:6

*He answered him, "Do not be afraid any longer; only believe,
and she will be made well."*

LUKE 8:50

Jairus, the ruler of the synagogue, believed that his daughter could
be healed—if only Jesus would come by. How difficult for a man
with authority, who cared for the spiritual needs of others, to feel
helpless at home. But he knew that with Jesus nothing is too hard.
He had seen miracles with his own eyes. So he asked! They were
on the way to his house when someone burst through the crowd
shouting loudly that his daughter had died and he should not trouble the Teacher anymore. Jesus answered, "Do not be afraid...;
only believe." Once inside the house, Jesus took her by the hand
and said, "Child, arise" (Luke 8:54). And she did.

A teen in today's society received healing from Jesus too. Completely broken, friendless, and poverty stricken, sometimes wish-
ing she could die, she came to a point of surrender. She sincerely
kneeled and prayed one word, one often thrown around by her
peers. But she spoke it prayerfully: "Whatever!" She really meant
it! She explained through her tears that nothing mattered anymore
but what God wanted. When she gave up, let go of her longings and
strategies, God changed her and gave her a brand-new life. She later
married and had three children. If "whatever" describes where you
are, Jesus heals.

---

*God proved His love on the Cross. When Christ hung, and bled,
and died, it was God saying to the world, "I love you."*
ATTRIBUTED TO BILLY GRAHAM

Do not be afraid, little flock, for your Father has chosen gladly
to give you the kingdom.

LUKE 12:32

Your Father has chosen you! These are the most comforting of
words in Scripture! To think that God looks down upon a troubled
heart and says, *You belong to me!* This truth, to me so precious, to
some may bring fear and confusion. *Am I called? If not, can I come*
to Him? These promising words become a curse if you think there
is no hope! But if you ever wonder if you are called, then aren't you
being called? Your wondering reveals God's calling. He always calls
before you seek.

After years of confusion about this prominent theme of God's
Word, light broke through my cloudy sky one summer when I took
my children to camp. As I turned onto the tree-lined driveway
to enter through the wrought-iron gate, I noticed a sign attached
above it stating: Whosoever Will May Come. After the boys settled
into their dorm and I prepared to go home, I drove once again to
the gate. From inside the campgrounds, the sign bore another message: Chosen in Him Before the Foundation of the World. The two
signs said it all. For the unbeliever the message is always "Whosoever Will"; after we believe in Him and are living safely in the
camp, we grasp the wondrous reality of being "Chosen in Him."

He chose us in him before the foundation of the world, that we
should be holy and blameless before him.

EPHESIANS 1:4

Peace I leave with you; My peace I give to you; not as the world gives do I give to you. Do not let your heart be troubled, nor let it be fearful.

JOHN 14:27

- Our God is the God of peace: "Now the God of peace be with you all" (Romans 15:33).
- Jesus is the Prince of peace: "His name will be called ... Prince of Peace" (Isaiah 9:6).
- The Fruit of the Holy Spirit is peace: "But the fruit of the Spirit is love, joy, peace ..." (Galatians 5:22).
- God speaks peace to His people: "He will speak peace to ... His godly ones" (Psalm 85:8).
- God ordains peace: "LORD, You will establish peace for us" (Isaiah 26:12).
- Divine wisdom is the way of peace: "And all [wisdom's] paths are peace" (Proverbs 3:17).

In Scripture you can find hundreds more verses, prophecies, sermons, proclamations from angels, writings of disciples, and statements by converts concerning peace. Christians are people of peace, called by the God of Peace, saved through the Gospel of Peace, chosen to publish Peace among the nations, told to pray for Peace, and filled with Peace by the Holy Spirit. Peace becomes ours when we believe, guides us in our walk, and keeps us daily.

There is no other religion like the Christ-one.

Take courage! It is I. Don't be afraid.

MARK 6:50 NIV84

There is always much piled atop our faith. At times the deeper part of us can hardly find air for it lies buried beneath the physical, emotional, and mental stress of everyday life. Reaching the core of ourselves where courage and faith abide requires disciplined choices. Slow your rapid pace. Quiet your heart. Open the pages of Scripture. Listen to Jesus. Exercise the faith of a child.

One young girl with a growing faith reached deep and caught hold of more courage than most adults can imagine. At eleven, she had been abused by someone she and her parents trusted. While working through the trauma afterward, she came to an amazing realization. One day in a counseling session, she asked, "Do you know that Jesus was sexually abused?" In a speechless moment, the counselor and her mother waited, until in a reverent tone the girl added, "When the soldiers hung Him on the cross, they took off his clothes." That truth, one that must have come straight from the heart of God, caused fear to loosen its grip on her heart. Through additional counsel from an older woman, using gentleness and love, and a shared faith, she became completely whole.

When fear happens today, she smacks it down with words of truth. It is the only weapon promised to free all who are bound.

You will know the truth, and the truth will make you free.

JOHN 8:32

Now, gird up your loins and arise, and speak to them all which I
command you. Do not be dismayed before them.

JEREMIAH 1:17

Jeremiah, the prophet known for teaching spiritual truth with
visual aids, is here using the cumbersome garments of the day to
picture things that complicate our work for God—including fear
and dismay. Can you imagine trying to care for your family and
work hamstrung by cumbersome robes, shawls, scarfs, and sandals? Today, we don't have to worry about stumbling over our
clothing—we have gone to the other extreme! But to his people,
Jeremiah said to gird up those garments, bundle them above the
knees. Having made his point, Jeremiah continues by telling them
to "arise and speak." These are two good solutions for depression
or "dismay."

Arise! Get off the couch and do something. Get up, get dressed,
go see your mother or someone else who loves you, visit a needy
friend, vacuum the living room. Muster up all the energy you've got
and don't whine and wallow.

Speak! Ask the Lord what He wants you to say, and while you
visit others, walk near your home, or mill around outside, open
your mouth and speak to those nearby. As you put these strategies into action, fear and depression disappear, and the sunshine of
grace shows up with a smile on its face.

Let us also lay aside every encumbrance and the sin which so
easily entangles us, and let us run with endurance the race that
is set before us.   HEBREWS 12:1

And about the time of her death the women who stood by her
said to her, "Do not be afraid, for you have given birth to a son."
But she did not answer or pay attention.

1 SAMUEL 4:20

The birth of a child brings immeasurable joy, inexpressible love, and in this case comfort. The Philistines had killed thirty thousand Israelite soldiers and sent those left running to their tents. Eli the priest sat by the roadway in Shiloh eagerly watching, his heart trembling for a glimpse of the Ark of God. Finally someone arrived with news. Israel had fled before the Philistines and there was a great slaughter; Eli's two sons were dead, and the Ark of God had been taken. Eli fell backward, his neck broke, and he died. Meanwhile his wife, Phinehas, was in hard labor, ready to deliver the baby.

Life is interesting, is it not! Thousands in Shiloh were overcome with grief. Defeat, death, and the capture of the Ark had thrown Phinehas into a fit of despair. In this state, the difficult birth proved too much for her. As she slipped away, the last words she heard were: *"Do not be afraid, for you have given birth to a son."* Did the words bring comfort? Yes, but her physical and spiritual needs prevailed. In one sense, she had lost God too. She named the baby Ichabod—"the Glory has Departed."

There are times in life when all we really want is the Glory of God—with us, around us, filling us, completing us. Whatever your grief today, whatever your fear, seek Him.

Arise, for it is your task, and we are with you; be strong
and do it.   EZRA 10:4 ESV

"Turn aside, my master, turn aside to me! Do not be afraid."
And he turned aside to her into the tent.

JUDGES 4:17–18

What a woman! Jael—fearless, aggressive, physically fit, and available—engaged Sisera, the commander of the Canaanite army. His troops had been routed by Israel's smaller army in a miraculous victory. And she saw the cowardly officer running toward the City of Refuge. The final victory would be won by a woman. As he passed near her tent, she invited him in, offering typical Near Eastern hospitality—a bowl of yogurt and a place to rest. Covering him with a blanket, she spoke the words we all need when life gets tough: "Do not be afraid."

While the drama played out front and center, the major plot had been developing for more than twenty years behind the scenes. With nine hundred iron chariots and multitudes of soldiers, evil Sisera had oppressed Israel. All along, the Israelites had been crying out to the LORD. In His time, God answered with an ingenious plan. Jael accomplished it—in the most difficult and gruesome way. Every Bedouin woman knew how to pitch tents, so Jael used what she had—a tent peg and a hammer—to kill the commander (a radical breach of Near Eastern hospitality!).

Why did God allow such brutality; why did He use a woman to do it? Were the men exhausted, too analytical, fearful, or proud? Jael accomplished the unexplainable, no matter the offense to her delicate sensibilities! Those are the women Yahweh uses.

> *"Don't be afraid," Samuel reassured them. "You have certainly done wrong, but make sure now that you worship the Lord with all your heart, and don't turn your back on him."*
>
> 1 SAMUEL 12:20 NLT

I count on the "but God" factor in my life. For I, like those Samuel addressed, have "certainly done wrong." I make all kinds of mistakes, wrong choices, and missteps. Do you? But God intervenes, but God turns our sin into something good, but God protects those we love from words that might hurt them, but God takes our sin and buries it in the deepest sea, but God brings those that He has forgiven to repentance and changes our hearts, but God instills love and grace into our souls.

What would we do, what would we become, were it not for the "but God" moments of life? For all of us *"have certainly done wrong, but...now..."*

Once we see our sin, it is time to put the wrong, the evil, the ugly behind, move forward, and *"worship the Lord with all your heart."* That one imperative helps us forget the past, stops our self-incriminating thoughts, releases the fear of condemnation, and frees us to live blessedly in His presence.

When, like a naughty child, you want to turn your face in shame, "Do not be afraid!"

> *The Lord will not abandon his people, because that would dishonor his great name. For it has pleased the Lord to make you his very own people.*
>
> 1 SAMUEL 12:21–22 NLT

Do not be afraid, Daniel, for from the first day that you set your
heart on understanding this and on humbling yourself before
your God, your words were heard, and I have come in response
to your words.

DANIEL 10:12

Daniel's heart was right, his mind set upon understanding, and
he had humbled himself before God. Then why did God delay in
answering his prayers? As he waited, there was nothing but silence.
Do you ever think God is slow to answer your prayers? Do you wonder why He waits? Do delays test your faith? Increase your doubt?
Cause your fear? Thoughts may be the very reason for a Divine
Pause, but in this case, there was more.

As soon as Yahweh heard Daniel's prayer, He dispatched
Gabriel. But between his departure from the courts of God and his
arrival at Daniel's feet, Gabriel encountered a host of fallen angels
led by a spiritual enemy, the King of Persia. The king opposed
the prayers of Daniel for twenty-one days. How fascinating! How
frightening! Until God intervened by sending Michael the Archangel with his heavenly host who pushed through the enemy lines led
by the Archenemy Satan and won the victory! The battle was one
that would change the course of the world. We may never know
why answers to our prayers may be delayed. But you can count on
a divine reason and God's perfect timing. Keep praying until the
answer comes.

Submit yourselves therefore to God. Resist the devil, and he will
flee from you.   JAMES 4:7 ESV

O man of high esteem, do not be afraid. Peace be with you; take courage and be courageous!

DANIEL 10:19

Encouraged by the appearance of the Archangel, Michael, Daniel doesn't linger in the valley of fear. He prayed, asking the LORD to speak and thanking Him for the strength that He had so graciously given. It was the angel who answered, "Do not be afraid...I have come in response to your words" (Daniel 10:12). When the angel touched him, Daniel was empowered by divinely dispensed grace, strength, and hope.

God will never ask you to do something that requires an extra measure of strength and not supply what you need. Daniel felt helpless in the presence of God. He was weak after a three-week fast, terrified by the vision he had seen, fearful of the future, and alone. No wonder he needed reassurance!

But he knew what to do: He rested, and waited upon God until he heard His voice again. The angel touched him as he trembled on his hands and knees, teetering on weak legs and tired feet. He touched his lips, heard Daniel's confession, and revealed God's love to him.

Why do you think the LORD so carefully prepared His beloved servant for this message? What have you experienced before as you prepared to serve God? His love always trumps fear.

And as he spoke to me, I was strengthened and said, "Let my lord speak, for you have strengthened me."

DANIEL 10:19 ESV

Joseph, son of David, do not be afraid to take Mary as your wife;
for the Child who has been conceived in her is of the Holy Spirit.

MATTHEW 1:20

Joseph had every right to be afraid. The appearance of the Angel of
the Lord, was really an appearance of the pre-incarnate Jesus. He
had appeared to Joseph in a dream delivering a message that would
cause even the most dedicated follower of Yahweh to be afraid.
Mary, a virgin, the young woman he loved, was pregnant. He heard
clearly—"Do not be afraid to take her as your wife."

This supernatural visitation of Jesus has happened several times
in history to relay an important message. On this day, Joseph
needed assurance that Mary's child was of the Holy Spirit. Divine
revelation was the only way the news could be delivered. The God-
Man Jesus was destined to become flesh, be born of woman, raised
by human parents, live as a man, and sacrifice himself on a cross to
take away our sin. Only God can do that!

Have you ever had a dream that frightened you or have you
experienced an event so holy, so incomprehensible, so life altering
that it alarmed you? Then you may know a bit of what Joseph felt.
To even unexplainable fear, our LORD responds with compassion,
grace, and help.

For the mind set on the flesh is death, but the mind set on the
Spirit is life and peace.

ROMANS 8:6

Therefore do not fear them, for there is nothing concealed that
will not be revealed, or hidden that will not be known.

MATTHEW 10:26

When I am traveling, I love to think that God knows exactly where
I am. He doesn't need OnStar or cellular data to keep up with me.
There is nothing concealed! But there have been other times when
I felt uncomfortable knowing that He sees me. I don't relish the
thought that He saw the price tag on a particular purchase, heard
that outburst of anger, listened in on the lie I told a police officer,
or watched me manipulate a certain situation. I am not above sin
though I wish I were, and, at times, it bothers me that God sees it
all. It's a truth both comforting and frightening, but He remains El
Roi, the God Who Sees Me!

The benefits of knowing El Roi far outweigh the negative feelings we sometimes have. Aren't you glad that He never slumbers,
or sleeps, and is always aware of all the circumstances we are in?
El Roi sees when a person has been used or mistreated by someone
they trusted, or when they stumble and need help. Whether you
need vindication or forgiveness, you may rest in the promise that
everything concealed will be revealed and all brokenness will be
healed. It is a certainty, in God's time!

God saw it! There is forgiveness but there is also a day of
judgment. And it will be a righteous judgment for He saw it all.

KAY ARTHUR [12]

But immediately Jesus spoke to them, saying, "Take courage, it is I; do not be afraid."

MATTHEW 14:27

Remember Zacchaeus? He knew Jesus was coming, saw the crowds gathering, and began standing on tiptoes to get a glimpse of Him, when suddenly, impulsively, he began to climb a nearby tree. He found a comfortable fork in the branches and hid among the leaves. Perfect! While the crowd pushed toward the clearing, he nestled there in obscurity, waiting for Jesus to come near. As he sat, he must have been thinking, *Who is this man who draws such attention?*

Interrupting his thoughts, the crowd moved closer and closer to the tree. Zacchaeus held his breath. Jesus, whose plan was simply to pass through Jericho, paused beneath the tree, looked up, and spoke directly to the man lodged in its limbs. He called him by name and issued His call. Come! "Zacchaeus, hurry and come down, for today I must stay at your house" (Luke 19:5). Zacchaeus slid out of the tree, and later at his own dwelling, he listened, repented, and believed. I wish I could have been at the home of that hated, ostracized tax collector as he and Jesus shared a meal. But there is really no reason to envy such a visit. He is available today to join you at lunch or on a walk, anytime, anyplace, whenever we welcome His open invitation. The best antidote for fear is our nearness to Him in prayer and biblical meditation.

> *When the disciples heard* this, *they fell face down to the ground and were terrified. And Jesus came to them and touched* them *and said, "Get up, and do not be afraid."*
>
> MATTHEW 17:6–7

What happened to terrify the disciples? Jesus was "transfigured" right before their eyes. Imagine three disciples trekking up a high mountain with Jesus leading, garments hiked to the knees, dusty sandals laced tightly, hot sun beaming overhead, sweat dripping, muscles aching. Then Jesus stops, turns toward them, and as they wiped their faces, He begins to change, from a rugged man of the sea and mountains into an otherworldly, ethereal, holy being. What Scripture calls "transformation" the dictionary calls "metamorphosis." Like the metamorphosis of a caterpillar into a beautiful butterfly, Jesus the man appeared as the Holy Son of God. The Bible says that "His face shone like the sun, and his clothes became white as light" (Matthew 17:2).

If you had stood there with them, would you have been afraid? Have you ever been in a place of worship, in a quiet place of prayer, or with other believers when God came very close? Did you feel like shouting or bowing, lifting your hands or kneeling? Did you jump for joy or were you afraid?

If God comes down, if Jesus comes close, if the Holy Spirit moves, only a few things will be certain. He will do it according to His Word, in His time, and you will be changed!

> *The Lord is near to all who call upon Him, to all who call upon Him in truth.* PSALM 145:18

You shall not fear man, for the judgment is God's.

DEUTERONOMY 1:17

Moses prayed with the words and tone we all use when we're overwhelmed. It could have been like the world's shortest prayer: "Help!" And it was enough. God answered with a pragmatic solution—delegate. The great fault of having the gift of leadership is thinking that we can handle *everything*, we can do it *best*, and it must be done *our way*. But Moses had to learn, as we do, that when you ask God to increase your ministry and He answers one thousand–fold, the result will be more work!

Our only recourse is to yell "help" and accept God's answer as Moses did—"the thing which you have said to do is good" (Deuteronomy 1:14). Next, the Lord addressed Moses' fear of man, reminding him that His hands are behind the scenes, directing the action, protecting His plan, and making sure nothing goes awry. Don't we all need to be reminded of that truth? "You shall not fear man, for the judgment is God's." Remember that His name is El Roi, the God Who Sees, and Jehovah-Jireh, the God Who Provides.

Whatever your responsibilities for today, or this week, or this semester, there is a Hidden Hand orchestrating plans and holding on to you.

Keep your eyes on Jesus, *who both began and finished this race we're in. Study how he did it. Because he never lost sight of where he was headed . . . And now he's there, in the place of honor, right alongside God.*

HEBREWS 12:1–2 MSG

Do not be afraid; go and take word to My brethren to leave for
Galilee, and there they will see Me.

MATTHEW 28:10

These words calmed the women who appeared at the tomb, and
they proceeded to Galilee to tell the disciples. Jesus was not in the
grave but had risen! They were afraid, but filled with joy that He was
alive. It was not the nail-biting fear of worry or despair, but wonder,
reverence, and an unexplainable awe that shook them from scarf to
sandal. It is the kind of fear we experience when something occurs
totally outside our sphere of comprehension, when we see power
beyond the realm of our finite minds, when we behold holiness that
overwhelms. Jesus understands. Moving quickly past their feelings,
He gave them important work to do.

Don't be afraid: Go! Take my word to the brethren. The women
obeyed by heading off to Galilee to meet with the disciples. Work
is the best remedy for fear, both then and now. Slip your hand into
His and obey. With a significant task to accomplish, fear slips quietly to the back of your mind. Don't pacify yourself with busywork
but choose a meaningful errand, a job that must be done well, and
the focus of your mind shifts from fear to the divine task at hand.
Jesus will accompany you throughout the assignment and escort
you to the finish line. It is impossible for fear to occupy the space
in which He dwells.

Prove yourselves doers of the word, and not merely hearers who
delude themselves.

JAMES 1:22

His appearance was like lightning, and his clothing as white
as snow. The guards shook for fear of him and became like
dead men.

MATTHEW 28:3–4

The guards were so afraid, their knees knocked and buckled. They wanted to run, but fell on their faces, breathless, immobile, "like dead men." All over the appearance of an angel! Whenever one shows up, fear does too. The extent of fear depends upon the heart of the one who sees and the purpose of the angelic visitation. This angel was an awesome sight, a huge muscular form whose mission was to move the huge stone that blocked the entrance to the tomb. The stone was not removed so that Jesus could get out, but so the disciples could get in. By the time the angel arrived, Jesus was already on His way to Galilee.

The guards who shook like jelly in the presence of the angel pulled themselves together and headed for the chief priest and elders. There they had been paid a large sum of money to lie. Their concocted story claimed that Jesus' disciples came in the night and stole his body while they slept. Guards actually admitted sleeping on the job? How foolish!

Picture the scene on resurrection morning—three women, several guards, and one angel gathered in the garden. From those few, word of Jesus' resurrection spread—to the disciples, to the chief priests, to the elders, to residents of Galilee, and onward. And so it goes today.

Christ died and lived again, that He might be Lord both of the
dead and of the living.

ROMANS 14:9

But as for you and your servants, I know that you do not yet fear the Lord God.

EXODUS 9:30 ESV

There is a wholesome fear—one full of respect, honor, and awe—that looks Godward and sees Him as He really is. It may take some time to develop a healthy fear of God. Knowing Him comes first. Knowing God on a deeper, more familiar level depends upon how much time you spend together and how widely you open your heart to Him.

The relationship we long for is not something tossed out like candy from a parade float. We must seek Him like deep-sea divers seek treasure. In the writings of Jeremiah, we find: "When you come looking for me, you'll find me. Yes, when you get serious about finding me and want it more than anything else, I'll make sure you won't be disappointed" (Jeremiah 29:13–14 MSG). May we come to Him like David "to behold the beauty of the Lord, and to meditate in His temple" (Psalm 27:4).

The character of Christ is transferred by beholding. Behold His face, study at His feet, and little by little, day by day, a beautiful friendship grows along with a rapturous fear of Him.

To fall in love with God is the greatest of all romances.

ATTRIBUTED TO AUGUSTINE

The secret of the Lord is for those who fear Him, and He will make them know His covenant.

PSALM 25:14

But fear not, O Jacob my servant, nor be dismayed, O Israel, for
behold, I will save you from far away, and your offspring from
the land of their captivity.

JEREMIAH 46:27 ESV

We all long to be loved. And we *need* to be loved. Without love pree-mies fail to thrive, babies disassociate, children withdraw, teens rebel, and the aged despair. With love, men and women, animals, and even plants thrive and flourish! Superior to the unexplainable emotion of love expressed by human beings stands the matchless love of God. Perfect, unconditional, ceaseless, everlasting. A love that finds us when we are far away, loves us all the way home, saves us for eternity, and keeps us close forever.

There is no other chapter in the Bible that tells us more about the concept, the need, the meaning, and the result of pure love than the Apostle John's first letter written to his "little children" in the faith. He treats sin as a childlike offense toward a loving Father, speaks of adoration in spite of wrongdoing, reveals mercy in dealing with sin, and demonstrates the grace of forgiving.

While we will never find perfect love in human relationships, nothing hinders His paternal love for children like you and me. God wants us to know Him intimately so that we may live eternally, fearlessly, in Him.

By this the love of God was manifested in us, that God has
sent His only begotten Son into the world so that we might live
through Him.   1 JOHN 4:9

*There is no fear in love; but perfect love casts out fear, because
fear involves punishment, and the one who fears is not perfected
in love.*

1 JOHN 4:18

"Perfect love casts out fear." Fear and love do not go together—
fear does not fit with love and does not abide where love dwells.
When God's love fills our hearts completely, there's no dark corner
where fear can hide. It simply vanishes away. "There is no room
in love for fear. Well-formed love banishes fear. Since fear is crippling, a fearful life—fear of death, fear of judgment—is one not yet
fully formed in love" (1 John 4:18 MSG).

As Amy Carmichael, a beloved missionary in India for more
than fifty years, wrote, "There is no need for you to plead that the
love of God shall fill our heart as though He were unwilling to fill
us. He is willing as light is willing to flood a room that is opened
to its brightness, willing as water is willing to flow into an emptied
channel. Love is pressing round us on all sides like air. Cease to
resist, and instantly love takes possession."[13]

Rest in the love of Jesus, bask in the light of His glory, rejoice in
Him. Become "fully formed in love," and do not spend one more
minute fearing fear.

---

*We have come to know and have believed the love which God
has for us. God is love, and the one who abides in love abides in
God, and God abides in him.*

1 JOHN 4:15–16

*Fear not, O Jacob my servant, nor be dismayed, O Israel, for
behold, I will save you from far away and your offspring from
the land of their captivity. Jacob shall return and have quiet and
ease, and none shall make him afraid.*

JEREMIAH 46:27 ESV

After forty years under the reign of Nebuchadnezzar in Babylon,
God's people were afraid and homesick. Then Jeremiah the prophet
spoke the words they had longed to hear from God: "Fear not, O
Jacob . . . I will save you from far away." God would make a full end
of the nations where His people had been driven, but He would not
make an end of His own. They were promised a safe return home.
Have you ever been away from home for far too long?

Home! Where your roots grow deep and memories hover like
clouds—white fluffy clouds, and perhaps a few foreboding, flood-
threatening ones. Whatever the picture that comes to mind when
you think about home—a cottage warmed by grace and love, a
cabin where icy winds whistle through cracks, a downtown flat,
or a house in the suburbs—home calls your name and draws you
back. Home-going is part of living. We always go back! To celebrate, to reflect, to deal, as we move onward to the perfect home—
one eternal in the heavens.

---

*I would have despaired unless I had believed that I would see the
goodness of the LORD in the land of the living.*

PSALM 27:13

*Fear not . . . declares the L*ORD*, for I am with you . . . I will*
discipline you in just measure.

JEREMIAH 46:28 ESV

"It is not fair!" If you have children, you've heard it. Maybe you
have uttered the words yourself. For we live in a world that's off kil-
ter! Justice is a vague concept, truth is relative, evil dominates, and
fear prevails. According to a chaplain in Marketplace Ministries,
one in three people in today's workforce has an anxiety disorder.

Into this situation, the LORD says, "Fear not! I am with you."
Peace and freedom from anxiety and fear describes our hearts
when we know that our lives are in the hands of a patient, gracious
God. He is always fair because He is in His very character a completely fair and just God. While sin taints the world we live in, He
calls us out, cleans us up, and gives us purpose and a plan. Someday justice will reign! It will, as Martin Luther King, Jr. declared,
roll "down like waters, and righteousness like a mighty stream."[14]
We have to wait, moving on in step with Jesus, but wait nonethe-
less for that amazing day when rights will be honored, discipline
will be just, and no one will sigh, "Life is not fair!"

Every valley shall be exalted and every mountain and hill
brought low; the crooked places shall be made straight and the
*rough places smooth; the glory of the L*ORD *shall be revealed,*
*and all flesh shall see it together; for the mouth of the L*ORD *has*
spoken.

ISAIAH 40:4–5 NKJV

Come forth from her midst, My people, and each of you save yourselves from the fierce anger of the LORD.

JEREMIAH 51:45

Jeremiah was warning God's people to leave Babylon, to escape the fierce anger of God. By obeying Him, they would find peace and eliminate fear. Today, when you find yourself in fearful circumstances, remember Jeremiah's warning. God still guides His people. When fear assails you, do you listen to Him or to the news channel? Do you find His plan or make some of your own? What are we to do about our fear?

Consider these words from *The Gospel According to Job* by Mike Mason: "Fear of other people, fear of demons, fear of the world and of ourselves, fear of sickness and pain, fear of living and of dying—all these phobias must be rolled up into one big ball and pushed up the hill to Calvary. For like other kinds of suffering fear will never be completely alleviated in this life. Only as we bring our fears before the cross of Christ can their sting be extracted, their poison neutralized, their utter groundlessness exposed."[15]

It is Yahweh who gives us the imperative—No Fear! It is one of more than 365 other warnings about fear given by our God. But He also tells us that there is a time *to fear.* Fear the Lord.

But I will show you whom you should fear: Fear him who, after the killing of the body, has power to throw you into hell. Yes, I tell you, fear him.

LUKE 12:5 NIV84

David was afraid of the Lord that day, and he said, "How can the ark of the Lord come to me?"

2 SAMUEL 6:9 ESV

They recaptured the Ark and joy overtook them! So much so, they forgot how to handle the treasure! Instead of carrying it by its rods and handles, they placed it on an oxcart. Heading toward Jerusalem, the ox stumbled, the chest tipped and almost slipped into the dirt. One man put out his hand to stabilize it. And the reaction cost him his life. To understand the wrath of God and the grip of David's fear, you must know how revered this chest and its contents were. The holiest of artifacts including the tablets of the Law inscribed by the finger of God were inside.

But more important than the objects within was the Presence that dwelt on top between the golden cherubim. A Presence so weighty and thick that the Ark was called "the Name, the very name of the Lord of hosts" (2 Samuel 6:2). It was more than a chest; it was God. And He could not be looked upon, much less touched. When David saw what happened, he crumpled in fear and refused to carry the Ark one step more.

Today we don't talk much about God's holiness. We joke and with loose language call unclean things holy. Holiness is the most often mentioned attribute of God, the most frequent description of His character, the only quality of His nature spoken in triplicate, yet we remain flippant and careless.

Oh, worship the Lord in the beauty of holiness!

PSALM 96:9 NKJV

The fear of the Lord, that is wisdom.

JOB 28:28

Mike Mason in *The Gospel According to Job* claims we soften the fear of God when we call it awe or reverence when in reality it is still fear, plain and simple. Fear is fear whether accompanied by feelings of respect and reverence or not. I understand that kind of thinking!

When I was growing up, I feared my dad. He seldom punished a single one of his six children. He didn't have to, because we feared that he might, and knew that he could. While I often wished for a dad with a cozy disposition, my fear of him and my respect for his authority kept me in line. He was not a perfect daddy, but he was perfect for me. He put the fear of God in me long before the love of God took hold.

"We fear God because, even though we are secure in His eternal love for us . . . there are many parts of our lives that are not yet purified and made holy," Mr. Mason wrote. "Jesus compared the Kingdom of God to 'yeast that a woman took and mixed into a large amount of flour until it worked all through the dough' (Matthew 13:33). In other words, the salvation that has already taken root deep in our spirits must continue to advance into all areas of our flesh . . . We should not be surprised to find our flesh trembling and quaking before the relentless march of God's Holy Spirited yeast inside us."[16]

The angel of the LORD said to Elijah, "Go down with him, and don't be afraid of him." So Elijah got up and went with him to the king.

2 KINGS 1:15 NLT

Elijah was told by an angel to deliver a message to the king. It was literally Yahweh Who had spoken. Elijah would be attended by the angel, and God's power would protect them. So the prophet got up and went. Standing fearlessly before the king, he declared that because of the king's failure to seek God and act boldly, he would be deposed and face death. Soon afterward, the king died from the injuries he sustained in war—just as the LORD had said.

The message for you and me today is a powerful one. It is safe for us to stand before the most influential, significant, mal-adjusted, fearsome leader on earth and speak the truths of God, when accompanied by the LORD. It always requires the power of His might to face down fear and exude strength. Putting ourselves into His sovereign hands, following Him closely, and speaking His Word, we become His hands and feet and mouth. Then we are completely equipped to carry out the Great Commission of Jesus Christ.

Go therefore and make disciples of all the nations, baptizing them in the name of the Father and the Son and the Holy Spirit, teaching them to observe all that I commanded you; and lo, I am with you always, even to the end of the age.

MATTHEW 28:19–20

Don't be afraid . . . for there are more on our side than on theirs!
                                    2 KINGS 6:16 NLT

I've known times when friends were few, when relationships were strained, and, most hurtful of all, when my closest spiritual ties, even those in the church where I had grown and flourished, pulled away and cast aspersions. Then a woman whom I respected read these words to me:

> For it was not an enemy that reproached me; then I could
> have borne it:
>   neither was it he that hated me that did magnify himself
> against me;
>   then I would have hid myself from him:
>   But it was thou, a man mine equal, my guide, and mine
> acquaintance.
>   We took sweet counsel together, and walked unto the
> house of God in company (Psalm 55:12–14 KJV).

I was not alone in my suffering. David, author of thousands of poems and many books, a man after God's own heart, the one who confronted his sin and learned to know God, had been exactly where I was. If he had found grace to express his hurt, acknowledge his fear, and write on, then I could too.

In this, as in all things that cause pain and fear, God was doing something good. He was changing me from a young woman who feared rejection more than she feared God into someone stronger. He was drawing me close to Jesus, who was also "wounded in the house of my friends" (Zechariah 13:6).

A Prayer: *Lord, may I listen to Thee intently, hear Thee correctly, and obey Thee perfectly.* Amen.

*Do not be afraid; for I know that you are looking for Jesus who
has been crucified. He is not here, for He has risen, just as He
said.*

MATTHEW 28:5–6

After I believed in Jesus, I often wished I could have been a disciple, or one of the women who visited at the tomb, the one who gave Him water, or, best of all, one of the two people who walked with Him on the road to Emmaus. What a joy to have been walking home and suddenly realizing that the unknown man accompanying us was Jesus! But as I matured in my faith, I realized this breathtaking truth: Jesus is more with me now than he could have ever been with me then! It is true because of the resurrection! He is alive! He lives in me. He is closer than a whisper.

When we believe in Him, we do not simply accept a doctrine, adopt a belief system, or change our behavior. Not only do we "believe," but we "receive" Him (John 1:12). He takes up residence in our hearts. He's not only with us, but in us; we not only walk in His steps, we traverse this world in union with Him, responding to His words, knowing His inner promptings, and we are never, ever, even for one moment alone.

---

*It is to your advantage that I go away; for if I do not go away, the
Helper will not come to you; but if I go, I will send Him to you.*

JOHN 16:7

If they have called the master of the house Beelzebul, how much more will they malign those of his household. So have no fear of them.

MATTHEW 10:25–26 ESV

Have you ever been bullied? Has anyone maligned your character? Have accusations, gossip, or slander caused you to be afraid? Maybe it will help to know that our Lord was called names too. The Savior of the world, the Prince of peace, the Giver of life, the Lover of our souls was called "Beelzebul"! It is one of the names of Satan, the prince of evil spirits. A name that could not be more contradictory, more wrong, or more hurtful to the purest of men—the man with the name above all names. Did it cause Him to fear? No! He recognized the source and took it in stride. When it happens to us, we must not fear!

Jesus said that we students are not greater than our Teacher. Since he was called the prince of demons, it is possible that we may be called even worse names. Being accused is to be expected! If you follow Him, teach as He did, love others in like manner, take a stand for what's right, you will be maltreated just like He was.

Until he is cast into the lake of fire, the accuser will be busy trying to disrupt, defeat, and destroy the testimony of Christ any way he can—including name-calling!

He who listens to me shall live securely and will be at ease from the dread of evil.

PROVERBS 1:33

But don't be afraid of those who threaten you.

MATTHEW 10:26 NLT

Threatened means "to be told that someone will harm you or do something unpleasant or unwanted, especially in order to make you do what they want." One way to know the difference between the voice of God and other voices is this: God does not threaten. He does not accuse. He doesn't correct by intimidation. On the other hand, evil voices use these methods profusely in an effort to undermine truth, and make you fear.

Accusation says, "You are weak, foolish, sick, and hopeless." Conviction says, "This weakness is wrong but can be overcome." Threats yell, "Do that again and I will destroy you, cast you away, punish you." Conviction comes alongside and says, "I love you too much to allow that sin, repent and I will give you grace." While our enemy threatens, sneers, scoffs, derides, our Lord convicts, compels, calls, directs, leads, speaks through His Word, and, in goodness and grace, draws us to Himself.

Our best defenses against Satan's accusations are the four verbs in the following verse: "*Submit* therefore to God. *Resist* the devil and he will flee from you. *Draw near* to God and He will draw near to you. *Cleanse* your hands, you sinners; and purify your hearts, you double-minded" (James 4:7–8, emphasis mine). Submit, resist, draw near, cleanse. With these four actions fear is overcome and threats lose their power.

There is now no condemnation for those who are in Christ Jesus.

ROMANS 8:1

*And they were on the road, going up to Jerusalem, and Jesus
was walking ahead of them. And they were amazed, and those
who followed were afraid.*

MARK 10:32 ESV

The disciples were afraid, so Jesus took them aside and explained,
again, what would happen. He would be betrayed, sentenced to
die, and handed over to the Romans. Jesus presented detail hard to
comprehend. He would be mocked, spat upon, flogged, and killed,
but after three days he would rise again.

The Scripture says the disciples were amazed and afraid.
Amazed literally means "astonished" or "terrified." The atmosphere
surrounding this group of Jesus-followers was supercharged with
caustic, destructive, overwhelming fear. Enthralled by thoughts of
a kingdom where Christ would reign and they would occupy a significant role and enjoy a blessed life, the disciples were now hearing the Master talk of excruciating pain, total rejection, and death.

We all want to know what to expect in the future but not to be
preoccupied and afraid. Worry about the future is futile, like trying to breathe tomorrow's air. We can't cope with even one future
day, so it's best to leave tomorrow in Omniscient Hands. Before it
arrives, circumstances may change, help may come, prayer may be
answered, or a dramatic change of heart may occur. The truth is so
simple it sounds trite. We will find sufficient strength one day at a
time, step by step.

---

*Therefore do not be anxious about tomorrow ... Sufficient for
the day is its own trouble.*   MATTHEW 6:34 ESV

Zechariah was troubled when he saw him, and fear fell upon him.

LUKE 1:11–12 ESV

Interesting concept—"fear falls"! That happens when emotion comes embodied in a person or spiritual being. On this occasion the writer is speaking of the "fear of God" conveyed by the Holy Spirit. Fear fell upon Zechariah when an angel of the Lord appeared at the altar in the synagogue. I understand how troubled the man was! Why, even though we pray for God to be near us when we gather in our places of worship, if He or one of His emissaries actually did appear and become visible or spoke out loud, most of us would be scared to death.

The Holy Spirit comes and the congregation is surprised! What an indictment upon today's church. We really don't expect His presence, do we?

It was Palm Sunday and five-year-old Johnny stayed home from church because of a sore throat. When his brothers and sisters returned home, they were carrying palm branches. "What are those?" he asked. "Palm branches," his older brother explained. "People held them over Jesus' head as he walked by." Johnny fumed, "Wouldn't you know it. The one Sunday I don't go, Jesus showed up!" May this touch of humor be the catalyst for you to pray that Jesus will show up at your church. Do not be afraid when He comes.

The LORD is in his holy temple; the LORD's throne is in heaven; his eyes see, his eyelids test the children of man.

PSALM 11:4 ESV

*Do not be afraid, Zechariah, for your prayer has been heard,
and your wife Elizabeth will bear you a son, and you shall call
his name John.*

LUKE 1:13 ESV

Zechariah and his wife, Elizabeth, had been praying for a child, and the angel had come to reveal God's answer. The older couple would have a child. It would be a son, and they would name him John. After the pronouncement, Gabriel began to mention several aspects of his character. As Zechariah listened to the news, learned the child's name, and heard of his godly character, all fear vanished.

The child would be the source of joy and gladness for his parents, and the multitudes.

He would be great in the eyes of the Lord.

He would never drink wine or alcoholic drinks.

He would be filled with the Holy Spirit even before his birth.

He would turn many Israelites to the Lord their God.

He would be a man with the spirit and power of Elijah.

He was a man with a mission—specific and grand.

What parent would not be ecstatic knowing that much about their child before he arrived! Today, as you thank God for your own children, remember how very well our Heavenly Father knows each one. And He knows it all from conception.

And he came to her and said, "Greetings, O favored one, the
Lord is with you!" But she was greatly troubled at the saying,
and tried to discern what sort of greeting this might be.

LUKE 1:28–29 ESV

Gabriel was busy making pronouncements early in the first century. And every time he appeared, fear and anxiety accompanied.
Mary was "greatly troubled" and afraid. No wonder! With the
healthy temperament and inquisitive mind of a Jewish teen, she
began asking questions. Gabriel answered with the most intimate,
personal information about a subject she had only discussed with
her mother. It went something like this: Even though you're a virgin, you will conceive and bear a son! You will name Him Jesus, the
Son of the Most High. He will sit on the throne of David and reign
forever. God is with you! You are blessed above all women!

Disclosure of the message did not soothe her troubled heart—
until she reached deep into her soul and drew from her endless
supply of faith. Then she answered, "Behold, I am the servant of
the Lord; let it be to me according to your word" (Luke 1:38 ESV).

Of course she would follow Yahweh completely! May we too find
grace to believe as she did—even when the circumstances seem
unbelievable!

The Holy Spirit will come upon you, and the power of the Most
High will overshadow you; and for that reason the holy Child
shall be called the Son of God.

LUKE 1:35

Do not be afraid, Mary, for you have found favor with God.

LUKE 1:30 ESV

Mary and Elizabeth—two women with unquenchable faith, stead-fast love, and much grace, obeyed God and found favor with Him. Both conceived a son, exceeding all expectations—Mary was a virgin, Elizabeth beyond menopause. This, once and for all time, proved beyond any doubt that "nothing will be impossible with God" (Luke 1:37 ESV).

With this miraculous bond in common, the two became the closest of friends. Imagine the conversations between these kin-dred spirits—talk about their husbands, discussion of the baby boys developing within them, the idiosyncrasies of pregnancy, sharing recipes, sampling vegetables, discussing health needs, and caring for each other. Think about the spiritual discussions they must have had—the visitation from Gabriel, knowing the presence of God, their testing of faith, their communion with the Holy Spirit.

There is nothing sweeter than fellowship between two sisters in the faith. "Koinonia" is the Greek word writers of the New Testa-ment used to define this blessed state. It goes beyond friendship and commonality, literally meaning "communion, communication, agreement of spirit, when two walk together in harmony." Do not neglect getting together with a committed friend, mentor, or spiri-tual guide. For two are always better than one.

For I long to see you, that I may impart to you some spiritual gift to strengthen you—that is, that we may be mutually encouraged by each other's faith, both yours and mine.

ROMANS 1:11–12 ESV

I sought the Lord, and he answered me and delivered me from all my fears.

PSALM 34:4 ESV

The testimony of David is this: "I sought the Lord, and he answered me," and as he waited before God, he was delivered from every fear. Dismissing his troubling circumstances and finding refuge in God, it only took one taste for him to declare "that the Lord is good" (Psalm 34:8 ESV).

Begin your day with this psalm: "I will bless the Lord at all times; His praise shall continually be in my mouth" (Psalm 34:1 ESV). No matter what happens, in every circumstance, in all situations, we can reach the heights of the psalmist. Whether we are full of fear and anxiety, or peace and contentment, we can still bless the Lord. Ask yourself, *Will I have the faith and courage to bless the Lord, to magnify His name, to exalt Him . . . at all times . . . beginning today?*

"My soul makes its boast in the Lord" (Psalm 34:2 ESV). Such boasting is not mere words that roll off the tongue easily but comes from within. David's boasting comes from the soul—his mind, will, and emotions—the mind gathering truth, the will choosing joy, the emotions bursting forth into verbal expressions that extol the Lord. When we speak words of praise, when our soul boasts in the Lord, joy overcomes fear.

O fear the Lord, you His saints; for to those who fear Him there is no want . . . But they who seek the Lord shall not be in want of any good thing.

PSALM 34:9–11

*Be anxious for nothing, but . . . let your requests be made known
to God.*

PHILIPPIANS 4:6

How did we come to the wrong conclusion that good Christians
should be able to handle everything without help? Who taught us
not to cry? Who said that to be truly strong means never admitting
a need? Not one time in Scripture are we told to deny reality or
to deny our feelings! If you can talk about your difficulties, if you
can express your feelings, you are doing well! "Let your request be
made known." How can we find grace to help in our time of need if
we do not bring our needs into the light?

Paul had no difficulty feeling his feelings or expressing his
needs. He didn't have false guilt. He didn't need to keep secrets
and didn't act as if he had life all together. He put it all out there,
revealing his need of grace to those who would pray. Paul, the one
dramatically converted near Damascus, the one who had celestial
visions, the man who wrote two-thirds of the New Testament, was
also afraid—just like you and me.

When we let our requests be made known, we receive grace to
help in our time of need. Let grace have its way. Rest in grace. Trust
in grace. Bask in His grace and reflect grace-light wherever you go.

---

*We may come near, then, with freedom, to the throne of the
grace, that we may receive kindness and find grace—for
seasonable help.*

HEBREWS 4:16 YLT

*In a certain city there was a judge who did not fear God and did
not respect man.*

LUKE 18:2

How much faith do you have in the justice system in America
today? Are verdicts ever influenced by fear, politics, racism, jury
tampering? Do our judges "fear God and respect man"? Most of
us are not judges, but we do judge. So, how do you evaluate people? What factors do you consider when you see another's faults or
weaknesses? For one person you may be prone to say it was a mis-
take, plain and simple, maybe a fault, but the same behavior from
another is downright sin! We are inconsistent.

Consider these words of Paul: "Do you have any business crossing people off the guest list or interfering with God's welcome? If
there are corrections to be made or manners to be learned, God
can handle that without your help" (Romans 14:4 MSG). Be honest
in your appraisal. A few words of criticism aimed at us can get our
backs out of joint, but we don't feel a thing when we criticize somebody else. Why can't we get along? At work, on the playground, at
the gym, in church, at home. There seems to be no end to the number of occasions and places where we want everything our way.

---

*I am not what I might be, I am not what I ought to be, I am not
what I hope to be, but I thank God I am not what I once was.*

JOHN NEWTON[17]

Even though I do not fear God nor respect man, yet because this widow bothers me, I will give her legal protection, otherwise by continually coming she will wear me out.

LUKE 18:4–5

Does persistence really pay off? Are you more likely to get an answer or to get one quicker if you are persistent? It seems wrong that an approach that is a lot like nagging will get results where patience will not. Thankfully this is one story that Jesus interprets for us. First thing He does is reveal the main point: "to show that at all times they ought to pray and not to lose heart" (Luke 18:1).

He encouraged them to press on, exercise faith, continue seeking, and not give up or lose heart until God answered. What he *did not* say was that God operated on the same level or in the same way that the unjust judge did. Instead, he presented a contrast. If the unjust judge would give in to a woman just to stop her continual asking, how much more would a righteous God give out of His love and grace? He does not give to placate but to satisfy longings, quench thirst, erase fear. He is more interested in spiritual needs than physical or material desires.

Prayer is not about getting things, it is about knowing God, connecting with Him, entering into communion with Him who is the Desire of your heart. When you have Him, you have everything you need.

Whom have I in heaven but You? And besides You, I desire nothing on earth.

PSALM 73:25

I know that it will be well for those who fear God, who fear Him
openly. But it will not be well for the evil man and he will not
lengthen his days like a shadow, because he does not fear God.
                                        ECCLESIASTES 8:12–13

Ecclesiastes holds nothing back as Solomon considers the futility
of the world. In my study Bible, the book is introduced: "Life seems
inconsistent, unpredictable, and unfair. No matter the generation,
no matter the time in history, the righteous and the wicked have
the same experiences, face the same trials, grapple with the same
problems. And all end up in the grave."[18] That is the tone with
which Solomon writes. And to the struggling Christian or the confused seeker, it makes a lot of sense.

Comparing the evil and the righteous person, the author
explains the behavior of those who fear God and those who do not:
"The evil man...will not lengthen his days...because he does not
fear God," and "I know that it will be well for those who fear God,
who fear Him openly." In an issue so serious, a topic that includes
length of days and quality of life, we should ask ourselves where we
stand on the matter. Do you really fear God? Is your life an example
of respect and honor for Him?

The only way to develop an honest fear of the Lord is to seek
Him in prayer and follow His Word. The fear of God comes with
knowing Him.

I will be with him in trouble; I will rescue him and honor him.
With a long life I will satisfy him and let him see My salvation.
                                        PSALM 91:15–16

As for you and your servants, I know that you do not yet fear the
Lord God.

EXODUS 9:30

To what lengths Yahweh will go to convince men that He is to be
feared! "I will send all My plagues on you and your servants and
your people, so that you may know that there is no one like Me in
all the earth" (Exodus 9:14). On the human side of the equation,
to what great lengths people will go to maintain their pride! We are
engaged in a battle of fears—the fear of God and of yielding the self
to Him versus the fear of losing our personhood. Dying spiritually,
set against dying physically. Spirit-filled against self-centered.

After the seventh plague, Pharaoh continued to harden his heart
against God. He had already endured six devastating assaults on
his people and land. Still he persisted, mustering strength, gathering intelligence from his soothsayers and magicians, consulting his
gods, mobilizing armies, and taking a stand against Yahweh. He
would do so an eighth, ninth, and tenth time, until death took the
firstborn son of every family including his own.

Fear is a good and valuable human emotion. There are times
when God-given fear kicks in followed by respect and times when
we overcome illegitimate fears by faith. By faith, put away any
human fears that hinder your walk with Christ.

May your unfailing love be with us, Lord, even as we put our
hope in you.

PSALM 33:22 NIV

Be strong and courageous, and do the work. Don't be afraid or discouraged, for the LORD God, my God, is with you. He will not fail you or forsake you.

1 CHRONICLES 28:20 NLT

The Spirit of God had revealed to David specific and detailed plans for the building of the temple and its furnishings. To ensure the work would be done right, David recorded every detail that he had received in a heavenly revelation. He encouraged his son Solomon to be strong and courageous, not afraid or discouraged because God was with him. David called Him the LORD God, Jehovah Elohim, my Elohim, and said that He would oversee the work and the workers, making certain they would finish the Temple correctly. With God firmly in charge, all fear about the project vanished.

You will probably never build something as grand and with such required precision, but there is much building to be done for the LORD. We never have to worry, be anxious, or fearful when we carefully follow His blueprint and do what the carpenter demands. For whether it is a building of wood or stone, the building of character, building a family, or building a life, God oversees. He will not fail or forsake you. He will see that your work for the LORD is finished correctly.

Unless the LORD builds the house, those who build it labor in vain. Unless the LORD watches over the city, the watchman stays awake in vain.

PSALM 127:1 ESV

Martha, Martha, you are anxious and troubled about many things.

LUKE 10:41 ESV

Two sisters, Mary and Martha, both loved Jesus, but they had different temperaments and very different ways of demonstrating affection. They may have been on different levels spiritually, but that is not the point of the story. Jesus was coming to their house, and both girls got busy. Martha began preparing food, sweeping floors, and making beds, and Mary started looking for a pen and notebook to record what Jesus might say. How can sisters be so different from each other? And Jesus knew them both so well!

No sooner had He arrived and settled in a chair than He noticed the two assuming their accustomed roles without giving thought to what He really desired. At that moment, food was far less important than having their attention. Eager to share words of truth and life, His heart must have been set upon encouragement, fellowship, rest.

Jesus didn't hold back an opinion, "Martha, Martha! you are anxious and troubled." He paused before complimenting Mary for her soft-hearted attentiveness. His words did not demean household chores nor imply that Mary was a better Christian. But there had been a decision for the sisters to make, and Mary had chosen best. Fear or fussiness would not dampen her joy on this special day. She knew that paying attention to Jesus was the most important thing in life. And so it is today.

Mary has chosen the good part, which shall not be taken away from her.

LUKE 10:42

Don't be afraid of him. I'm making a present of him to you, him
and all his people and his land.

NUMBERS 21:34 MSG

"Don't be afraid of him," Moses said as he handed over the enemy
they feared. "I'm making a present of him to you." God's gift on
that day was not more land or more people, but removing from
their trembling hearts all traces of their fear. Always He is more
focused upon the heart than any outward need. He loves you
enough to defeat every fear that opposes your faith.

One morning our adult son began questioning the need for an
already scheduled biopsy possibly followed by immediate surgery.
Dreading the procedure and fearing the results, he said, "I am one
patient among hundreds. The doctor enters the examination room,
reads the chart, makes a decision based upon one test, and sug-
gests something that could change my life forever. I don't know
what to do." After a long discussion with the family, he made a
hard decision and found peace. He chose to wait for more testing
before consenting to surgery.

Afterward, my thoughts turned to the Great Physician who
always knows what's happening, the One who cares ceaselessly,
lovingly, who demonstrates in hundreds of ways that we are the
object of His affection! We can rest assured in His love and wisdom. He affirms it constantly in His Word.

My beloved is mine, and I am his.

SONG OF SOLOMON 2:16

God will give ear and humble them, because they do not change and do not fear God.

PSALM 55:19 ESV

Humility is the characteristic that Andrew Murray calls "the root from which all graces grow."[19] Though it is impossible to achieve humility on our own, Scripture teaches us to pursue it. "For everyone who exalts himself will be humbled and he who humbles himself will be exalted" (Luke 14:11). But it seems the harder I try to be humble, the prouder I become of myself. That's when I remember this statement by an unknown author: _"Humility is that grace that, when you know you have it, you have lost it."_ Is it possible to humble oneself and still try to be the best you can be?

It depends upon _why_ you want to be your best. Are your efforts self-promoting, man-pleasing, or God-honoring? Think about one of your best days. You gain a measure of prestige, accomplish a significant task, reach a long-sought-after goal, and you are rightfully proud. Congratulations are in order. But before you take a deep breath and stand up straight, you start thinking, _I am one creative being—a near genius. Look at what I have done!_

Examine yourself! God's ears are open, and He will humble those who do not fear Him.

Clothe yourselves, with humility toward one another, for God opposes the proud but gives grace to the humble. Humble yourselves, therefore, under the mighty hand of God.

1 PETER 5:5–6 ESV

*I tell you, my friends, do not fear those who kill the body, and
after that have nothing more that they can do.*

LUKE 12:4 ESV

One of our children uses a whiteboard in his room to record
appointments and upcoming events. He also writes quotes and
words of wit and wisdom. For several months this statement stayed
put: "What is the worst thing that can happen?" I asked him about
it. "Well, the worst thing that can happen would be if it killed me.
But if it kills me, I am in a better place and the list doesn't matter
anymore." We laughed as I noticed another quote on the board:
"What doesn't kill you makes you better." Truth all over the place,
though some are spoken in jest!

The one-liners in our son's bedroom and the verse written above
have much in common. As you deal with your fears, don't focus on
the one that can only kill the body; focus instead on the one that
can do even more. Sometimes we become entangled in thoughts of
each day, but not for long, eternity is in our hearts and never really
leaves our minds.

Our fear should be focused upon God alone. There is nothing
more consoling when we are pressed by problems than remember-
ing that God is outside this realm. His throne is above the world
and outside of time. He is the everlasting God.

---

*Let us come before His presence with thanksgiving, let us shout
joyfully to Him with psalms.*

PSALM 95: 2

Indeed, the very hairs of your head are all numbered. Don't be afraid; you are worth more than many sparrows.

LUKE 12:7 NIV84

"It occurred to me one day that though I often worry about whether or not I sense the presence of God, I give little thought to whether God senses the presence of me," wrote Philip Yancey in his thought-changing book called *Prayer*. "When I come to God in prayer, do I bare the deepest, most hidden part of myself? Only when I do so will I discover myself as I truly am for nothing short of God's light can reveal that. I feel stripped before that light, seeing a person far different from the image I cultivate for myself and for everyone around me."[20]

What is the image you have cultivated for yourself? Do you think you are near perfect? Do you feel inept, inadequate, or unskilled for the work you do? Do you see an image in the mirror that does not measure up to the one you desire? Perhaps now would be a good time to consider, to pray, to "bare the deepest, most hidden part" of yourself. In that quiet place, in the company of the Creator, the One who designed you for His purposes, will you find a true picture of who you really are.

When I remember You on my bed, I meditate on You in the night watches, for You have been my help, and in the shadow of Your wings I sing for joy.

PSALM 63:6–7

SUMMER

The moon is at her full, and riding high,
Floods the calm fields with light.
The airs that hover in the summer sky
Are all asleep tonight.

WILLIAM C. BRYANT

No, do not be afraid of those nations, for the LORD your God is among you, and he is a great and awesome God.

DEUTERONOMY 7:21 NLT

This is one of those times when the LORD just says, "No! Do not be afraid!" I need to hear His "nos," don't you? Sometimes we just need to stop! Stop the sniveling, quit the whining, tie your shoe, and start walking. Walk in the truth that you know. The LORD your God is among you. "And He is a great and awesome God."

God chose Israel as His beloved possession for one reason—because He loved the Israelites. They were set apart to sanctify the earth since it had been polluted by sin. His choice was never meant to be a source of pride. It was a mystery, for there was no special goodness, greatness, or purity to warrant such a calling. His choice was based upon the covenant He had made with Abraham, Isaac, and Jacob. He had vowed to make them a great nation and to give them Canaan. He was faithful to His Word. And He always is!

When you realize that you are one of His beloved, that He has chosen and drawn you to Himself, certain truths bind us there: The LORD alone is God. He is the Faithful God, and we are partners in His Covenant of Grace.

This is my comfort in my affliction, that Your word has revived me... Your statutes are my songs in the house of my pilgrimage.

PSALM 119:50, 54

> *God heard the boy crying, and the angel of God called to Hagar*
> *from heaven and said to her, ". . . Do not be afraid; God has*
> *heard the boy crying as he lies there."*
>
> GENESIS 21:17 NIV

Hagar prayed for her son dying in her arms, addressing God as "El Roi"—God Who Sees Me. And He answered! A twenty-first-century mother prayed for her son too—on her knees, throughout busy days, and in sleepless nights. "Lord, change him. I'm afraid! Do you hear me?" Her anguish reached crisis point when his long battle with alcohol threatened his life. His liver was failing; he had chest pains. Her prayers became Hagar-like, frantic: "Please! Help! I can't do this anymore." She even offered God an idea. "Let me trade places with my son. Give me his addiction and set him free. Take my life and save his." Exhausted, she sank into her pillow and wiped her tears.

In the stillness, God spoke: "If I were to take your life, you would have to trust me to take care of your son. Why not trust me now?" Faith bubbling like an eternal spring brought a fresh understanding of God's ways. He'd been waiting for her to let go, to get out of the way, so He could do something better than she could imagine! She let go of her most precious possession, and God gave restful sleep. She awoke with hope. Later her son yielded his life to God.

> *She also said, "I have truly seen the One who sees me?"*
>
> GENESIS 16:13 NLT

Do not be afraid! . . . Go to him and comfort him, for I will make
a great nation from his descendants.

GENESIS 21:18 NLT

It challenges common sense, motherly instinct, and our concept of Christian compassion. But sometimes "letting go" of another person or problems is the kindest act of all. We know that every person is responsible for their own spiritual growth. We can't make choices for somebody else. But our actions fail to support our belief. Most of us are "fixers" struggling with the "let go and let God" concept.

We can't let go because we don't know what it really means. Being solution-oriented and pre-programed to *do something*, we jump in headfirst. But we must be careful that *our doing* doesn't interfere with *His doing*. Help, in this situation, is not really about *doing* anything. It's about *not doing*. It's taking our hands off, allowing God to handle the situation as He pleases, in His time. Life's twists and turns, ups and downs, stumbles and falls, accompanied by fears too big to handle are the very things God uses to bring about a change of heart in those we love. They are also the things we prevent by our giving and doing. Our over-involvement and lack of wisdom just complicate matters, delaying the person's willingness to yield to God.

We just cannot fix this for someone else. We are not that powerful! It is time to let go and leave our fear in the hands of the Almighty.

Everything you want is on the other side of fear.

JACK CANFIELD[21]

The LORD is the one who goes ahead of you; He will be with you.
He will not fail you or forsake you. Do not fear or be dismayed.

DEUTERONOMY 31:8

When it comes to helping an addicted loved one, our part should be easy, like opening a closed hand to free a captive butterfly or releasing a loaded backpack from our shoulders. If a mother could fix a child by loving him, or a wife could save a husband by yelling, there would be no addicts! We all try! But there are not enough words, not enough new ideas, not enough money to change even one person. But God can heal! "Commit your way to the LORD, trust also in Him, and He will do it" (Psalm 37:5).

"Commit" literally means "to roll" or "to roll away." Another Bible translation reads: "Roll on Jehovah thy way, and trust upon Him, and He worketh" (Psalm 37:5 YLT). "Worketh" is in the present tense and means "beginning now"—literally the minute you let go. Notice the three verbs in sequence. "Roll"—like rolling a ball downhill, trust—lean into Jehovah, then (and only then) He "worketh." The psalmist wrote, "He will do it!"

Perhaps it's time to "trust upon Him." Uncurl your clenched fingers and fear rolls away like a boulder rolling downhill. Do not fear or be dismayed.

Roll on Jehovah thy way, and trust upon Him, and He worketh,
and hath brought out as light thy righteousness, and thy
judgment as noon-day. Be silent for Jehovah, and stay thyself
for Him.

PSALM 37:5–7 YLT

*Do not let your heart be troubled; believe in God, believe
also in Me.*

JOHN 14:1

Have you ever had a really bad year? One in which you experienced
several tragedies or losses? A time when you were really afraid? A
year when you may have feared stepping outside because something might just drop out of the sky and hit you on the head? Sometimes it happens for no other reason than this: God loves you so
much that He trusts you with pain and sorrow. In the Scriptures it
is called "filling up what is lacking in Christ's afflictions" (Colossians 1:24).

The suffering of Jesus on the cross was completely sufficient for
our salvation. The verse is not talking about that! This word for
Christ's affliction has a different meaning, like pressure, tribulation, or distress. And as long as the church is active in our world
and we are a part of it, we will be the recipients of His affliction.
Since the church is His body, when it suffers, He suffers too. It is
our privilege to suffer willingly in His place for His glory.

He delights in you enough to take you to a deeper place with
Him. He desires your attention so much that an invitation goes out
requesting you get to know Him better, asking you to participate in
something so holy, so life-changing, so absolutely out of this world
that it will bond you forever to Him.

---

*That I may know Him and the power of His resurrection and the
fellowship of His sufferings.*

PHILIPPIANS 3:10

Sarah obeyed Abraham, calling him lord, and you have become her children if you do what is right without being frightened by any fear.

1 PETER 3:6

"Without being frightened by any fear." Well, that's asking a lot of us. See or hear something that ties you in knots and just put a lid on it? Declare the thing delightful and press on? Is it even possible to be unafraid when something is really frightening? The word "frightened" in Greek is "phobia," and "any fear" means the person, place, or thing that produced the fear. Do not fear the fear! Could it simply be encouraging you to keep doing good and ignore the fear, and never let it keep you from obeying the Lord?

Sarah had confidence in her husband and had no problem recognizing his position of leadership in the family. She called him lord. Obedience is easy, when you believe in the one who leads. Even when your confidence is shaken, you can have faith in God who stands beside, protects, and guides through the one in charge. God is a God of order, and He does all things well. If we continue to do what is good and trust God, we enjoy being called the children of Sarah. And with that status comes great security and peace.

Obey your spiritual leaders, and do what they say. Their work is to watch over your souls, and they are accountable to God.

HEBREWS 13:17 NLT

If you should suffer for the sake of righteousness, you are blessed.
And do not fear their intimidation, and do not be troubled.

1 PETER 3:14

Intimidation happens, sometimes to the experienced, to the most confident among us, even to the one who is called, equipped, and certain of his mission. It's the pebble in a rock-climber's boot, the flea that torments a service animal, or the mosquito that buzzes under my desk and bites my feet while I am writing devotionals. Intimidation can also come from an enemy, a naysayer, a nitpicky octogenarian, a cranky baby, or a man with a headache. Even when nothing is verbalized, the downward curl of a lip, a cockeyed grin, or a snarky comment can intimidate just as well. It won't kill me! It won't even stop me from doing my work. But it does frustrate plans, impede progress, disrupt thoughts, and sometimes makes me stomp my feet and shout, "Devil, get lost."

The word "intimidate" is most often interpreted "fear," sometimes "dread" or "that which strikes terror." And that means different things to different folks! We all have different histories, which set us up for different failures and unique fears. But, praise be to God, Jesus delivers us from all of them.

For everyone who has been born of God overcomes the world.
And this is the victory that has overcome the world—our faith.

1 JOHN 5:4 ESV

We will not fear, though the earth should change and though the mountains slip into the heart of the sea.

PSALM 46:2

We put a lot of confidence in the earth. For many, it is the one thing that provides stability. For as long as we've been occupying this planet, it has not ceased to turn upon its axis, rotate around the sun, display its one moon, and provide a safe place to gaze at the stars. While I do my part to protect and preserve it, I am not afraid of what might happen to the earth itself. I'm content to leave it in the hands of God, allow scientists to worry, and pretty much get lost in my little corner of the world.

What if "the earth should change"? What if the mountains begin to slip into the sea? Honestly, I think that would expose a huge problem with fear! With no place to run, no mountain to climb, no sea upon which to sail away, would people cry out for God?

Knowing that God is good and does all things well is enough to illuminate the darkest parts of our world. If the earth shifts beneath our feet, we can hold on to the truth that encouraged the psalmist. He said, "I will not fear" because his confidence was in God alone, not even in something as sturdy as the planet earth.

———

They who dwell in the ends of the earth stand in awe of Your signs; You make the dawn and the sunset shout for joy.

PSALM 65:8

*Have no fear of them, nor be troubled . . . always being prepared
to make a defense to anyone who asks you for a reason for the
hope that is in you; yet do it with gentleness and respect.*

1 PETER 3:14–15 ESV

What is the reason for your hope? If your hope is built on anything
other than Christ the Rock, you may be compared to the "foolish man who built his house on the sand" (Matthew 7:26). That
house could not withstand rain and floods, wind and storms. And
when it fell, the destruction was great. Christ, the Solid Rock, is
our hope, our confident expectation of eternal life, our firm foundation. There is hope when our faith is in Him.

Hope is akin to faith. Most of us hope for salvation, redemption,
and spiritual growth. We have faith that God will complete the
work He has begun in us. We hope for it, plan for it, and when problems come, we seek quick solutions. Closure, a trendy word spoken
often in today's friendship circles, shows how much we like everything fixed, cleaned up, and figured out in a way that makes sense.
Hope takes us much deeper. It is a grace that enables us to walk
on, without resolution, being content, feeling complete because we
have faith in a Source Who is beyond and above ourselves.

----

*Therefore, having been justified by faith, we have peace with
God through our Lord Jesus Christ, through whom also we have
obtained our introduction by faith into this grace in which we
stand; and we exult in hope of the glory of God.*

ROMANS 5:1–2

I am afraid of my lord the king, who has appointed your food and your drink; for why should he see your faces looking more haggard than the youths who are your own age?

DANIEL 1:10

Daniel knew the dangers lurking in the shadows of the king's court, but he found a way to take a stand for what was right. He submitted to the teaching of those who held him captive, including the study of literature and language. But he would not eat a diet that was not kosher. Being a faithful Jewish boy, he wanted to follow the law he'd been taught. Look how he handled the fearful situation. He politely appealed and suggested an alternate plan, saying something like this: "Would you allow me and my friends to eat the diet we're familiar with, the one commanded by our people, and then see if we are equally healthy than those who eat the rich meats and wine offered at the king's training table?" The king agreed and they passed the test!

We would do well to follow Daniel's example when challenges come. Especially when we don't agree with a spiritual leader's expectations. Daniel made up his mind based upon God's Word. He sought permission and God granted grace. Being resolute and taking a stand doesn't mean being obnoxious or stubborn. It looks for an opportunity to be creative and compliant, drawing upon God's wisdom. By graciously handling this life-threatening situation, he saved himself, his friends, and the wise men of Babylon as well.

Grace is God's power to do what I cannot do.

UNKNOWN

*In the fear of the LORD there is strong confidence, and his
children will have refuge.*

PROVERBS 14:26

I have to admit there are times I slip into the same muddled
thoughts that I've heard from others. *If only I were good enough, pretty
enough, smart enough, then God would love me more.* I'm tempted by
the craziest things, have made a gazillion wrong choices, and there
are days I don't have a clue what God wants me to do. Some may
think, *If I just hadn't made so many mistakes, if only I had done this
thing, or had not done that.* So how can we, fearful beings that we
are, be accepted by a perfect holy God?

While we may feel unacceptable, the truth is our Heavenly
Father delights in loving the unlovely, the flawed, and the broken.
He is pleased with us simply because we belong to Him. We are His
children, warts and all. While we might give our lives for someone
who is nice, for our children, for a person we love, Jesus willingly
laid down His life for the likes of you and me. Some of us simply
don't think we measure up. Others may have been neglected, hurt,
or abused in ways that make it even harder to believe we are loved.
His unconditional love is easy to accept once we grasp that "Christ
died for the ungodly" (Romans 5:6).

----

*The LORD will be your confidence and will keep your foot from
being caught.*

PROVERBS 3:26

There is no fear in love.

1 JOHN 4:18

Our Father knew we would be searching for the real meaning of love, so He inspired a comprehensive description of it in the New Testament. Here is 1 Corinthians 13 written in the everyday, easier-to-grasp language of *The Message*: "Love never gives up. Love cares more for others than for self. Love doesn't want what it doesn't have. Love doesn't strut, doesn't have a swelled head, doesn't force itself on others, Isn't always 'me first,' doesn't fly off the handle, doesn't keep score of the sins of others, doesn't revel when others grovel, takes pleasure in the flowering of truth, puts up with anything, trusts God always, always looks for the best, never looks back, but keeps going to the end."

Author Eugene Peterson claims, "The two most difficult things to get straight in life are the meaning of love and the nature of God. More often than not, the mess people make of their lives can be traced to failure or stupidity or meanness in one or both of these areas."[22]

Have you ever loved one single person with that kind of love you just read about? Have you been loved that much? Ask God to answer your questions and allow His love to fill the empty places in your heart.

*Have a reputation for helping out with children, strangers, tired
Christians, the hurt and troubled.*

1 TIMOTHY 5:10 MSG

In families that function well, we come together in an ever-
widening circle bringing our needs, prayers, and problems. To
share joys and sorrows, to ask questions and celebrate answers,
to seek advice and find insights, to reveal fear and find peace. And
to meet one of life's most basic needs, having connection and feeling loved. Our churches are a family too, for the same reasons. We
need each other.

In *What Is a Family?*, author Edith Schaeffer wrote: "A family is
a mobile—a human art form. Within the framework of family each
individual is moving, changing, growing, or declining—affecting
each other intellectually, emotionally, spiritually, physically, and
psychologically. The grouping of toddlers with young schoolchil-
dren, of ten-year-olds with teenagers, of young married couples
with middle-aged couples, of grandparents with two generations
coming along under them, is an amazingly real, vivid, and living
mobile."[23]

As part of a living art form, we are not helpless or inadequate. A
family provides extra sets of arms, more hearts in union, and lots
of shared information. It is a safe place to be honest about fear, and
overcome anxiety. Most are not perfect, but we can do our part to
make ours better. We all need a safe place to fall and a secure place
to rest.

*Walk with me and work with me—watch how I do it. Learn
the unforced rhythms of grace. I won't lay anything heavy or ill-
fitting on you.*

MATTHEW 11:29 MSG

Have you ever accepted a position of leadership because you
wanted to please somebody other than God? Maybe you said yes
for a good reason—to fill a vacant position, to help a leader you
admire, or maybe to simply find important work to do. Jesus not
only said, "Work with me" but also "walk with me"—bringing
work and walk together into a meaningful relationship between
Master and apprentice.

Not to learn better methods or develop leadership skills, but to
"learn the unforced rhythms of grace." Jesus says, "Learn of me."
In the original language the words mean "disciple." He is saying be
My disciple. Follow me.

In Matthew's gospel, Jesus singles out two qualities that we may
duplicate, "for I am gentle and humble in heart" (Matthew 11:29).
How interesting that He doesn't say imitate me because "I am powerful, I am eloquent." Instead He says to be like Him in gentleness
and humility. Gentleness toward others is the quality He imparts
to His disciples as they work together serving others; humility is
the attitude of heart Jesus demonstrated to His followers as he
leads them into total selflessness. He is the Leader we will follow to
the ends of the earth.

---

*Stand by the ways and see and ask for the ancient paths, where
the good way is, and walk in it.*

JEREMIAH 6:16

Do not be afraid of them . . . for I have given you victory over them. Not a single one of them will be able to stand up to you.

JOSHUA 10:8 NLT

Joshua was God's chosen leader as His people entered the Promised Land. He was not the oldest or the most mature, but he was full of the Spirit and had a heart for God. Think about your personal criteria for a leader, teacher, or minister. Do your views differ from God's?

We may think the job requires . . .

- someone who's strong—having inner strength, physical energy, and good health;
- a person with an impressive educational background, educated in the best schools and universities—preferably Christian schools;
- one who is self-confident and has a vibrant personality;
- a person who loves God supremely, wholeheartedly.

When God looks for a person to lead His people, He looks for someone with qualities that may seem completely upside down to us. He seeks . . .

- someone who knows he's inadequate, so he will depend on Him;
- one who realizes his weakness, so he will find strength in God's resources;
- one who may or may not have a college education but who values spiritual truth;
- a person who is not self-confident but Christ-confident (secure and complete in Him);
- someone who knows her own heart, who can confess her need for growth in Christ.

Is anyone here afraid or worried? If you are, you may go home before you frighten anyone else.

DEUTERONOMY 20:8 NLT

Fear is both infectious and contagious. Like yelling "fire" in a theater, an outburst of fear from just one individual catches on quickly and spreads like a virus. It moves through a family, contaminates a group, infests the church, and affects a nation. No wonder Moses wanted to stop the infection before the entire mission failed. So he said something like this: *If anyone is afraid or worried, run along home before you frighten someone else.* Fear is the flu pandemic of 1918. Nothing can stop its spread but a period of quarantine and lots of rest.

When it comes to faith, the polar opposite of fear, the cure is the same. Quarantine yourself in a quiet place—your office with a closed door, your favorite chair in a secluded room, the pier on a placid lake, or walking along a scenic pathway without counting steps or adding up miles. The goal is to be quiet. Listen. Speak God's Words back to Him. Guard this special time as if it were pure gold. Rest until He has restored your soul.

He humbled you and let you be hungry, and fed you with manna which you did not know, nor did your fathers know, that He might make you understand that man does not live by bread alone, but man lives by everything that proceeds out of the mouth of the LORD.

DEUTERONOMY 8:3

Whom have you so dreaded and feared that you have been
false to me, and have neither remembered me nor pondered
this in your hearts?

ISAIAH 57:11 NIV84

The question is who do you dread, who do you fear more than you fear God? How could you, a person who once honored God, become more afraid of someone else far less important and much less powerful? What kind of fear would lead a person who loves Jesus to deny Him? How deep the extent of fear! How soul-saturating the disease called dread! Does it have any influence over you? Is it strong enough to make you become false with God?

Today would be a good time for us to examine ourselves, to ponder this in our hearts and bring it into the light. There is no condemnation to those who are in Christ Jesus. His grace is sufficient—even for our fear! God never told us to hide from Him. Instead He said to talk to Him, revealing all our needs and requests. Come to Him today as Hezekiah did, spreading it all out before the Lord, then offering prayer. See him bowed, hands resting upon the pages as he seeks wisdom (see 2 Kings 19:14–15).

God is waiting for you to lift the shade, open the windows of your soul, and allow the fragrant flow of His Holy Spirit to wash over you.

————

The LORD is near to the brokenhearted and saves the crushed
in spirit.

PSALM 34:18

Is it not because I have long been silent that you do not fear me?

ISAIAH 57:11 NIV84

Israel had forgotten God because He had "long been silent"! Into that void rose apathy and discontent. The people drifted from the truth and forgot God's goodness. What fear had supplanted their fear of God? God has said He will never accuse nor always be angry (see Isaiah 57:16). But sometimes He is silent. Have you ever known the silence of God? What could possibly be His purpose?

A few days after back surgery, my temperature soared, pain increased, and fear threatened. What was happening to me? I prayed and expected a quick answer from my Father. Instead, a distressing ominous silence prevailed.

The doctor said an infection was spreading close to my spine. Another surgery to clean the previous wound was scheduled. I did not doubt God's existence, but I did wonder about His love. I felt lonely and afraid. After the second surgery and six weeks of IV antibiotics, I finally recovered.

I awoke one morning to bright sunshine filtering through my windows. I picked up my Bible and held it close. In the stillness, I understood the *why*. By leaning into the truth I knew, by trusting His presence even when I did not feel it, I had actually grown in my faith. Isn't that what faith is all about?

Faith is not that I see God, but that I know God sees me; that is good enough for me. I will run out and play—a life of absolute freedom.

OSWALD CHAMBERS[24]

And which of you by worrying can add a single hour to
his life's span?

LUKE 12:25

Most of us are skeptics—we believe what we can see and feel, while
God wants to bring us to a place of blind faith and dependence. Do
you honestly think that by worrying about having a longer productive life, you can increase your days on this planet? Can you by worrying add one inch to your stature? Of course not! Worry can make
us insane! Still, when we don't feel the presence of God, worry and
fear can slip in and displace faith. Either we believe and hang on, or
we give in to frustration and give place to fear. Issues both large and
looming and small but disconcerting are settled by faith.

One of my sons was about fourteen when he realized that he
was shorter than all the boys in his class. He envied and worried. It
only added weight to his backpack of fear. But eventually the cure
came by faith, accompanied by good works! I marked his height on
the doorframe going into our kitchen. Whenever the subject sur-
faced, I asked him to deal in reality.

We'd head to the kitchen and measure his height. Every time
we drew a line above the ruler, there had been growth—an eighth
of an inch, a fourth, or more. Bit by bit, he was getting taller. Eventually height was not an issue. Neither was worry and fear. When
he reached his senior year he also had reached his goal! He had
become the exact size written in God's eternal plan before he was
even conceived.

My frame was not hidden from you when I was made in secret.

PSALM 139:15

For God hath not given us the spirit of fear; but of power, and of love, and of a sound mind.

2 TIMOTHY 1:7 AV

The word "fear" in this verse is translated cowardice, fearfulness, or timidity. Timothy had a spirit of fear or an element of fearfulness in his character. It was a natural disposition that was detrimental to his ministry as a church leader. He needed power, love, and "a sound mind." Some of the disciples had the same kind of fear. Jesus defined it as having little faith. They were fearful instead of faithful. There is another word for the fear which we all experience at times. The Greek word looks and sounds like our English word "phobia."

Seems to me there are three kinds of fear. Proper fear, which means fearing God, having reverence, being in awe of what is Holy. Real fear: the normal run-for-your-life kind of fear because there is cause to be afraid. And false fear: a phobia that can be described as false evidence appearing real.

False
Evidence
Appearing
Real

Examine your own soul. Do you need to deal with fear so it will not hinder your ministry? Confess it to God and ask Him for the Timothy solution—renewed power, love, and discipline or sound thinking. Allow the Holy Spirit to fill your heart with the sun-ripened fruit of love, joy, and peace.

*Their protection has been removed . . . and the LORD is with us;
do not fear them.*

NUMBERS 14:9

God had promised to give the land of Canaan to Israel, but the
Israelites were afraid. So Moses sent an advance team of twelve
men to spy on the land and the people. Once there they found the
land to be beautiful and bountiful. But they saw the residents living in walled cities—the Israelites lived in tents, open to attack.
The people were giants—the Israelites were small. Their faith
began to waver.

No wonder that author Erwin Lutzer wrote in *Failure: The Back
Door to Success* about what he calls shedding the Grasshopper
Complex. Of the twelve spies who went out, ten were "shaken with
fear, the fear of failure. The result? The majority report read, 'We
were like grasshoppers in our own sight, and so we were in their
sight' (Numbers 13:33 NKJV). Conclusion—failure is inevitable.
Grasshoppers don't win wars!"[25]

Seems the spies had forgotten God's promise that He would be
giving the land to them! Only two believed God. Not a good ratio, is
it? Two would follow God; ten would doubt and instigate a church
split. How destructive is fear! Unresolved, it always leads to failure.
When the spies saw themselves as grasshoppers, they assumed the
Canaanites thought the same. But the Canaanites were afraid of
Israel! They had heard about God parting the Red Sea.

Are there giants in your land? If so, the "Grasshopper Complex"
can be overcome by your persistent faith.

I saw a dream and it made me fearful; and these fantasies as I
lay on my bed and the visions in my mind kept alarming me.

DANIEL 4:5

Picture King Nebuchadnezzar strutting back and forth on his
balcony surveying his many accomplishments. He had acknowledged the God of Israel, but he couldn't resist congratulating himself: "Is this not Babylon the great, which I myself have built as a
royal residence by the might of my power and for the glory of my
majesty?"(Daniel 4:30). I myself? My power? My majesty? That was
enough! God's voice boomed earthward, reverberating on celestial
airwaves until it connected with his intended receiver—the ear
of the proud king. "Sovereignty...has been removed from you!"
(Daniel 4:31).

Crazed by fear, Nebuchadnezzar wandered into the fields where
he lived for seven years, eating a unique variety of humble pie—the
dew-drenched grasses of his pasture. Accustomed to marble pools,
he washed himself with dew. His hair grew long "like eagles' feath-
ers and his nails like birds' claws" (Daniel 4:33). Who would not be
terrorized at that—especially considering that hair and fingernail
thing!

Eventually the king wandered back home and his reason
returned. Could it be that pride is a kind of temporary insanity—
a craziness that claims we do not need God, that we are self-
sufficient? Is it possible that reasonably sane people could lose our
minds as the good king did? That should strike fear in every proud
human heart.[26]

*When your dread comes like a storm and your calamity
comes like a whirlwind, when distress and anguish come upon
you . . . "Then they will call on me."*

PROVERBS 1:27–28

Relationships become complicated because of our inherent
differences—in every cell, in personality, innate sin patterns,
our genetic code, in our blood and bones, we are creatively and
uniquely designed by God—knit together in our mother's womb
like carefully sewn embroidery (see Psalm 139:13). Widely different gifts, talents, and abilities develop. Indelible impressions alter
the way we think. With distinct personality types and a few personality disorders, we function and dysfunction in our own way.

With all that God-given diversity, He tells us to live in unity!
What a great sense of humor! As we stretch toward the goal of one
heart and mind, we must accept each other. Our differences give
perspective and balance, and serve to complete the body of Christ.

Other struggles happen because of stress, anxiety, and fear.
With all these factors mixed together, we need liberal doses of
compassion and forgiveness. Forgive is a compound word: FOR
and GIVE. Forgiveness is not a feeling but a conscious decision. It's
saying I choose to be FOR you and I am willing to GIVE to you. I
will offer up my opinions and position on this matter and yield.
Seems there will always be opportunities in this life to forgive.

———

*Therefore, accept each other just as Christ has accepted you so
that God will be given glory.*

ROMANS 15:7 NLT

Jonathan . . . arose and went to David . . . and encouraged him in
God . . . "Do not be afraid . . . you will be king over Israel and I
will be next to you."

1 SAMUEL 23:16–17

David was chosen by God to be the king, and Saul feared him. Saul's fear was rooted in jealousy, instigated by the devil, but always in the sovereign control of Elohim. So full of evil was Saul that his son Jonathan had to choose between a relationship with his deeply spiritual friend and the deteriorating relationship with his father who was operating under the influence of demons.

Jonathan made a good choice, even though it was a difficult one. Family ties are strong, even among those who are wicked. To his friend, Jonathan had said, "Whatever you say, I will do for you" (1 Samuel 20:4). These two friends shared family problems, even the truth about Saul's evil intent. Jonathan and David were united with each other in a covenant of friendship, entered into with an oath before God, and anchored in the lovingkindness of the LORD. Do you have a friend like Jonathan? Are you that kind of friend to someone else?

Friendship is . . . willingness to serve the other person faithfully even at great cost.

Friendship is . . . based upon and centered in relationship with God.

Friendship is . . . available in good times and bad, has mutual goals, and is willing to risk.

The LORD will be between me and you, and between my
descendants and your descendants forever.

1 SAMUEL 20:42

Do not fear, for I will surely show kindness to you for the sake of your father Jonathan.

2 SAMUEL 9:7

How can David, a man who killed tens of thousands of people using dreadful methods, also be full of compassion and gripped by grace? Why would he seek a descendant of Saul, the man who tried countless times to murder him, just to show him kindness? We can more easily understand revenge, one who goes to great lengths to find the survivor or the perpetrator, and put him to death. This story is upside down to the human mind. It can only be written when the heart of the lead character knows God's love—love shed abroad by the Holy Spirit.

Mephibosheth, the son of Jonathan, was five when his father and grandfather were killed. As he and his nurse fled the bloody scene, the child was injured in a disastrous fall. Years later, David approached Ziba, an elderly servant of Saul, and asked if there was anyone left of the house of the king. And there was! "There is still a son of Jonathan who is crippled in both feet" (2 Samuel 9:3). David sent for him, calmed his fear, and gave him his grandfather's land and treasure. He ate at the king's table regularly as one of his sons.

David is a picture of Jesus—One who loves you and me with our crippled feet and broken lives, simply because He wants to show us kindness. We are invited as sons and daughters to His table laden with bountiful grace and mercy.

Love—there is no greater power on earth.

Don't be afraid... God in his goodness has granted safety to
everyone sailing with you.

ACTS 27:24 NLT

Healthy relationships depend upon good choices. So, who are your friends? Who are you sailing with? It is an important question and one worth consideration, for those who accompany you have a great influence upon your life. In this situation, Luke's sailing companions reaped the benefit of being closely associated with Jesus. Because they made that choice, God granted them complete safety.

Solomon, the wise son of King David, wrote the book of Proverbs after years of making wrong choices about relationships:

- "Faithful are the wounds of a friend, but deceitful are the kisses of an enemy" (Proverbs 27:6).
- "Oil and perfume make the heart glad, so a man's counsel is sweet to his friend" (Proverbs 27:9).
- "Iron sharpens iron, so one man sharpens another" (Proverbs 27:17).

These words by author Linda Dillow lift my thoughts about friends to a higher plane, taking it out of the ordinary associations of life into the holiest of relationships: "A friend is clothed with Seraphim wings, running ahead of me shouting, 'Holy Holy, Holy,' pushing me into the presence of God. The Spirit of Aaron and Hur clothes a friend, running behind me, she sets me on a rock, holds up my weary hands and waits with me in silence while the Lord fights my battles."[27]

*Furthermore, men are afraid of a high place and of terrors on
the road.*

ECCLESIASTES 12:5

Psychologists say that men and women are different in every cell
of our bodies. We are different in other ways too. Different ideas
about television channels and the snacks we share, whether it is
cold or hot, what time to go to bed, and whether the child was
wrong or just being a boy. The differences extend outside the home
as well. It gets in the car with us on local errands and every road
trip. I am willing to admit that while I am checking my lip gloss,
the man I travel with is focused upon "terrors on the road."

It is an irrational fear, but one that's very real to him. He knows
I am a good driver with an almost perfect record and proficient
at multitasking, but emotions get the better of him. Obviously the
perspective is different from the passenger's seat; from that side
of the car, the guardrails seem closer and the speedometer reads
incorrectly.

I continue to be patient and offer opportunities for him to practice self-control. Meanwhile, God is using his fears for good, just
as He has promised. Recently I heard him praying as I pulled onto
the highway. He gripped the handle above the window and said,
"Lord, I feel very close to you right now."

---

*Keep fervent in your love for one another, because love covers
a multitude of sins.*

1 PETER 4:8

Be subject to one another in the fear of Christ.

EPHESIANS 5:21

This is my favorite verse when it comes to marriage. It applies to newlyweds and oldyweds, pregnant moms and moms at work, dads with computers, and men in trucks. It works when having babies, raising kids, filling an empty nest, and facing retirement. Absorb its all-encompassing wisdom: "Be subject to one another in the fear of Christ!"

That is Relationship 101. If we want to get along with anybody, it's the key to success. In the military, being subject to another would mean arranging the troops under the command of a leader, but we are talking family here! Biblical order has nothing to do with one parent being commander in chief. It is easier than that. It's about two people with the same goals, in different roles, who love each other. It means giving in to the needs of another, yielding wants, embracing new ideas, and listening to advice.

It is easy when you integrate the final phrase of the verse: "in the fear of Christ." Christ is the head of the family, the object of our devotion, and the one we fear. After you submit to Him, it's easy to yield to someone else who also submits to Him. When we function in the fear of Christ, we have no other fears.

But I want you to understand that Christ is the head of every man, and the man is the head of a woman, and God is the head of Christ.

1 CORINTHIANS 11:3

Work out your salvation with fear and trembling.

PHILIPPIANS 2:12

If salvation is a gift of God's grace and completely free, then why does this verse say we must "work it out"? We're not only told to work, but to work hard—with "fear and trembling." This sounds serious and scary. Thankfully we become unafraid, as we put the verse in context. "It is God who is at work in you, both to will and to work for *His* good pleasure" (Philippians 2:13).

It is God who accomplishes His purposes in our lives from inside out. Since He is working out His plan on our behalf, then why must we do anything at all? The disciples also questioned these seeming contradictions. "What must we do to do the works God requires?" Jesus answered, "The work of God is this: to believe in the one he has sent" (John 6:29). That sounds easy, until you come across other verses that teach obedience and discipline.

In challenges like this, doubts and fears disappear as we learn to handle the Word of truth more accurately. There is a great difference in working *for* our salvation and working *out* our salvation. Working it out is obedience, for we are all saved *unto* good works. And our deepest joy is found in knowing God's will and pleasing Him.

For we are His workmanship, created in Christ Jesus for good works, which God prepared beforehand so that we would walk in them.

EPHESIANS 2:10

Stand firm in one spirit, contending as one man for the faith of the gospel, without being frightened in any way by those who oppose you.

PHILIPPIANS 1:27–28 NIV84

Paul faced an uncertain future. Would he ever see his friends in Philippi again? Was he going to be killed for his faith? But his main concern was for the younger, inexperienced members of the body of Christ. He wanted them to continue in a lifestyle that would represent the truths of the gospel of Christ. As he focused upon those who'd grown through his teaching and upon those still faithfully serving the Lord in the church, his heart must have filled with love and compassion. They would face persecution as surely as he had. They would need his words of encouragement just as he wanted the same from them. Just as you and I need today.

"Stand firm!" he wrote. It's a charge Paul issued at least thirty times in his letters. In the midst of opposition, there's no need to argue and confront. It's enough to keep standing, to persevere in faith, to remain in a spirit of unity. The Holy Spirit will sustain you and bind you together so you can follow the next admonition: "Contend as one." It literally means to become one-souled. With unity, fullness of Spirit, and one-souled obedience, we will not be "frightened in any way by those who oppose."

For freedom Christ has set us free; stand firm therefore, and do not submit again to a yoke of slavery.

GALATIANS 5:1 ESV

Those who continue in sin, rebuke in the presence of all, so that the rest also will be fearful of sinning.

1 TIMOTHY 5:20

"There has never been one sin committed on this earth for which the man who committed it did not suffer," wrote author and teacher Henrietta C. Mears.[28] Her words are contrary to what most people think today. We laugh at sin, tease each other, wink at it, or don't recognize it at all. Yet sin is the reason Jesus had to die. It is also the reason we are afraid!

We dress up sin by calling it some other name, preferring "sleeping with" or "borrowing" instead of biblical words. But when God speaks of sin, He uses clear words, easy to understand, that can be found in any dictionary. We do not have to wonder what He is talking about. He gets specific. If the Lord mentioned only general categories or used softer words, we might think our sins were just mistakes, understandable problems, or excusable faults. The mirror of the Word of God is painfully clear.

Jesus paid for your sins—the just for the unjust—and absolution requires death. Blood was shed in the Garden when God killed a lamb and clothed man and woman with bloody fur; blood flooded the trenches at Tabernacle sacrifices. Blood overflowed the basins in the Temple court. Blood flowed from the Christ at Calvary. There is no sin committed on earth for which the unthinkable price was not paid.

———————

Without the shedding of blood there is no forgiveness of sins.

HEBREWS 9:22 ESV

> *But Jesus overheard them and said . . . "Don't be afraid. Just have faith."*
>
> MARK 5:36 NLT

When He said, "Just have faith," Jesus actually meant "*keep on believing.*" Sometimes things get lost in translation. The faith of Jairus needed perseverance, a faith that not only *had* believed but *kept on* believing. Jesus was on the way to heal his daughter when He was interrupted by a woman who also needed healing. As he watched Jesus turn to help her, Jairus was afraid they would not get to his daughter in time. People in the crowd were saying, "Your daughter is already dead; do not trouble the teacher anymore."

Did Jairus "keep on believing"? Or did he succumb to fear? Jesus met him in that fearful place where death and life intersect, saying, "Do not be afraid; keep on believing!" For a moment Jairus had allowed reason to prevail. It was logical; he could hear wailing and loud voices as he neared his house. His faith wavered. But he took a bold step and, with Jesus beside him, walked into his house to the girl's bed.

When Jesus is present, there is always hope. With serenity, grace, and kindness, He told the child to arise. And she did. Jesus also knows what is killing you! Picture Him today, taking you by the hand and with great authority and limitless power saying: "*Talitha kum!*" (which translated means "Little girl, I say to you, get up!") (Mark 5:41).

Faith is reason at rest in God.

ATTRIBUTED TO CHARLES SPURGEON

Do not worry about your life, as to what you will eat; nor for
your body, as to what you will put on.

LUKE 12:22

Jesus said, "Do not worry." But the words He used could have also been interpreted as "take no thought," "do not be anxious," "do not be troubled," or "do not fear." And what was the subject of the anxiety and fear He warned about? Clothing and food! The Bible is certainly relevant today! When we get an invitation to some special event, the first thing we worry about—and I am speaking here of men, women, daughters, sons—is *what will I wear?* Will I have to rent a tux, do I have the right dress, can I wear jeans?! The list goes on before our mind switches to *what will we eat?*

Thankfully the Lord redirects our thoughts by reminding us of what's really important about life. He uses two of the most beautiful and sometimes forgotten natural creations—grass and lilies—to show that He takes very good care of what belongs to Him. He speaks of our value and how much He cares for every single one of His creations. And He promises to supply everything we need to have a blessed life. "Do not be afraid, little flock, for your Father has chosen gladly to give you the kingdom" (Luke 12:32).

The key to an abundant life today requires only one shift in focus—from things that give temporary happiness to things that bring eternal joy in His kingdom.

———————

For life is more than food, and the body more than clothing.

LUKE 12:23

"Don't be afraid. I am here!" Then they were eager to let him in.

JOHN 6:20–21 NLT

The disciples were afraid and a bit flabbergasted. Jesus had just walked on the water to get to them. And from that day to this, "walking on water" has become a catchphrase. Girl meets guy and to her he is *really perfect.* "He can walk on water!" Businessman lands a good deal, carpenter constructs a great building, preacher leads his church to a blessed future, woman becomes a CEO or runs for president, and some will proclaim that person can "walk on water"! Have you ever wondered why that particular miracle, more than all others, has come to describe things that are above and beyond expectations?

Maybe because it is unexplainable, unquestionable, and absolutely unique—done only once by one person—the One and Only, Jesus. While some mimic other miracles, I've never seen anyone feign walking on top of a turbulent sea—not a magician, soothsayer, overly eager preacher, false prophet, or demonic spirit. Water-walking is a one-of-a-kind wonder and unequivocally divine.

But what is impossible in the physical realm is possible in the spiritual. When life becomes turbulent, it is altogether possible to become unsinkable and totally buoyant. We can step out upon the icy waters of fear and stand steadily upon defeat, fear, and anger. We too can "walk on water" with our eyes upon Jesus.

The steps of a man are established by the LORD, and He delights in his way.

PSALM 37:23

*I am leaving you with a gift—peace of mind and heart. And the
peace I give is a gift the world cannot give. So don't be troubled
or afraid.*

JOHN 14:27 NLT

We receive His peace and pursue peace whenever we can. Jesus
said, "Blessed are the peacemakers" (Matthew 5:9). Let these six
insights guide you toward making and receiving peace today.

1. Let go of grudges. "Be kind to one another, tender-hearted,
   forgiving each other, just as God in Christ also has forgiven
   you" (Ephesians 4:32).
2. Let go of past failures. "...forgetting what *lies* behind and
   reaching forward to what *lies* ahead" (Philippians 3:13–14).
3. Let go of self-pity. "I have learned to be content in whatever
   circumstances I am" (Philippians 4:14).
4. Hold on to life—do not withdraw, embrace Godly
   friendship. "Two are better than one because they have a
   good return for their labor" (Ecclesiastes 4:9).
5. Hold on to biblical virtues. "Now for this very reason also,
   applying all diligence, in your faith supply moral excellence"
   (2 Peter 1:5).
6. Hold on to something bigger than yourself—God Himself.
   "The steadfast of mind You will keep in perfect peace,
   Because he trusts in You" (Isaiah 26:3).

Fear not, for I have redeemed you . . . when you pass through the
waters, I will be with you; and through the rivers, they shall not
overflow you. When you walk through the fire, you shall not be
burned, nor shall the flame scorch you.

ISAIAH 43:1–2 NKJV

Don't you love these promises? You will not drown when you pass through deep waters. You may wade into roaring rivers without being swept away. Your path may lead you into fiery and fierce trials, but you will not be seriously burned, not scorched on the surface, and not even smell like smoke. Our God is always standing ready to help, encourage, point out new directions, and cover you with love and grace during the most serious or complicated issues of life.

Isaiah's solution for deep-seated fear was this: Remember you are redeemed. Do these words console you? If not, perhaps you need to take a closer look at the meaning of redemption—to buy or purchase. Jesus paid the price or the ransom for our sins, buying us back from the power of another. Redemption frees us from the law so that we may live by grace. Redeemed, we are free from sin, free from lawlessness, free from the bondage of self-will, delivered from tradition, released from man-pleasing, and free to be led by the Spirit, by grace, through faith.

It is for freedom that Christ has set us free. Stand firm, then,
and do not let yourselves be burdened again by a yoke of slavery.

GALATIANS 5:1 NIV84

Do not be afraid of serving the Chaldeans; stay in the land and
serve the king of Babylon, that it may go well with you.

JEREMIAH 40:9

How would you feel if the Lord told you to stay in the land, serve the enemy, and honor the king when everything within you tells you to run home? This was the state of God's people in Jeremiah's day. What if God asked you to stay in America when the tax code is outdated and you are losing money, stay in the church when it is fragmented, stay in the university when teachers challenge your way of thinking, stay in your marriage when your spouse is selfish, stay in a friendship when you don't see eye to eye on important issues? Are you willing to stay put, simply because it is the will of God?

What would you do if God told you not only to stay but to honor the one in authority? Honor the teacher, the husband, the wife, the pastor, the president, the governing body, the church leadership? Does the Lord ever ask such difficult and unexplainable choices of His children? He asks for even more. What if He tells you or me to serve the offender?

We can because when we honor God's appointed authority, we honor God. We can serve the least as if we were doing it unto the Greatest. We can wash another's feet, bring soup, bow while disagreeing, and love with a grace far beyond ourselves. Listen carefully to your heavenly Guide and do not be afraid.

> *"Do not be afraid of the king of Babylon, whom you are now
> fearing; do not be afraid of him," declares the LORD, "for I am
> with you to save you and deliver you from his hand."*
>
> JEREMIAH 42:11

O Babylon! The war taking place today in the twenty-first century
is in the same place; with the same people; for the same reason as
the battles of the fifth century BC. Only the strategies and tech-
niques of fighting have changed—from horses, swords, and stones,
to the best technology, equipment, and highly trained soldiers. Will
there always be war? Will it always be in that part of the world? The
answer is yes. Scripture tells us that wars and rumors of wars will
not cease in that area in our lifetime (see Mark 13:7). It is enough to
frighten us all. We must look to El Elyon, the Most High God, the
Deliverer, to find peace even as war rages around us.

Kay Arthur in *LORD, I Want to Know You*, wrote: "If God is not
Sovereign, if He is not in control, if all things are not under His
dominion, then He is not the Most High and you and I are either in
the hands of fate (whatever that is), in the hands of man, or in the
hands of the devil."[29]

God's intentions cannot be frustrated by the plans of man.
What He decides stands.

———————

My counsel shall stand, and I will accomplish all my purpose.

ISAIAH 46:10 ESV

His heart is upheld, he will not fear.

PSALM 112:8

This psalm begins "Praise the LORD!" It means "Hallelujah!" Praise is a topic mentioned frequently throughout the book of Psalms, often in contrast to the fear that seeks to depress us. In light of the multiple times praise-words are used in Scripture, I wonder if we as God's people emphasize enough the importance of praise. How often do we say Hallelujah? Do we praise Him frequently? Occasionally? Seldom? Not since the "Jesus People" of the 1970s left town? Have we substituted giving thanks for praise? These are questions worth asking because the Lord is worthy of our praise!

Have you ever praised the Lord because your heart is "upheld"? Because your heart is "fixed" or "stayed" upon Jehovah? It is not fixed upon him because you fixed it there yourself; it is not stayed upon the Lord because of your own staying power. I know this because the words are written in a way that indicates "continually being done to us or for us." Your heart and mine are constantly being upheld, sustained, and established by a power greater than our own.

While we *cannot* uphold our own heart, *we can* accept God's support, receive grace, lean in, and stay put. Holding on to Him, we will cease living fearful lives, and we will continually be praising the Lord. Hallelujah!

———————

Stayed upon Jehovah, hearts are fully blessed, finding in His presence perfect peace and rest.
FRANCIS HAVERGAL, "LIKE A RIVER GLORIOUS"

When I walk in a valley of death-shade, I fear no evil, for Thou [art] with me, Thy rod and Thy staff—they comfort me.

PSALM 23:4 YLT

David, the tenderhearted shepherd, the man after God's own heart, the King of Israel, the prolific writer of songs and poetry, also knew how it felt to slip into sin, to feel defeated, guilty, stained, and worthless. So he wrote from his own experience. In praise of God's Word, he penned the magnificent Psalm 119—a poem of 176 verses, written in eight stanzas using all twenty-two letters of the Hebrew alphabet. Each verse in a stanza began with the same letter proceeding from A to Z—well, actually from aleph to tav. That in itself reveals David's bright, orderly mind and his steadfast heart.

It is a creative work that would take most of us a year or more to understand even with a computer and Bible software. A masterwork of beauty and form, Psalm 119 blesses all who walk through its garden cupping eternal blossoms in human hands. Ageless, helpful, stress-relieving, thought-inspiring, spirit-motivating words for every seeking heart. The Word of God liberates us from fear and leads us in righteous paths. Today, focus on these promises:

- "I shall delight in Your statutes; I shall not forget Your word" (Psalm 119:16).
- "Your testimonies also are my delight; *They are* my counselors" (Psalm 119:24).
- "I shall delight in Your commandments, Which I love" (Psalm 119:47).

*To this day they do according to the earlier customs: they do
not fear the LORD, nor do they follow their statutes or their
ordinances or the law, or the commandments.*

2 KINGS 17:34

The Israelites had every reason to be afraid. Their land had been
invaded by the Assyrians, their king captured, and the entire
nation exiled to the cities of the Medes. You'd think that would
be enough to turn their hearts back to the LORD but it was not.
They continued practicing pagan customs while shunning God's
statutes, ordinances, laws, and commandments. No wonder fear
permeated their lives! This one chapter in 2 Kings mentions fear a
dozen times. They feared false gods and did not fear the True God.

Why is so much emphasis put upon their fear? Because of their
sin, which included erecting sacred pillars, bowing before hand-
carved Asherim poles, constructing high places, burning incense
to the gods of the land, making golden calves, sacrificing their own
children in fire, and doing "things secretly which were not right" (2
Kings 17:9).

This made God very angry. And that was only their outward sin.
Inwardly their attitudes became vain, they broke their covenant
relationship with God, forsook His words, laws, and commandments and, most significantly, did not believe Him. No wonder
they were afraid. Have you ever done something secret or tried to
hide from the Omniscient God?

A Prayer: *Father, we pray for mercy when we deserve justice,
for grace when we choose custom over commandments and
tradition over truth.* Amen.

The LORD is my light and my salvation; whom shall I fear? The
LORD is the stronghold of my life; of whom shall I be afraid?

PSALM 27:1 ESV

When we are afraid, no matter the reason, it is time to turn to the "stronghold" of our life. Stronghold—"a fortified place, a place of security or survival." David expressed great confidence in the LORD, for He was not only his stronghold, but his light and salvation.

David was facing a large group of enemies who were threatening his life, and he needed courage. When we are in a situation that causes great fear, we must reach down, deep inside, to the very core of our being, into the depths of our soul, grab hold of courage, and pull it to the surface. "Take courage!" the Lord says. Take it, as if it were a thing easily displaced or covered up. Beth Rudy, author of *A Prayer Pal*, wrote, "David encountered many frightening people and situations, but wasn't provoked by a sinful fear of men. When you're afraid, do as David did, turn to your King. Open your Bible and enter into the holy presence of our great, big God. Your perception will change when you seek His power, peace, and protection. What scary person or situation requires you to trust in God today?"[30]

_____

If you abide in Me, and My words abide in you, ask whatever
you wish, and it will be done for you.

JOHN 15:7

But I will warn you whom to fear: fear him who, after he has killed, has authority to cast into hell. Yes, I tell you, fear him!

LUKE 12:5 ESV

There is a best seller in bookstores today that declares on the cover that "Heaven is for Real!" Of course heaven is for real! It is mentioned in more than four hundred verses in the Bible. I don't need a personal revelation or an ambiguous story to convince me. Do you? Read the book if you want to read the child's personal experience. But don't take everything in it as the gospel truth. The Holy Spirit–inspired canon of Scripture is complete! And the only person who got a glimpse into heaven and lived was warned not to talk about it.

If you are one who wonders about eternity and feels afraid of what may occur after death, maybe you should read what the Bible says about it: "Do not let your heart be troubled; believe in God, believe also in Me. In My Father's house are many dwelling places; if it were not so, I would have told you; for I go to prepare a place for you" (John 14:1–2). Jesus is not a way or one way; "Jesus said to him, 'I am the way, and the truth, and the life; no one comes to the Father but through Me' " (John 14:6).

No eye has seen, no ear has heard, and no mind has imagined what God has prepared for those who love him.

1 CORINTHIANS 2:9 NLT

*Be strong and courageous. Do not be afraid or dismayed before
the king of Assyria and all the horde that is with him, for there
are more with us than with him.*

2 CHRONICLES 32:7 ESV

Hezekiah was king and he did what was good, right, and true before
the LORD. In fact, the Bible says that he did every work according
to the law and commandments of God and that he sought God
with all his heart (see 2 Chronicles 31:20–21). What an epitaph
that last phrase would have been! He was a great, godly king whom
the people followed faithfully. Then they were tested by the Assyrians. Being warned, the people fortified their city, strengthened
their walls, and listened to the king. "Be strong! Be courageous! Do
not be afraid! There are more with us than with them."

Hezekiah was not talking about numbers here. He was talking
about a Power greater than the enemy's power. It was Yahweh Elohim, and with Him on your side, the largest horde is powerless. But
this is the thrilling part: God is with us *right now*, and whatever
the problem, how fierce the battle, how complicated the situation,
"there are more with us than them." Praise the Lord!

LORD, there is no one besides You to help in the battle *between
the powerful and those who have no strength; so help us, O LORD
our God, for we trust in You.*

2 CHRONICLES 14:11

It is a terrifying thing to fall into the hands of the living God.
HEBREWS 10:31

If you are one of His elect, there is nothing that can take you from Him. Still, the verse above was written to believers in Christ. We know this because the paragraph opens with "Therefore, brethren" (Hebrews 10:19). Later, the writer tells us the words were written to those with confidence to enter into the "Holy Place by the blood of Jesus" (Hebrews 10:19). He is writing to covenant people, those who come to Him by a new and living way made possible through the sacrifice of Jesus. So why did He tell those who believe, who have access to Him, who love Him, that it is terrifying "to fall into the hands of the living God"?

While we may not understand completely, we know for sure what this verse is *not about*! It is *not about* losing the faith we have in Christ, *not about* being sentenced to an eternity without Him, and *not about* punishment. But it does reveal the possibility of a believer willfully choosing to sin against God and for the sin to be so heinous that it insults the grace of God. And that is a terrifying thing. When a believer continually chooses to ignore correction, shrugs his shoulders, counts it a minor infraction, and pushes God away, He must judge the sin and correct the sinner. It is a fearful thing, but also a fine thing. God cares for every single one of His children more than any earthly father, and whom He loves He chastens.

For the Lord disciplines the one he loves, and chastises every son whom he receives.
HEBREWS 12:6 ESV

From the time that the Chest came to rest in Kiriath Jearim, a long time passed—twenty years it was—and throughout Israel there was a widespread, fearful movement toward GOD.

1 SAMUEL 7:2 MSG

The "fearful movement toward GOD" today might be called a widespread spiritual revival, when God's presence became obvious and people's lives were changed. It began with a new realization of the fear of God. Besides the hundreds of times the Bible tells us *do not fear*, there are many verses that say *do fear*—fear the Lord. This reference is a mix of both. God's people were afraid because they'd seen hundreds die at the hand of a wrathful God. But there was a reverence about their fear because of their love and respect for Him. Love coupled with fear; fear linked to honor and reverence.

The greatest longing of God's people was to have Him in their midst, to sense His nearness, and to have an appointed place to worship and pray. That longing resides in the heart of every person—an empty place that only He can fill. In every soul an inner search is always going on, pushed by an unmet need. The Israelites would feel better when the Ark of the Covenant rested in the Temple. Even though there would be no physical closeness, they would worship, wonder, and hope standing nearby in the outer court.

Be thankful today that you have a life-fulfilling, soul-satisfying, close relationship with Jesus Christ without even one curtain hanging between.

God . . . in these last days has spoken to us in His Son, whom He appointed heir of all things.   HEBREWS 1:1–2

Be strong and courageous, do not fear nor be dismayed.

1 CHRONICLES 22:13

Blessings come when we observe the statutes and ordinances which God commanded. As a nation, are we doing that today? Do we observe the statutes of God? Well...the Ten Commandments have been removed from some public grounds, our children are not allowed to pray in school, and Bibles are being removed from public places. We're not allowed to speak openly about our faith, while we yield the right of free speech to dissident groups. In our individual lives, do we honor the truth? Do businesses hold to His standards? In the marketplace, do vendors use just measurements and fair values?

What can one person do? "Do not fear or be dismayed," the verse says. We were not promised still waters or flowery beds of ease! We must stand strong and be courageous. Bow only to the King of Kings! Yield not to fearful leaders of apostate religions. Pray to be more like Daniel, who presented a creative alternative to those in authority. Pray to become more like Paul. Ask God to make you like Phoebe, a servant to the church.

I commend to you our sister Phoebe...that you receive her in the Lord in a manner worthy of the saints, and that you help her in whatever matter she may have need of you; for she herself has also been a helper of many, and of myself as well.

ROMANS 16:1–2

Steep yourself in God-reality, God-initiative, God-provisions.
You'll find all your everyday human concerns will be met. Don't
be afraid of missing out. You're my dearest friends!

LUKE 12:29–30 MSG

A student sometimes gave the change in his cup-holder or an extra dollar from his pocket to the beggars who gathered under the bridge near the university campus. But one morning a man stepped up to his car and tried to reach inside for a dollar bill he had spotted on the console. "I really need that money!" he insisted. Startled, the young man gave him the dollar, but pulled away quickly, and from that day on, he kept his windows closed at that corner.

Months later, he encountered a homeless man in a park where he was sharing lunch with a friend. A haggard old man approached and asked, "Can I have a dollar for food?" The young man was moved with compassion by his disheveled appearance and obvious pain. He faced him saying, "You don't want food, do you?" The man turned away, muttering, "I need a drink." The student called him back and gave him a dollar. "I will give you this because you told the truth. God loves you, man."

In God's great plan for the student, this exchange was His will. We do not have to always understand, we only have to obey.

And the King will answer and say to them, "Assuredly, I say
to you, inasmuch as you did it *to one of the least of these My*
brethren, you did it *to Me."*

MATTHEW 25:40 NKJV

Neither fear them nor fear their words, though thistles and
thorns are with you and you sit on scorpions.

EZEKIEL 2:6

Ezekiel, the prophet known for his rugged appearance and uncommon courage, recoiled in fear at the thought of thistles, thorns, and scorpions. Everybody has their limits! And their excuses! At a recent conference, the speaker read a list of excuses she had heard from women who didn't exercise: *I'm too busy, I'm depressed, I'm tired, it's raining, it's too hot, it's too cold, I need new shoes, it makes me sweat, I overslept, it ruins my hair!* The justifications are funny and pitiful. Unfortunately, the same words roll off our own tongues, much too easily, and not just about exercise.

Some highly esteemed Bible characters made excuses too. Abraham and Sarah said they were too old. David was too young. Moses was not eloquent. Gideon was afraid. And Peter blamed his denial of Christ on a girl. But still, these men and women encountered God, produced heirs, slew giants, wrote books, conquered enemies, and delivered captives.

When circumstances complicate your life and hinder you from accomplishing God's will, what do you do? Try rethinking the mess you're in and see it as a component of His will for you. After all, God is the manager of all circumstances.

———————

The LORD Almighty is the one you are to regard as holy, he is the
one you are to fear, he is the one you are to dread, and he will be
a sanctuary . . .

ISAIAH 8:13–14 NIV84

Let not your [minds and] hearts faint; fear not, and do not
tremble or be terrified [and in dread] because of them.

DEUTERONOMY 20:3 AMP

A man breaking the chains of alcoholism chose a one-word remedy which he posted in his garage—his so-called man-cave, where
he spent most of his leisure time. He chose the word Hope! Hope
painted on the walls, Hope on a plaque he purchased at Goodwill,
Hope painted on a sign discovered in curbside trash, Hope cut out
of lumber with a jigsaw. Every time he opened the door to his cave,
every way he turned, he saw the word "Hope." Amazing as it may
seem, the word came alive for him. He began to feel it, want it, and
desire to know all about it!

He expressed his longing to God. His prayers went something
like this: "Lord, give me hope. Restore the hope I used to have. Put
hope within me." And finally, "Lord, You are my hope." He started
to seek hope as David sought it: "My soul longs for your salvation;
I hope in your word. My eyes long for your promise; I ask, 'When
will you comfort me?'" (Psalm 119:81–82). Oh how we fear situations where we have no hope!

But hope is available in any circumstance. Seek it through the
Scriptures.

For whatever was written in earlier times was written
for our instruction, so that through perseverance and the
encouragement of the Scriptures we might have hope.

ROMANS 15:4

It is the LORD of hosts whom you should regard as holy. And He
shall be your fear, and He shall be your dread.

ISAIAH 8:13

Isaiah is saying don't fear anything that man can do to you, don't
fear one single enemy, do not fear circumstances, or any event that
might happen while you live here on earth. It is the LORD whom
you should highly esteem and He shall be your one and only fear!

In the most unusual of prophecies, Isaiah foretells the fall of
Israel, though there would be victories along the way. He used
one large visual aid, a scroll with the name of his soon-to-be-born
son. God named the tiny baby with the biggest name in biblical
history—Maher-Shalal-Hash-Baz—meaning "Swift is the booty,
speedy is the prey." It became the battle cry of the nation as they
fought their enemies even though they knew of another prophecy
which revealed their eventual, albeit temporary, doom.

Fear fades like a vapor when we keep our eyes on God's holiness. When we look toward deliverance, instead of focusing upon
the problems. When we look to Jesus, instead of giving place to
fear. Instead of dwelling upon what makes us fearful or upon some
worry about what might happen, let us wait expectantly upon the
Deliverer.

Don't be like this people, always afraid somebody is plotting
against them. Don't fear what they fear. Don't take on their
worries. If you're going to worry, worry about The Holy. Fear
GOD-of-the-Angel-Armies.

ISAIAH 8:12–13 MSG

Of whom were you worried and fearful when you lied, and did
not remember Me nor give Me a thought?

ISAIAH 57:11

Truth-tellers are an endangered species in our world. But Pinocchios are everywhere.

From the woodworker's shop to the marketplaces, theaters, pulpits, classrooms, and the house next door. In the United States it's just not acceptable to call them liars for that would not be politically correct. So we label them forgetful, absentminded, or misinformed. They make mistakes, misspeak, and are often misquoted. Oh, if only somebody would just speak the truth, come right out and declare, "I said it because I wanted the job, to be promoted, to make more money. I wanted you to like me. I needed to be included. I said it and I was wrong!"

Unfortunately, even writers can become loose with the truth. Some of us exaggerate, overestimate, and embellish, and I'm not talking about fiction writers. Sometimes it is amusing, but this is not a problem to be treated flippantly. Especially when handling God's truth. Like teachers and preachers, Christian writers have a greater responsibility to be truth-tellers.

Of whom are you worried? Whom do you fear? Do you remember God? Have you given Him one thought? Good questions! Convicting inquiries handled inaccurately might cause one's nose to grow. Our only recourse is to fall on our knees in reverential fear, and ask for grace.

———————

For there is not a word on my tongue, but behold, O LORD, You
know it altogether.   PSALM 139:4 NKJV

As the LORD, *the God of your fathers, told you. Do not be afraid;*
do not be discouraged.

DEUTERONOMY 1:21 NIV84

With two vital factors in your life, you will never be overcome by
fear or sink into a state of despair or discouragement! Factor number one—having a dynamic faith with roots pushing deep into the
knowledge of "the LORD, the God of your fathers." His names are
stacked one upon another revealing who He is. He is the Lord—
Yahweh, Essential Being, Essence of Life. He is God—Elohim,
God in plural form—Father, Son, and Holy Spirit. He is called *your*
God—a personal God that you can know. And He is "the God of
your fathers." He is not a god who came into being in the fifth century, not an image carved from stone or wood, not a human dignitary risen to significance out of the fallen masses. He is the Eternal
Jehovah Elohim! Know Him and you will not be afraid!

Factor number two—having passion for the Word of God. Do
you read it? Study it? Memorize it? Love it? Listen to it? Hear it
preached? We live our lives "adrift in an incredible ocean called
faith," said speaker Jeannette Clift George. "Hold on to what He
has said and what He has done."[31] Only then will we remain altogether fearless.

Not to us, O LORD, *not to us, but to Your name give glory*
because of Your lovingkindness, because of Your truth.

PSALM 115:1

Do not be in dread or afraid of them.

                                          DEUTERONOMY 1:29 ESV

Charlie Brown, the cartoon character of Charles Shulz, said, "I have a new philosophy. I'm only going to dread one day at a time." After reading that and having a good laugh, my thoughts turned more contemplative. I looked up "dread" in my 1959 version of *Webster's Dictionary* (a throwback to basic thought) and pondered its definition: "Great fear and continual alarm in anticipation of impending evil or danger; an overpowering horror or fright; one who or that which is feared or revered. 'Let him be your dread' (Isaiah 8:13)."

Moses told his people not to dread or fear *them*—indicating the giants of Anakim. There is only one way we can even come close to being calm while facing our giants. By faith! Faith—the exact opposite of fear. We can overcome dread and fear by faith in Jesus Christ. Faith comes and continues to grow as we closely follow the "perfecter" or "finisher" of our faith (see Hebrews 12:2).

Faith is a subject so huge, so important, that it's impossible to define though many have tried. My favorite is a well-known quote by Ralph Waldo Emerson, American essayist and poet of the 1800s, who said, "All that I have seen teaches me to trust the creator for all I have not seen."

Now faith is the substance of things hoped for, the evidence of things not seen.

                                          HEBREWS 11:1 NKJV

Do not be afraid . . . for I will protect you.

GENESIS 15:1 NLT

Only the Sovereign LORD can absolutely protect us. Our enemy has been granted power but only over evil and only for a limited time. But Jesus came "to destroy the works of the devil" (1 John 3:8). We are held securely by a power far greater than the limited power of the prince of darkness. Because we know God, are in Christ, and are filled with the Holy Spirit, we too are powerful, able to stand and overcome the forces of the enemy. The Word of God reassures us, "greater is He who is in you than he who is in the world" (1 John 4:4).

When I was a child, I was frightened by the darkness that surrounded my bed at night. In the stillness, with my daddy's snoring shaking the foundation of the small house we lived in, I would tuck the blankets tightly around my trembling body, pushing the corners under my feet and legs and shoulders so nothing could get to me. I needed protection. A blanket could not cover up my fear. I wish I had known then how secure and safe I was wrapped in the warm blanket of God's goodness. I am safe, and you are too. He escorts His children throughout life until He carries them over the threshold of Heaven's door into eternal life.

Trust in the LORD and do good; dwell in the land and enjoy safe pasture.

PSALM 37:3 NIV84

Be not afraid of their words, nor be dismayed at their looks . . .
you shall speak my words to them.

EZEKIEL 2:6 ESV

Ezekiel headed out on his mission speaking God-given words—a healing balm to every troubled soul. Does God still provide the right words to ordinary people today? It was the Apostle Peter who told each of us that we should always be prepared to answer those who ask by giving a reason for our hope. He went even further, declaring that when we speak, we should do so as "one who is speaking the utterances of God" (1 Peter 4:11).

Is it possible that we, like Ezekiel, could be so filled with truth that it would flow through us to the timid souls we encounter? What if our spoken words literally dropped like God-words from our lips to those parched and thirsty? How would our lives flower and bloom if from every pinprick of pain, unkind cut from a friend, or knife-jab of fear, truth would flow from the open wound? What if the balm of Gilead cleansed away our knee-jerk responses and produced new responses bursting with life?

With the tourniquet of fear loosened, clogged veins restored, and divine words pumping, we would produce the fruit of the Spirit in today's world. Lives would change. And there would be no room for fear.

Your words were found and I ate them, and Your words became
for me a joy and the delight of my heart; for I have been called by
Your name, O LORD God of hosts.

JEREMIAH 15:16

You shall not be afraid of them; you shall well remember what
the LORD your God did to Pharaoh and to all Egypt.

DEUTERONOMY 7:18

How easily we humans forget. Like the disciples, we are fed miraculously with a few loaves and fishes, and the next time we gather
we worry about what we will eat. Like Ezekiel, we are provided
a campsite near a river that flows freely in the drought and birds
deliver food every day, but when we're told to move on, we fear we
will die of hunger! Like Hagar, we miraculously find a stream in the
desert, and when God sends us back home, we fear dehydration.
Like Moses, we follow a way of escape through a deep river, and we
are terrified the next time we face troubled waters. *Father, help us*
not to succumb to spiritual Alzheimer's!

We do not have to be afraid! When your son is on a ventilator,
when your daughter runs away, if your husband leaves, if you lose
your job, if your friend gossips about you, if you wreck your car
and the airbags deploy, or if the oxygen masks on the plane don't
inflate. What will you do then? God grant that we may stand like
an oak and drink deeply from the fountains You provide. May our
faith be unquenchable, our strength sufficient, our love unwavering. And may we always remember well what the LORD our God has
done!

I count all things to be loss in view of the surpassing value of
knowing Christ Jesus my Lord.

PHILIPPIANS 3:8

*Fear nothing—not wild wolves in the night, not flying arrows
in the day, not disease that prowls through the darkness, not
disaster that erupts at high noon.*

PSALM 91:5–6 MSG

Our faith grows as we digest the truth of God's Word. There is no
other way to know His heart, understand His plan, and live in fellowship with Him. His Word is our spiritual food, the means of our
spiritual growth. How often we get sidetracked!

Like a hungry baby, we chew our fists and suck on our fingers,
when the pure milk of the Word of God sits ready to be opened
and digested. We have tasted truth and know it is sweeter than
honey, but in times of testing we nuzzle, and whine, and cry, but
still do not eat. Some have made the right choice. Ezekiel wrote,
"So I opened my mouth, and he gave me the scroll to eat...so I ate
it, and it tasted as sweet as honey in my mouth" (3:2–3 NIV). "When
your words came, I ate them," Jeremiah said. "They were my joy
and my heart's delight, for I bear your name, LORD God Almighty"
(Jeremiah 15:16 NIV).

---

*Like newborn babies, long for the pure milk of the word, so that
by it you may grow in respect to salvation.*

1 PETER 2:2

*I am God, your God. Don't for a minute be afraid of the gods of
the Amorites in whose land you are living.*

JUDGES 6:10 MSG

Today in America we are taught to be tolerant of many religions,
different traditions, unique and sometimes bizarre rituals, and
other gods! Tolerance may seem nice and polite to many. But there
is still only One God. The One who said, "Thou shall have no other
gods before me" and wrote with His finger into tablets of stone,
"Thou shalt not make any graven image or bow down to them."
That God! The God of the Ten Commandments (see Exodus 20:
3–17 ASV).

Sometimes I wonder why we Americans are so afraid. Have we
twisted the meaning of the word "tolerate" into a term that means
"total acceptance"? Do we tolerate every other religion, while Christians get no tolerance at all? Tolerate means "to allow, to endure, to
stomach." Now, we can do that. We can be tolerant because we
respect the free will God has given to every person; we can be tolerant because Jesus has told us to love each other, but we must not
embrace a false religion, and by God's grace neither will we bow
down to them. Would you join me in making that choice?

---

*Go therefore and make disciples of all the nations, baptizing
them in the name of the Father and the Son and the Holy Spirit,
teaching them to observe all that I commanded you; and lo, I am
with you always, even to the end of the age.*

MATTHEW 28:19–20

Say to those with anxious heart, "Take courage, fear not.
Behold, your God will come . . . He will save you."

ISAIAH 35:4

The prophet Habakkuk is my favorite example of faith. In three chapters he wrote deep insights and at least one verse that you are familiar with, perhaps without knowing it came from his pen: "But the righteous will live by his faith" (Habakkuk 2:4). What Habakkuk wrote is a major theme of the Bible. And it is the way to overcome fear.

He was able to write clearly about faith because it was the story of his life. Faith helped him overcome fear and answer his eternal why. Unafraid of asking questions, he endlessly queried God and waited patiently for answers. He prayed in a watchtower, a place beyond the reach of clamoring crowds and complicated problems. A place above confusion, where he could commune with God and still see what was going on in the land. Do you have a watchtower, a place where you sit with God? How often do you rest there?

Most of us can identify with Habakkuk. He looked at circumstances and was confused, but when he waited upon God he rejoiced. In addition to being a prophet who connected with God on complex issues, he was also a Levite singer in the temple. How interesting—a singing prophet. I can't wait to meet him and maybe join him on the chorus!

Yet I will exult in the Lord, I will rejoice in the God of my
salvation.

HABAKKUK 3:18

No chastening seems to be joyful for the present, but painful;
nevertheless, afterward it yields the peaceable fruit of
righteousness.

HEBREWS 12:11 NKJV

"Nevertheless, afterward..." Even though being disciplined by God is painful and fearful, there's comfort in knowing there will be an afterward. We fear the chastening might never end, but God says, "Do not be afraid." Trials come only if "needs be" and only last for "a little while" (see 1 Peter 1:6). The Bible is full of examples.

After their son was murdered by his own brother, Adam and Eve were blessed with another son guarding the lineage from which the Savior came. Eve said, "God has granted me another child in place of Abel" (Genesis 4:25 NIV). After Ruth's husband died, she married Boaz, the kinsman redeemer, a man who said, "I will do for you whatever you ask" (Ruth 3:11). Hannah struggled with infertility, depression, and fear that she might never have a child, but she gave birth to Samuel. She said, "For this child I prayed, and the Lord has granted me my petition that I made to him" (1 Samuel 1:27 ESV). After many trials including a near-fatal illness, "The LORD blessed the latter part of Job's life more than the former part" (Job 42:12 NIV).

The disciples watched Jesus die and lost all hope of a kingdom, but Christ arose, the Holy Spirit came, and the disciples' relationship with God became closer than before. Whatever your problem today, you can expect a harvest of righteousness and grace afterward.

When you were weary and worn out, they met you on your
journey and attacked all who were lagging behind; they had no
fear of God.

DEUTERONOMY 25:18 NIV

Fear crouches like a hungry lion ready to devour weary prey. Fear
has no mercy. It stalks the weak who are "weary and worn out." At
least we have been warned!

I received a phone call one day that our son was in the hospital's ICU. The doctors had induced a coma and put him on a ventilator. Three days passed and I had not been able to go to him. I
am a mom, and that's where I wanted to be—if only to watch him
breathe. I opened my Bible and read, "Because he has loved Me,
therefore I will deliver him; I will set him securely on high, because
he has known My name" (Psalm 91:14). In my mind, that "he" was
the name of my son! As I thought of him "sitting securely on high,"
my fear fled, the darkness lifted, and a plan came together.

My niece offered an airline ticket, and we flew to his bedside,
where I smothered him with mama-kisses, prayer, and the words of
Psalm 91. Even the comatose can hear! Do you know someone who
needs to hear God's Word? It is the balm of Gilead for any troubled
soul!

By the way, my son completely recovered and is doing fine!

Is there no balm in Gilead? Is there no physician there? Why
then has not the health of the daughter of my people been
restored?

JEREMIAH 8:22

*Do not be terrified by them, for the L*ORD* your God, who is among you, is a great and awesome God.*

DEUTERONOMY 7:21 NIV84

Our God is an awesome God. Overwhelming, breathtaking, splendid, and awe-inspiring. These are only a few of many synonyms of "awesome." But even a word like that doesn't describe Him well enough. Perhaps that is why He is described more completely by His names. You may be surprised at how many names He has. Every time you encounter one—in Scripture, in a sermon or Bible study, or from a framed picture in a gift store—your life is impacted.

Recently I was shuffling through the shelves in such a store in our community. My thoughts were focused upon finding a special decoration for a certain spot in our home. I was not centered upon God, much less thinking about His name, until I picked up a vase and moved a plaque to one side. Suddenly I was captivated by an elegantly framed, unfamiliar, hard-to-pronounce word. I recognized it as one of the names of God. In elegant Edwardian script painted in bright gold and edged in brown velvet were the words "Jehovah-Mekoddishkem"—the Lord Sanctifies You.

Suddenly I realized that He was "sanctifying" me by reminding me of His name even while I was nonchalantly digging among all sorts of contemporary treasure. He is always aware of me—whatever I am doing, wherever I may be, on this very day.

———

A Prayer: *Lord, I praise You today for who You are. I want to know You by name. Amen.*

Jesus came over and touched them. "Get up," he said. "Don't be afraid."

MATTHEW 17:7 NLT

When Jesus was transfigured, His garments became glistening white and His face took on an ethereal glow, shining like the sun. The experience was amazing, dazzling, and life-changing. Three disciples witnessed the change in their Lord from a dust-of-the-earth man who liked to sail and fish to a Spiritual Being clothed with His eternal purpose. Yes, the disciples were afraid, but that was before He touched them. With that touch came peace, renewed energy, reflected light, and a longing deep in the hearts of his disciples to please Him. Of course they wanted this holy moment to linger. They wanted to rest in the Presence of Jesus forever.

As they continued to bask in the warmth of God's presence, Moses and Elijah appeared—the same Moses who went up on Horeb and disappeared and the same Elijah who drove his chariot right into the clouds where God escorted him into heaven. On the mountain, the men were talking. Wouldn't you love an evening to linger and fellowship with this group? No wonder Peter wanted to build three tabernacles and stay!

But their time had not yet come. There was much to do Earth-side before their eternal rest. Following Jesus' touch, came His words: "Get up. Don't be afraid." Both then and now we are to leave trouble, anxiety, and fear behind and press on without fear.

Be exalted above the heavens, O God; let Your glory be above all the earth.   PSALM 57:5

When Saul saw that he was prospering greatly, he dreaded him.
But all Israel and Judah loved David, and he went out and came
in before them.

1 SAMUEL 18:15–16

Sometimes it troubles a person in authority to see another leader "prospering greatly." It is then that the green-eyed monster pops out of the abyss and says, *Pay attention.* In this case he appealed to Saul with sinister thoughts that made him envy David. Saul was also afraid! His position was in jeopardy, his associations threatened, and his grip on power slipping.

Had he forgotten that Jehovah-Sabaoth, the Lord of Hosts, the one who exalts kings and destroys kings, was his only real "dread"? His fear was misdirected! Saul's problem was not David but his own insecurity and sinful attitude coupled with his refusal to believe the Lord of Hosts.

Have you ever, on some level, faced the kind of angst that Saul faced in those days? Do you ever feel threatened by someone more successful or seemingly more self-confident? It is a common occurrence because of the condition of our flesh. But in Jesus we are fearless, secure, and strong. He fulfills all our needs. Author C. S. Lewis is quoted as having said about our endless questions: "I know now, Lord, why you utter no answer. You are yourself the answer. Before your face, questions die way."

It is He who changes the times and the epochs... He gives
wisdom to wise men and knowledge to men of understanding.

DANIEL 2:21

Stay with me; do not be afraid, for he who seeks my life seeks your life . . . you are safe with me.

1 SAMUEL 22:23

David graciously fought with his beleaguered people against their nemesis, the Philistines, leading them to a regional victory. But instead of being grateful, they betrayed his hiding place to Saul. Have you ever been betrayed by someone you trusted? By someone you considered a friend? If so, you understand how David must have felt. Disloyalty hurts and brings about multiplied fears.

While David's fear increased, Saul's mood deteriorated—from jealousy, to hate, to craziness, then to a place where he tried to murder the young heir to the throne. That is how sin works; it sinks deep into the unrepentant soul and from the dregs of depravity is born a beast that is never satisfied. It drags its victim down into the mire of wickedness. *First a thought, then an action, then a behavior, then a character.* After that, character dictates every reaction—whether good or evil.

Thankfully there is a cure for the human heart and the injustice that sin causes. When David had an opportunity to retaliate, he recognized Saul as God's anointed and waited for God's timing to be granted the crown. In every battle, Jehovah-Nissi, the Lord is My Banner, stands on the side of righteousness.

The flesh sets its desire against the Spirit, and the Spirit against the flesh; for these are in opposition to one another.

GALATIANS 5:17

Do not be afraid, because the hand of Saul my father will not
find you, and you will be king over Israel and I will be next to
you; and Saul my father knows that also.

1 SAMUEL 23:17

David and Jonathan were friends—their spiritual ties closer than
the physical ties of father and son. "Blood is thicker than water,"
they say; but one may add, "Spirit is thicker than blood." Have you
ever been in a relationship with a friend, teacher, disciple-maker,
partner, protégé, brother or sister in Christ, creating a spiritual
connection deeper than the bond of flesh and blood? Jesus makes
that possible. Think on these words from the pen of English author
and writer of another era Dr. J. Sidlow Baxter:

> O Lord thou hast made Thyself to me
> A living, bright reality.
> More present to faith's vision keen
> Than any outward object seen,
> More dear, more intimately nigh
> Than e'en the closest earthly tie.[32]

How precious, how delightful is a friendship that takes us closer
to the most intimate fellowship of all. Abraham was called a Friend
of God, and Jesus calls us His friends.

Abraham believed God, and it was counted to him as
righteousness—and he was called a friend of God.

JAMES 2:23 ESV

You are my friends if you do what I command you.

JOHN 15:14 ESV

The king said to her, "Do not be afraid; but what do you see?"
And the woman said to Saul, "I see a divine being coming up out
of the earth."

1 SAMUEL 28:13

Saul sank to a new low when he consulted a medium—the witch of Endor. Looking for spiritual advice, he asked that she reach out to the departed Samuel. When Samuel actually appeared, the medium was surprised and had to admit this was the work of God. Her reaction proved the deceptive wiles of fortune-tellers. She knew that she could not really connect with any man, certainly not a man of God. The only power the witch had, the only power witches have today, is a satanic ability to produce counterfeits. No believer in Jesus should tamper with that kind of evil power—not then, not now. It is asking for a truckload of fear, anxiety, and distress to be dumped on your shoulders. How foolish!

If you ever have an urge to conjure up some wise leader or inspired writer of Holy Scripture, instead, just read their books! All the counsel, advice, wisdom, and direction you need is recorded for you in the Bible. Which reminds me of a message T-shirt I spotted recently. The words were those of speaker Justin Peters: "Want to hear God speak to you? Read your Bible. Want to hear God speak audibly? Read it out Loud!"

Let the words of my mouth and the meditation of my heart be
acceptable in your sight, O LORD, my rock and my redeemer.

PSALM 19:14 ESV

*The earsplitting words and soul-shaking message terrified them
and they begged him to stop . . . they were afraid to move. Even
Moses was terrified.*

HEBREWS 12:20–21 MSG

Amazing things happened on mountaintops, with significant
meaning to us today! On Calvary, Christ died. And on Calvary, our
spiritual journey began. We too must die to our old way of life and
begin a new life in Him.

On the Mount of Olives, He arose from the grave. Afterward
He walked to Galilee to meet His disciples and trod the earth for
forty days. Now we live in joyous union, walking with the risen
Lord. Upon a mountain, Jesus was tempted by the devil. There He
showed us how to handle the enemy with the Word of God.

Jesus climbed to the heights in Judea to commune with His
Father in solitary places upon the mountain. Finding a solitary
place to worship God should be our highest priority.

God gave the law on Mount Sinai and revealed His grace on
Mount Zion.

From Mount Olivet, He ascended to heaven, and someday He
will descend back to earth planting his feet again on Olivet. When
He comes He will set up His Kingdom and reign a thousand years
with His saints including you and me.

---

*Who may ascend into the hill of the LORD? And who may stand
in His holy place? He who has clean hands and a pure heart,
who has not lifted up his soul to falsehood and has not sworn
deceitfully.*

PSALM 24:3–4

As for the promise which I made you when you came out of
Egypt, My Spirit is abiding in your midst; do not fear!

HAGGAI 2:5

The people had returned from exile to rebuild the temple in Jerusalem, but upon arrival decided to take care of their own houses
first. It made sense. Where would they wash their hands and have
supper, where would they sleep and gather with their own families?
But year after year, they just couldn't find time to give themselves
to the community. Even more seriously, they didn't find time to
pursue God, fulfill His purposes, or build His house.

Can you relate to these distracted Jews? Seems most of us get
caught up taking care of the urgent and forget the important. Before
we know it, fifteen years have passed. Their delayed obedience
might have lasted longer had Haggai not heard from the LORD. Haggai in turn relayed His prophecy to the people. He issued a rebuke
and a challenge, spoke courage into fearful souls, comforted discouraged hearts, and promised future blessings. It was not easy to
move a fearful nation to step up and build on the sixteen-year-old
foundation, but Haggai persisted, and the project was finished in
four years. With the new temple in place, God began to bless and
restore His people, just as Haggai had promised.

"The latter glory of this house will be greater than the former,"
says the LORD of hosts, "and in this place I will give peace."

HAGGAI 2:9

Then the earth shook and quaked; and the foundations of the mountains were trembling and were shaken, because He was angry.

PSALM 18:7

We don't like to think about the wrath of God or even consider that He becomes angry with those He created. We are confused by a God who reveals anger and much prefer talk about His love and grace. But to ignore this facet of His personality would be wrong. I recently heard that the wrath of God is mentioned in the Scriptures more than the love of God—an astonishing 580 times.

God's wrath is different from the wrath of man because it is connected with His justice. We all want to see justice prevail, wrongs made right, holiness prevail, and rewards be given. But those actions would never take place without God's wrath being revealed first.

In the book of Romans, Paul begins giving reasons for God's wrath in the very first chapter: He becomes angry when we refuse to honor Him by suppressing the truth that He has made known to every person. His wrath is obvious when we dishonor His commands by continuing to disobey even when we know the truth. He is full of wrath when we despise His love and grace and treat lightly the depth of His kindness and patience. But if we respond honestly to His wrath, we may know His mercy and grace.

We will fear future wrath or love present grace.

AUTHOR UNKNOWN

And who of you, being anxious, is able to add to his age one cubit?

MATTHEW 6:27 YLT

The entrance into life is a precious gift; and the last enemy that shall be conquered is death. Between those two realities, there is no need to be anxious or to fear. No one, not the most devout Christian or the most powerful enemy, has a say in how many days lie between our birth announcement and our eulogy. Only the Alpha and the Omega knows. What we do know for sure is that our days are numbered; that we are all appointed to die once; and, for the Christian, death ends in resurrection.

We are encouraged to live one day at a time. It is a theme picked up by wise men and women, counselors, preachers, teachers, and business leaders. When will we ever learn? "Each day has enough trouble of its own" (Matthew 6:34). Sometimes even one day is too much to handle. It is then that we walk with God one step at a time. And when you get to the point that you are too tired or life is too complicated to take even one step, you are carried by faith—the kind of faith described by these words from an unknown author: "Faith is knowing that when we have reached the end of all the light that we know and are about to take the next step into the darkness of the unknown, there will be something solid to stand upon—or we will be taught how to fly."

About clothing why are ye anxious?

MATTHEW 6:28 YLT

My brother was hunting when a bird that he'd shot landed in a cluster of cactus. He managed to dislodge it without being stuck by thorns, but his hand was smeared with deep reddish purple, a beautiful royal color. It came from little white webs spotting the cactus ears.

Discovering and appreciating nature is the best part of hunting for him. He poked a finger at another white spot and his finger became brightly colored. He wanted to know exactly what this was, thinking, *How can something white, when mashed, turn maroon?*

Back at home, he learned there is a cochineal insect that lays its eggs on a cactus ear and folds a silk web around them to await hatching. When he had mashed the sack, it crushed the eggs, released the color called carmine, stained the silk, and dyed his hand. Today in the Canary Islands, cactuses are seeded with this insect, and the eggs are harvested, dried, and crushed to make dye.

As I heard this story, my thoughts turned to the future when we all will wear royal colors and sit beside the King of Kings in glory. But before we don our robes, we live much as the tiny insect does—clinging to our spiritual host until the day of harvest comes.

He has made us to be a kingdom, priests to His God and Father—to Him be the glory and the dominion forever and ever. Amen.

REVELATION 1:6

Why are ye anxious? . . . "If the herb of the field, that to-day is,
and to-morrow is cast to the furnace, God doth so clothe—not
much more you, O ye of little faith?"

MATTHEW 6:28, 30 YLT

Instead of becoming anxious about the external components that complicate our lives, why don't we concentrate on something worth our time and energy? Let us be concerned about our faith. If you are prone to worry, fret about having "little faith." Get serious about growing your faith. Feed it well on truth and grace. Give it large doses of the love of God and sow seeds of kindness to everyone you meet. Spend your life floating in the tranquil sea called faith, anchored by what He has said and what He has done.

Stuart Briscoe in *What Works* wrote, "The fact of the matter is that I take refuge in the Lord. Unashamedly I run to Him. In fact, if it were not for the ready access I have to Him, I would never survive the ministry. The pressures would be more than I could take. I hide myself away with Him. I crawl into a corner and talk to Him. When the pressure is on, I pull the drapes and commune with Him. I take refuge in Him."[33]

―――――――――

Do not fear, for I am with you; do not anxiously look about you,
for I am your God. I will strengthen you, surely I will help you,
surely I will uphold you with My righteous right hand.

ISAIAH 41:10

Therefore, let us fear if, while a promise remains of entering His
rest, any one of you may seem to have come short of it.

HEBREWS 4:1

"Let us"—what a soft way to issue an imperative. But linked with
the word "fear" it is more than a gentle reminder. It is a serious
directive meant to move us out of lethargy and into action. It's time
to seize the promise given to Christ-followers in that day and this.
It is possible for all of us to enter His rest. To come short of it would
be an unthinkable tragedy, considering how busy and tired we
Christians become.

Apparently we come short of rest by our lack of faith, by disobedience, or by not being "diligent to enter" his rest (Hebrews 4).
Other translations tell us to "make every effort to enter that rest"
and "labour to enter it." Sounds like rest involves hard work, and
that just doesn't make sense. What kind of effort does resting
require? Must we work at not working?

The work being explained here is being diligent, making every
effort, laboring to put ourselves in a place where the Word of God
can have an effect on us. There is really no other way to find rest, to
diminish fear, or find peace than knowing and honoring the living,
active Word of God.

"Come away by yourselves to a secluded place and rest a while."
(For there were many people *coming and going, and they did*
not even have time to eat.)

MARK 6:31

Do not fear . . . but make me a little bread cake . . . and make one for yourself and for your son.

1 KINGS 17:13

Elijah lived by the stream with everything that he needed abundantly provided. But eventually the brook dried up and the ravens stopped their daily flyby. Elijah didn't wring his hands. Instead he sought God and waited until divine directions came.

He gathered his stuff and moved into a village where he met a compassionate widow. When he asked for food, she acted in faith even though she wondered where her own next meal would come from. She made bread for him, herself, and her child from the dregs of her oil jug and the last handful of grain. The next morning there was enough to do it again. That one miracle calmed every fear, but God's provision had just begun. For many days she continued to make bread by pouring oil from an empty jug and scooping up grain from a crumpled bag. The food multiplied miraculously until the famine was over.

Has God, our Jehovah-Jireh, ever made something out of nothing for you? He is able!

Though the fig tree should not blossom and there be no fruit on the vines, though *the yield of the olive should fail and the fields produce no food, though the flock should be cut off from the fold and there be no cattle in the stalls, yet I will exult in the L*ORD.

HABAKKUK 3:17–18

I confess my iniquity; I am troubled by my sin.

PSALM 38:18 NIV

The Psalms are full of emotion, and not just joy and praise. Pain, pathos, and fear are conveyed by David and other writers with heavy hearts in complicated situations. No wonder the book of Psalms is so popular. Not one of them fails to speak of something we are now or will soon be going through. However, living in the New Testament era, we know that God's forgiveness can wipe our sins clean. We do not live under the same fear as the saints of old, always wondering if their sacrifice was enough or if it was presented properly.

Forgiveness and grace make a way for us to be free from the power of sin. Do we fail? Do we sometimes respond in sinful ways? Do we at times yield to temptation? Unfortunately, yes! But that does not mean that we must bear the weight of it, wallow in a pit of regret, or try to compensate by working harder to attain godliness. We know that we are free indeed because the perfect, sinless, Lamb of God was sacrificed, paying the only acceptable and completely sufficient price for sin, including those we commit today.

We appropriate the forgiveness purchased on the cross when we confess our sins to our Great High Priest.

He does not need to offer sacrifices every day. But Jesus did this once for all when he offered himself as the sacrifice for the people's sins.

HEBREWS 7:27 NLT

Don't be afraid, little flock. For it gives your Father great
happiness to give you the Kingdom.

LUKE 12:32 NLT

Pulling away from the crowd, Jesus focused on His disciples and
began to teach them and to warn them. He begins by warning
them of the leaven of the Pharisees and continues with a dozen
cautions about anxiety, fear, and worry. He speaks tenderly to His
flock and describes the Father's happiness in giving them the Kingdom. One sure way to conquer fear is to contemplate future blessings. Every problem may not be solved, every disease healed, every
dysfunction corrected in this world, but you can be sure that they
will change.

Years ago, a teacher was asked to write a statement that would
always be true in every situation and would help people live successfully. He wrote: "This too will pass away." Nothing remains
forever the same. People change, new people are introduced, situations improve, and certain things are added and removed. Change
happens.

"This too will pass away"—the words make us sad as we fear
some loss, but at other times they make us glad. The pain will not
last forever, the broken relationship will be forgotten, sin is forgiven, fears disappear, needs are supplied, or the need changes.
Rest in the reality of this simple but profound truth and look up;
you too will inherit the Kingdom, and Jesus will sit on the throne.

The LORD has established His throne in the heavens, and His
sovereignty rules over all.   PSALM 103:19

I am sending you out as sheep in the midst of wolves, so be wise
as serpents and innocent as doves... Do not be anxious.

MATTHEW 10:16, 19 ESV

Sheep in the midst of wolves? What a predicament! Yet sometimes we are sent into a wilderness occupied by ferocious animals! You are nothing more than food to them. Is there a way of escape?

Sheep are weak, skittish, easily frightened, prone to wander, and wear a coat that's easy to sink a claw into—versus wolves, which are aggressive, with armor-thick skin, and lethal weapons built into their paws and mouths. Imagine a one-on-one encounter between these two enemies. The wolf open-jawed, canine teeth glistening, salivating with hunger, poised to jump on a placid sheep. Who do you think wins that battle?

The sheep! But only if it is "as wise as serpents and innocent as doves."

"Wise" can also mean "shrewd." Think of having wisdom with "street smarts." Are we actually being encouraged to be shrewd? Sheep are shrewd enough to know that wolves hang out in the wilderness and wise enough to realize they will survive only if they stay close to the Shepherd.

We who are sheep in God's pasture may walk unafraid through rough country knowing that we will soon rest in green pastures beside still waters.

I want you to be wise about what is good and innocent about
what is evil.   ROMANS 16:19

Peace I leave with you; my peace I give to you . . . Let not your hearts be troubled.

JOHN 14:27 ESV

When your heart is troubled, are you tempted to blame someone else? Maybe that is your first reaction. We always resist being the one at fault. Like brushing lint from the shoulders of our jacket, we sweep blame onto someone else. Sometimes we are tempted to blame God! But when we seek Him and ask Him to reveal our faults and cleanse our hearts, light comes in like sunshine through freshly washed windows. The only thing that can cloud our relationship with Majesty is the "sin which so easily ensnares us" (Hebrews 12:1 NKJV).

The moment we acknowledge our part—the sin part—we are no longer troubled or afraid. Peace flows like a river. It always accompanies repentance and obedience. An unnatural, unfathomable, unexplainable peace—recognizable as coming from Jesus. When peace fails to come, we need to wait upon God until He reveals the reason. His timing is all-important. Beware of getting ahead of Him and missing the principal message.

In *My Utmost for His Highest*, the well-aged wisdom of Oswald Chambers opened for me a new way of thinking. "Problems come as probes to keep the mind awake and amazed at the revelation of God. Any problem that comes between God and myself springs out of disobedience; any problem . . . that is alongside me while I obey God increases my ecstatic delight, because I know that my Father knows, and I am going to watch and see how He unravels this thing."[34]

You will not be afraid of the terror by night.

PSALM 91:5

The Hebrew word for "terror" means "fear, dread, or great alarm." Suffice it to say, the author of this Psalm addresses a really big fear, feelings bad enough to make you run for a flashlight or get up from the bed and have a cup of chamomile tea.

This is the time to run instead to El Shaddai. "El" means "mighty or strong" and designates God; "Shaddai" is a bit more complicated because scholars disagree on its root word. Some think it means "powerful in rule or judgment"—God Almighty. Others think it signifies His power to meet human need—God the All-Sufficient One. I'm thinking if scholars disagree, who am I to be dogmatic? But since the Hebrew word "shad" means "breast," more specifically "a woman's breast," it is easy for me to embrace El Shaddai as the many-breasted God, the "pourer forth or shedder forth of blessing." He is the One we run to for sustenance and comfort when we are afraid, especially when it's dark.

Next time you are afraid and don't know what to do, run into the arms of El Shaddai and from His bounty receive strength, security, and love. He invites us all to come to Him, lean upon His breast, and be succored by Him.

Because he has loved Me, therefore I will deliver him; I will set him securely on high, because he has known My name.

PSALM 91:14

For this reason my loins are full of anguish; pains have seized me like the pains of a woman in labor. I am so bewildered I cannot hear, so terrified I cannot see.

ISAIAH 21:3

When I hear one of the male species speak of the pain of child-birth, I usually shake my head and wonder, *How do you know? Pick another metaphor!* But knowing that behind the man with a pen is God inspiring the words, I have to pay attention and agree, *Isaiah was in great pain and fear—like labor pains!* What were the upsetting circumstances?

God had commissioned him to deliver the message that Babylon would be taken by the Assyrians, and it made the prophet's loins hurt, his mind spin, and his feelings burst out of control. Adding to Isaiah's anguish, everybody was in a festive mood, completely oblivious to impending disaster. Dread of delivering devastating news tormented him.

Have you ever had to make that kind of hard choice? To spare someone's feelings, you go to the party when it doesn't feel right. You say yes, when you think no. You grant permission so the child won't pout. You compromise to keep peace.

Pray for a heart like Isaiah's. He wanted to spare the people a message that would hurt, but he loved them enough to speak the truth. If you are on the receiving end of truth, find joy in knowing somebody really loves you.

―――――――

What I have heard from the Lord of hosts, the God of Israel, I make known to you.   ISAIAH 21:10

My heart is in anguish within me, and the terrors of death have fallen upon me. Fear and trembling come upon me, and horror has overwhelmed me.

PSALM 55:4–5

David felt "deep anguish" because of the betrayal of a close friend. For him it was the unkindest cut of all coming from someone he cared about and trusted. We do not know the details, but we can't stop our imaginations from playing out a dramatic scene, especially since David has made his feelings known. What could have caused such pain? He listed his fears—"anguish, terrors of death, fear and trembling, and overwhelming horror."

This kind of persecution could come only from the evilest of men or the fiercest of demonic forces. I can't help but think of the persecution of Christians today from those in other countries who do not know our God. It is not the first time in history that Christ-ones have been maligned, maimed, and killed in bizarre and humiliating ways—tortured, burned at the stake or torched in cages, beheaded by swords, dismembered with knives, crucified, and drowned. Could it be that David was facing that kind of terror?

He was also troubled by the soul-terrors that you and I face today—accusations, pressures, and threats. Thankfully David showed us his confidence in God and faith in prayer. He asked for clarity and that his enemies might be confused.

I said, "Oh, that I had wings like a dove! I would fly away and be at rest."   PSALM 55:6

The one who fears is not perfected in love.

1 JOHN 4:18

Have you ever loved someone with the 1 Corinthians 13 kind of love? Maybe you can say, "I know that chapter, and I have tried, but it seems impossible!" Perhaps you have managed to get it right on a few counts but failed miserably on others. You may have been successful in controlling your anger a few times and can honestly say you did not keep score. You may be able to claim you haven't given up—at least not yet. But on other points, you admit failure. Is it even possible to love another person like that as long as we live on this fallen planet? Still, most of us are trying.

Have you ever *been loved* that much? You may have been loved well by someone very special—a doting father, an adoring husband, a close friend, a soul mate. But others cannot make that claim. Most people are looking for love, some in the wrong places, and others fear they will never find it.

To all who are searching for love, it is found in Jesus. Jesus loves you! There's nothing you can do to keep Him from loving you—not your bad attitude, confusion, hurt, or problems. Nothing, and I do mean nothing, will ever separate you and me from the everlasting love of Christ. Abide in His love and be Unafraid.

[Nothing] will be able to separate us from the love of God, which is in Christ Jesus our Lord.

ROMANS 8:39

You will not be afraid of the terror by night... A thousand may
fall at your side and ten thousand at your right hand, but it shall
not approach you.

PSALM 91:5, 7

Whether this verse is about falling physically or falling spiritually, the resolution is the same. If a thousand fall by your side from some rogue, highly contagious virus, or if ten thousand fall in a massive tragedy or a war against terrorists, it shall not come near you. You have no reason to fear because the Lord is faithful and angels will "guard you in all your ways" (Psalm 91:11).

To calm your fear, these are the names and characteristics of God in Psalm 91.

His name is El Elyon, Most High God.

He is Almighty, El Shaddai, All-Sufficient God, the Great I AM.

He is the LORD Yahweh or Jehovah, Self-Existent God.

He is our refuge and fortress—a safe place to hide.

He is Elohim—the Father, Son, and Holy Spirit.

He is our shield and buckler—everything we need to fight and win.

He is my dwelling place—a place to abide and rest with Him.

He is my refuge—a place of security and peace.

He holds me fast in His love and has granted me salvation.

Because of who He is, there is no reason for you to fear. When you see thousands of others falling nearby, you can run into His arms and whisper His name. He is there for you.

*You will not be afraid... For you have made the LORD, my refuge,
even the Most High, your dwelling place.*

PSALM 91:5, 9

When El Elyon, God Most High, is our dwelling place, fear has
to find another place to live. He is the Ruler of the Universe. He
allows no unruly visitors or uninvited guest. You will not be afraid.

Writer Thomas Merton, in *Thoughts in Solitude*, expresses well
our own ups and downs as we struggle with faith and fear: "God,
we have no idea where we are going. We do not see the road ahead
of us. We cannot know for certain where it will end. Nor do we
really know ourselves, and the fact that we think we are following your will does not mean that we are actually doing so. But we
believe that the desire to please you does in fact please you. And we
know that if we do this you will lead us by the right road, though
we may know nothing about it. Therefore we will trust you always.
We will not fear, for you are ever with us, and you will never leave
us to face our perils alone."[35]

Do not worry about having enough faith. It is not faith itself that
conquers fear. It is Jesus himself who has borne our fear, anxiety,
and worry on the cross. Believe it and receive it!

———————

*Surely, just as I have intended so it has happened, and just as I
have planned so it will stand.*

ISAIAH 14:24

Do not be afraid…you meant evil against me, but God meant it for good in order to bring about this present result, to preserve many people alive.

GENESIS 50:19–20

Only God can take a dastardly deed done by a group of jealous brothers and turn it into an act that would save a nation. Only a God Who redeems can do that! Sovereignty means God is in control and rules over everything. The idea that He knows everything can be frightening. But when you stumble, when your child gets addicted, or someone you love suffers loss or faces death, God's sovereignty is the most comforting of His attributes.

Joseph, the favored son of Jacob, wore a coat of many colors and talked too much about his dreams. It kindled the flame of envy in the hearts of his brothers. They ganged up against him, tore off that coat, and threw him into a dried-up well. First came the deed, then the cover-up. They put goat's blood on the coat and showed it to his father to prove he was dead. But God is Sovereign. Joseph was rescued by the Egyptians, promoted to a place of authority, and he rescued his own people from famine.

Can you think of a time when God overruled events and rescued you? Has he turned evil into good for you? That is what God does every day of our lives.

———————

Just as I have intended so it has happened, and just as I have planned so it will stand.

ISAIAH 14:24

"So therefore, do not be afraid; I will provide for you and your
little ones." So he comforted them and spoke kindly to them.

GENESIS 50:21

Joseph did not retaliate! Instead, he comforted his brothers and
promised to provide for them and their descendants. He spoke
kindly to them. Have you ever thought that you would like to be
a more encouraging person, but when something bad happens
you don't know what to say, or what to do? The Apostle Paul wrote
something specifically for you: "The God of all comfort, who comforts us in all our affliction so that we will be able to comfort those
who are in any affliction with the comfort with which we ourselves are comforted by God...Our comfort is abundant through
Christ. But if we are afflicted, it is for your comfort and salvation;
or if we are comforted, it is for your comfort, which is effective in
the patient enduring of the same sufferings which we also suffer;
and our hope for you is firmly grounded, knowing that as you are
sharers of our sufferings, so also you are *sharers* of our comfort"
(2 Corinthians 1:3–7).

Comfort is the theme of the passage and something we all need
to practice. Who is the source of comfort? How can we comfort others? If you have suffered, you know what comforts and what does
not. Simply let the comfort of Christ overflow. The comfort we have
received becomes the comfort we give to others.

Even though I walk through the valley of the shadow of death, I fear no evil, for You are with me.

PSALM 23:4

Three times Jesus asked Peter if he loved Him, and he answered in the affirmative. The intriguing part of the story unfolds when you notice the distinctive words these men used. Jesus spoke first: "Simon, do you 'agape' me? In other words, do you love me unconditionally, enough to sacrifice yourself for me?" (see John 21:15–17).

"Yes, Lord! I 'phileo' you," Peter answered. "I am your friend. You know that I love you in a brotherly way. We share the same interests." Jesus asked again, "Simon, do you 'agape' me completely? Are you willing to sacrifice yourself for me?" Peter replied, "You know that I 'phileo' you. You are my friend! We have much in common." Jesus asked, "Simon, do you 'phileo' me? Are you my friend?" Simon Peter was grieved, because Jesus asked again and again and again. He also noticed that He uttered another word for love this time—the word that Peter used to define the relationship. "Lord," he answered, "You know all things. You see things from a perspective far above what men can comprehend. You are acquainted with me personally; and know by experience that I am your friend."

Put yourself in Jesus' place. Do you think He felt comforted, reassured, blessed? Have you ever said "I love you" and the other person answered, "Let's just be friends"? Today, can you speak the words He longs to hear? Jesus, I agape You.

Therefore, while the promise of entering his rest still stands, let us fear lest any of you should seem to have failed to reach it.

HEBREWS 4:1 ESV

The Word of God cuts like a sword through the superfluous, corrects our course, and points out new directions. Interaction with truth changes our perspective. We discern between things that are good and things that are better or best. This helps us eliminate urgent, time-consuming, or self-serving activity and concentrate on what's most important—the plans God has for each of us. It also makes a piercing distinction between soul and spirit—our mind, will, and emotions, and the things that come from our spirit—that place where God dwells, that part of us that wants only what He wants. Truth helps us discern between thoughts and feelings that come from self and those from God.

When we are open and honest about ourselves before God, we move through the complicated maze of human emotions into the light and freedom of truth. There we enter into his rest—rest in who we are, rest in relationships, rest in what we choose to do, rest while using our unique spiritual gifts and desires to serve God. So if finding rest requires work and the work we do for God is a matter of resting in him, what would a day in the life of Jesus' followers be like?

It is the Spirit who gives life; the flesh profits nothing; the words that I have spoken to you are spirit and are life.

JOHN 6:63

You will not be afraid... of the pestilence that stalks in darkness.

PSALM 91:5–6

A missionary doctor serving people with Ebola, a virus that kills 90 percent of its victims, became infected with the disease. His life in jeopardy, he was flown home to the United States, placed in isolation, treated with experimental drugs, and infused with vitamins and nutrients. In nineteen days, he was discharged from the hospital and reunited with his family, and now he is working on a cure for others. Recently he spoke to a large audience of missionaries and friends that included his wife and two children.

This report circulated on the Samaritan's Purse website afterward: "One of the most powerful moments of the service occurred unnoticed by many, when Dr. Brantly turned, looked straight at his young son on his wife's lap, and sang to him some of the opening words of Matt Redman's anthem 'Ten Thousand Reasons': 'Whatever may pass, and whatever lies before me, Let me be singing when the evening comes.'"

Do you wonder how Dr. Brantly survived? The medicine, the IV fluids, the doctors' care, being at home? Evidently God used all of the above. But it was the careful watch-care, the abiding presence, the unlimited power of Jehovah-Rapha, the Lord That Heals, who mixed all the ingredients together into a perfect balm. And to Him we offer glory and praise.

———————

Bless the LORD, O my soul, and forget none of His benefits;
Who pardons all your iniquities, Who heals all your diseases;
Who redeems your life from the pit, Who crowns you with
lovingkindness and compassion.   PSALM 103:2–4

No, my daughters, for it is exceedingly bitter to me for your sake
that the hand of the Lord has gone out against me.

RUTH 1:13 ESV

Exceedingly bitter! Naomi's words indicate grief, uncertainty, despair, and fear. She had lost her husband, grieved the deaths of two sons, and was now driven by fear of starvation to leave her daughters-in-law and go home, back to her people and their land. I wonder if her greatest fear was of loneliness.

But the story had only begun. The women wept and clung to each other for a final gathering of strength, and a decision. One chose to stay in Moab, where her husband was buried and his family lived among their pagan gods; the other mustered up all the courage she could find and chose a new God-directed adventure. The words Ruth said to Naomi are most often remembered at weddings and anniversaries. But they were first spoken by a daughter-in-law to her mother-in-law. Blessed are the women who can share such love and grace in a complicated relationship. There is no fear in love; there are no stereotypes in grace.

Ruth's words were more than a commitment to Naomi. They were her profession of faith in the true God. Ruth left Moab with Naomi and lived in Bethlehem where she was loved and protected by both Elohim and Boaz, her kinsman redeemer.

Entreat me not to leave you, or to turn back from following after
you; for wherever you go, I will go; and wherever you lodge, I will
lodge; your people shall be my people, and your God, my God.

RUTH 1:16 NKJV

AUTUMN

My Sorrow, when she's here with me,
Thinks these dark days of autumn rain
Are beautiful as days can be;
She loves the bare, the withered tree;
She walks the sodden pasture lane.
ROBERT FROST, "MY NOVEMBER GUEST"

*Do not be afraid or discouraged, for the Lord will personally go
ahead of you. He will be with you; he will neither fail you nor
abandon you.*

DEUTERONOMY 31:8 NLT

Wherever we go, whatever we do, Yahweh is going ahead, leading the way, lighting the path, and pointing out potholes. He will
always be with you; He will neither fail, nor abandon you. Do not
be afraid that your own ability to persevere will weaken. It does not
depend on your efforts, but upon your choice to walk in the light
surrounding Jesus.

"Dis-courage" means "without courage." Courage like that of a
great lion is yours as long as you stay close to the Alpha up front.
You may avoid being dis-couraged by carrying in your mind words
of encouragement from the Scriptures, words of prayer shared in
close-knit groups, or thoughts expressed by like-minded friends.
"En-courage" means "to give or infuse courage." When God uses a
personal conduit to give you courage, receive it, hold it close, and
be thankful.

Earlier this week the leader of a Bible study group texted a simple message: "I was encouraged today by Revelation 21:1–7, so I
will pass it on, maybe you will be encouraged too." My heart filled
with courage as I read the verses. May I encourage you to read them
today and don't forget to pass it on.

---

*Behold, the tabernacle of God is among men, and He will dwell
among them, and they shall be His people, and God Himself will
be among them.*   REVELATION 21:3

And my soul is greatly dismayed; But You, O Lord—how long?
PSALM 6:3

In the 1960s a technology expert reported information he'd heard at a meeting of IBM employees. The discussion had been highly motivational, focusing on the future of technology. Someone predicted that because of technical advances, within twenty years man's workload would be drastically reduced. Instead of the usual forty-hours-plus-overtime workweek, they could count on about half—a scant twenty to twenty-four hours. It would mean a totally new schedule of three or four days a week. That led to a lengthy discussion of what employees would do with their extra time.

But over the years and after major advances in technology, we are not sitting around wondering what to do with our excess time, are we? We are doing three things at once, pecking our next appointments into our smartphones or calling ahead to plan a meeting. My theory: Every day that we live our workload will increase as a result of the electronic gadgets that make it easier to accomplish more. We will work efficiently and faster until we melt, then we will join those who preceded us in heaven still carrying our smartphones.

Time is common to all. We each have the same amount and we can't manufacture more. But we can redeem the time we have. There is no reason to fear; instead, let's keep walking by faith and "making the most of every opportunity" (Ephesians 5:16 NIV).

> *Come to Me, all who are weary and heavy-laden, and I will give*
> *you rest.*
>
> MATTHEW 11:28

Three different definitions of "heavy-laden" offer a complete understanding of what Jesus meant. *"Come to Me, all who are carrying a heavy load."* Life's heaviest loads are the emotional ones including fear, worry, anxiety, and a wide range of bad feelings. *"Come to Me, all whose work is hard."* Is your work hard, difficult, or complicated—physically, mentally, spiritually? *"Come to Me, you who are overburdened by the commands which the teachers of the Law have placed upon you."* Are you under pressure, feeling conflicted, or confused?

Most of us have trouble admitting we are carrying a heavy load emotionally. With feelings raw from circumstances, we refuse to sound whiney! Some of us may not want others to know that our work is hard. We clam up. Some may not admit that they are troubled by legalism, but it is tough trying to live up to the unrealistic expectations of religious leaders.

But I have good news for all of you who will admit your need. The promise written to Jesus' contemporaries applies to you and me today. To all who choose to bring their burdens to the Lord, He promises rest—not just physical rest, but spiritual, emotional, and mental rest. "Come to Me and I will give you rest."

> *Are you tired? Worn out? Burned out on religion? Come to me.*
> *Get away with me and you'll recover your life. I'll show you how*
> *to take a real rest.*   MATTHEW 11:28 MSG

All who are weary and heavy-laden . . . My yoke is easy and My burden is light.

MATTHEW 11:28, 30

Most of us assume a yoke is heavy—it's carved from a large beam of wood. And a burden has to be weighty, or it would not be called "burden." So how can Jesus invite someone who is already weary and heavy laden to take on a yoke? Is He being real about the "easy and light" part? In a previous statement, He has told us to rest, then without a period between He adds, *Put on my yoke and let's get to work.*

Long before the days of air-conditioned tractors with power steering, there were oxen or mules and plows. I've seen pictures. The stronger, more knowledgeable, experienced animal became the lead. The other kept in step, balanced the trace, and added muscle. It is actually a good picture of you and me doing our part as we walk in tandem with Jesus. He does the work as we stay in the harness and keep the task moving forward.

We were not meant to go through life apart from God, separated from Jesus, or finding work independently of Him. He delights in partnering with His children and carrying the heavy end of the load. Then it becomes easy to leave behind the limitations of fear and weakness and move quickly into a place of rest and peace.

For thus says the Lord GOD, the Holy One of Israel: "In returning and rest you shall be saved; in quietness and confidence shall be your strength."   ISAIAH 30:15 NKJV

I was with you in weakness and in fear and in much trembling.

1 CORINTHIANS 2:3

Most of us know Romans 8:28, even though some of us quote it without the final phrase. God causes all things to work together for good to those who love God, to those who "are called according to *His* purpose." What a blessing to know that our salvation and spiritual growth into the likeness of Jesus Christ is a certainty and under the Sovereign control of God (see Romans 8:29). But that is just the start.

Paul continues: "And these whom He predestined, He also called; and these whom He called, He also justified; and these whom He justified, He also glorified" (Romans 8:30). Notice the strong verbs he used, all written in the past tense: predestined, called, justified, glorified—all similar but distinct in meaning, and each one coming out of the other. This is what the Almighty has accomplished for us. Simply put, from God's point of view, from eternity past to our eternal future, He sees us as a finished work because of His purpose and grace, not by chance or merit. He sees us seated in heavenly places with Him even as we live here on earth (see Ephesians 2:6).

May all your fear of not measuring up, of failing to be conformed to His image or not accomplishing His work in this world be dispelled by the amazing grace of our Lord.

My heart is confident in you, O God; my heart is confident. No wonder I can sing your praises!
PSALM 57:7 NLT

*Who among you fears the LORD and obeys his servant? If you are
walking in darkness, without a ray of light, trust in the LORD and
rely on your God.*

ISAIAH 50:10 NLT

Isaiah warned about times of spiritual darkness—times when you
can't see the light, even at the end of a tunnel! In that darkness, it
is time to trust in the LORD. Resist the temptation to light a fire of
your own, but keep walking by faith one step at a time. "Watch out,
you who live in your own light and warm yourselves by your own
fires...You will soon fall down in great torment" (Isaiah 50:11
NLT). Eventually the light of God's presence will illuminate your
pathway again. O for the steadiness of a faith that will make your
pathway clear even in the dark.

Isaiah was also speaking about a time, still in the future, when
light may be scarce and fear compounded. The Servant showed
those who will be alive in those extraordinarily challenging last
days how to respond. "He did not retaliate when he was insulted,
nor threaten revenge when he suffered. He left his case in the hands
of God, who always judges fairly" (1 Peter 2:23 NLT).

We must consider prayerfully whatever works we plan to do,
always asking, "Is this task God-given? Am I trying to please God
alone? Am I doing this simply because I can?" Remember that the
need is not the call.

---

*Wait for the LORD; be strong and let your heart take courage;
yes, wait for the LORD.*

PSALM 27:14

*Do not be terrified by them, for the LORD your God, who is
among you, is a great and awesome God.*

DEUTERONOMY 7:21 NIV84

Our God is an awesome God. Overwhelming, breathtaking, splendid, tremendous, amazing, and awe-inspiring. These are only a few of many synonyms that describe Him in that one word, *awesome*. In the Bible, He is described more completely by His names:

He is Elohim—Creator

El Elyon—God Most High

El Roi—God Who Sees

El Shaddai—All-Sufficient One

Adonai—the Lord

Jehovah—Self-Existent One

Jehovah-Jireh—the Lord Will Provide

Jehovah-Rapha—the Lord That Heals

Jehovah-Nissi—the Lord My Banner

Jehovah-Mekoddishkem—the Lord Sanctifies You

Jehovah-Shalom—the Lord Is Peace

Jehovah-Sabaoth—the Lord of Hosts

Jehovah-Raah—the Lord My Shepherd

Jehovah-Tsidkenu—the Lord Our Righteousness

Jehovah-Shammah—the Lord Is There

A Prayer: *Lord, I praise You today for Who You are. I want to
know you by name. Amen.*

*Hannah was in deep anguish, crying bitterly as she prayed to
the LORD... "I am very discouraged, and I was pouring out my
heart to the LORD."*

1 SAMUEL 1:10, 15 NLT

Hannah prayed with such emotion and pain that Eli the priest
accused her of being under the influence of wine, completely out
of control in the house of the LORD. Wracked with grief, fear, pain,
and heart-wrenching sadness, she stood in the presence of Yahweh and, in the truest meaning of supplication, pleaded for a child.
Such was her desperation that she vowed to give the boy back to
God for full-time Christian service—not when he was grown, but
as soon as he was weaned.

Hannah's husband was embarrassed by his wife's outburst of
feeling and did the first thing that came to mind—he invited her
out for lunch! Then he asked, "Am I not better to you than ten
sons?" (1 Samuel 1:8). Now I wonder: *What does that have to do with
anything!!* But she accepted the grace he offered and took control of
herself.

She managed her runaway feelings the same way you and I do.
Breathe, redirect our thoughts, and question the feelings. Is crying
helpful, does fear change anything? Then she cast it upon the LORD.

---

*O God, you are my God; I earnestly search for you. My soul
thirsts for you; my whole body longs for you in this parched and
weary land where there is no water.*

PSALM 63:1 NLT

But when he saw the wind, he was afraid.

MATTHEW 14:30 ESV

Wind represents many different things, including the things that happen in our lives above and beyond our control. Still we must not be afraid, for the LORD is in control and can always be trusted. "The LORD does whatever pleases him throughout all heaven and earth, and on the seas and in their depths...He sends the lightning with the rain and releases the wind from his storehouses" (Psalm 135:6–7 NLT). You may think it is only wind that stirs up, whips through, turns over, and dishevels. Sometimes it is the Holy Spirit—the Wind of God's Presence.

Wind is a fitting picture of the work of the Holy Spirit. He is not seen but felt; He has resistless power; and He cannot be controlled. He appears at times as a welcome balmy breeze and at other times as a whirlwind surprisingly fierce. "The wind blows where it wishes and you hear the sound of it, but do not know where it comes from and where it is going; so is everyone who is born of the Spirit" (John 3:8).

When Moses led God's people out of Egypt and into Canaan, the wind prepared the way to victory, just as the Spirit opens the way for us today. In the early beginnings of the church, there was the sound of rushing wind.

———————

Who is like You among the gods, O LORD? Who is like You, majestic in holiness, awesome in praises, working wonders?

EXODUS 15:11

Do not be afraid any longer, but go on speaking and do not be silent; for I am with you, and no man will attack you in order to harm you, for I have many people in this city.

ACTS 18: 9–10

Near the end of his Epistle to the Romans, Paul wrote, "Whatever was written in earlier times was written for our instruction, so that through perseverance and the encouragement of the Scriptures we might have hope" (15:4). That first word—"Whatever" or "everything"—reaches beyond his present writings to Rome to encompass all the words of God in both Old and New Testaments. Then he focuses on the truth that offers endurance, encouragement, and hope to all of us.

It was all written for our instruction, to teach us what we need to know. If the purpose was to teach, then we must be students. In the words of commentator Matthew Henry, "We must therefore labour, not only to understand the literal meaning of the Scripture, but to learn out of it that which will do us good; and we have need of help therefore not only to roll away the stone, but to draw out the water, for in many places the well is deep."[36]

We assimilate the truth in our hearts and minds as we persevere. It's where we do more than learn; we experience. "I know that Jesus Christ did not come to *teach* only," wrote Oswald Chambers. "He came to *make me what He teaches I should be.*"[37]

We will not fear, though the earth should change and though the mountains slip into the heart of the sea.

PSALM 46:2

When I was in danger of losing hope and cowering in a corner, I finally got it! Kay Arthur, while speaking to a group of Precept leaders, had ended a Bible study with a phrase that made me laugh: "Hangeth thou in there, O baby!" I would not be giving up anytime soon. A line from Romans had already grabbed me: "tribulation brings about perseverance" (Romans 5:3). A jolt of healthy laughter and a word of truth—two hooks that catch me every time. I saw my need to hang in there and persevere.

Later I looked up "perseverance"—it is the characteristic of one who is not swerved from his deliberate purpose and his loyalty to faith by even the greatest trials and sufferings. In its original form, *hupomeno* meant "to abide" or to "remain under" commitments, misfortunes, and trials, "to hold fast to one's faith in Christ, to bear bravely and calmly" even in great trials. With new understanding, I prayed for the grace I would need to *exult* in tribulations. Which, by the way, means more than "rejoice" but to "jump up and down with joy." It is our joy as Christ-followers, to stay put in the present circumstances that He has allowed, whether difficult or confusing, by grace, in faith, by the power of the Holy Spirit. We are not to recede, pull back, or flee.

In other words, "Hangeth thou in there, O baby!"

But we are not of them who draw back unto perdition; but of them that believe to the saving of the soul.

HEBREWS 10:39 KJV

"Draw back"—a two-word phrase that perfectly describes fear. Too afraid to stay put, stand tall, and carry on, we move back, away from the unknown like shrinking back from a hot stove. We tend to run from things that might do us harm. The opposite reaction is what this verse in Hebrews teaches—believe and keep on believing to the final and complete salvation of your soul.

What are we to do when there is no way to make sense of what happens? Throw up our hands and give up? Turn in a letter of resignation and quit? Or simply let God be God, and trust Him without terms? What we can never figure out by human reasoning, we are able to comprehend because of our faith. In Hebrews 11, the author lists in what's been called Faith's Hall of Fame many different crises and perplexing situations that come to good people. Almost every verse begins with the words "by faith." He lists problems and circumstances that nobody can accept apart from faith—God's people facing death, persecutions, disasters, mind-boggling circumstances, and hard-to-understand issues of life.

The truth is, there is much in life that doesn't make sense without faith. Today, we live our lives as Moses and the aforementioned heroes did: "he saw him who is invisible" (Hebrews 11:27 NIV).

The fear of the LORD is the beginning of wisdom, and knowledge
of the Holy One is understanding wisdom.

PROVERBS 9:10

Wisdom is available right here, right now as we deal with the complexities of life. Picture a gift wrapped in heavenly blue with ribbons trailing extended to you by the hands of someone you love. You reach, intrigued by the pretty package and charmed by the giver, and receive the gift. Upon opening the box you discover that wisdom is yours as you pursue it.

We study harder, only to discover that one may know the truth and not have wisdom. We seek to obey, until nagging doubt makes us wonder if we did it right or did enough.

Doing something physical did not fix your problem. Wisdom offers understanding then proceeds to explain what wisdom really is. It is knowing the "Holy One." Our pursuit is one of knowing God as supremely holy and that may stretch you again and again as you reach new heights of purest love and joy. Because the Word of God is a living thing, it has a life-giving and life-changing effect. It is impossible to know wisdom apart from the truth of God's word. It has the power to literally change your life.

———————

My mouth will speak wisdom, and the meditation of my heart
will be understanding.

PSALM 49:3

*Let us fear...Let us be diligent...Let us hold fast...Let us
draw near.*   HEBREWS 4

Four imperatives beginning with "let us" help us overcome fear and
find rest. Rest—both physical and spiritual—is available to every
believer in our Lord Jesus Christ. The first imperative is, "Let us
fear coming short of that rest" (see Hebrews 4:1). The rest of Salvation is pictured for us by the people of Israel who wandered through
deserts and fought endless battles in pursuit of Canaan, a land that
promised rest and abundance. But they could not enter because
of unbelief. Today, people waste years trying to earn salvation, or
make themselves fit for God's presence, while He tells us to simply
"believe." Salvation is a gift that we accept by faith, not self-effort.

The second imperative reveals that it is possible to miss rest by
refusing to enter. "Let us be diligent to enter that rest" (Hebrews
4:11). The Word of God opens the door to salvation by judging
thoughts and intentions, and by revealing and convicting us of sin.
We enter by taking one step of faith.

The third "let us" tells us to "hold fast our confession" (Hebrews
4:14). God's Word enables us to hold fast, to persevere. It judges
the thoughts and intentions of our heart. There is no creature hidden from God's sight; all things are open to His eyes (see Hebrews
4:12–13). The word is alive and active because it is synonymous
with God Himself. Jesus is called the Word.

The message concludes: "Let us draw near...to the throne of grace"
(Hebrews 4:16). He invites us to come to Him in prayer.

When we let God have His way in these four ways, we can joyfully expect to "receive mercy and find grace to help in time of need"
(Hebrews 4:16).

---

*You have made us for yourself, O Lord, and our heart is restless
until it rests in You.*   AUGUSTINE[38]

And you, son of man, neither fear them nor fear their words . . .
nor be dismayed at their presence . . . Listen to what I am
speaking to you; do not be rebellious like that rebellious house.
Open your mouth and eat what I am giving you.

EZEKIEL 2:6–8

In a life-changing moment, the Lord addressed Ezekiel's fear by saying: "Eat what I am giving you." With those few words, God put forth a principle that would guide the ministry of this deeply devoted, highly visual, slightly quirky prophet. "Behold, a hand was extended to me; and lo, a scroll was in it" (Ezekiel 2:9). Was the Lord saying he must eat parchment?

I can only imagine being in the presence of Yahweh—One so holy, so highly reverenced, having a name so packed with meaning that people feared speak it. I envision a breathless pause, Ezekiel's unsteady hand reaching forth, his trembling fingers encircling the roll. Then silence. What do you think happened next?

Picture him unrolling the scroll, tearing off one bite at a time, chewing, swallowing, and assimilating the truth physically, mentally, spiritually, until it actually became part of him—the Word of God transformed by his digestive system into blood that coursed through his veins and into the chambers of his heart. Even if you cannot imagine feasting on the Word literally, it is possible to fill our minds with truth, consume it regularly, absorb it until it becomes an integral part of our soul, and miraculous changes occur. Satiated with God's Word, we find ourselves ready to serve Him fearlessly.

Your words were found and I ate them.   JEREMIAH 15:16

You did not receive the spirit of slavery to fall back into fear, but you have received the Spirit of adoption as sons, by whom we cry, "Abba! Father!"

ROMANS 8:15 ESV

Having a "spirit of slavery" describes one who "disregards his own interests and gives himself up to another's will." A spirit of slavery may not have anything to do with a person's heart; or having a submissive will; some serve out of fear, without even considering a relationship with the Master. Slavery can describe a life of human effort and limited ability, accomplished because of outward pressure or a perfunctory obedience to the law. In contrast, receiving the spirit of adoption describes life motivated by the Spirit of God accomplished in union with the Holy Spirit.

"We have been set free to experience our rightful heritage. You can tell for sure that you are now fully adopted as his own children because God sent the Spirit of his Son into our lives crying out, 'Papa! Father!' Doesn't that privilege of intimate conversation with God make it plain that you are not a slave, but a child? And if you are a child, you're also an heir, with complete access to the inheritance" (Galatians 4:4–7 MSG).

The Father is your "Abba!" The name means much more than "daddy." It is a sacred name, a title of respect to a ruler, an elder, the author or beginner of a thing. It denotes a covenantal relationship that cannot be broken.

I am afraid of you, lest in vain I did labour toward you.

GALATIANS 4:11 YLT

The Galatian Christians were in danger of being led back into Judaism. They began by practicing familiar customs and rituals in their worship. They began to observe the mosaic calendar, to honor special days, weekly and monthly celebrations, and seasons like Passover, Pentecost, and Tabernacles. By doing this, the new believers thought they would gain the special favor of God. But Paul said that works could not be added to faith. He was afraid they would go back to their pre-Christ subservience to the law. He told them to imitate him. Once he met the living Christ, he had no desire to put himself back under the rules and legalism of the Jews.

Does this story apply to us today? Can legalism take root in our hearts after we have known the Lord? Is it possible to be drawn back under legalism? Can we actually prefer ritual to the reality of knowing Jesus? Perhaps . . . temporarily.

Maybe at the time you believed, somebody told you, "You are saved to serve." Perhaps in your own enthusiasm you wanted *to do* something as a sort of payback for the gift of salvation. Either way, the enemy of our souls would rather you tangle yourself in legalism than see you worship, pray, and obey.

Beware the barrenness of a busy life!

SOCRATES

Yet you, O Lord, are our Father. We are the clay, you are the potter; we are all the work of your hand.

ISAIAH 64:8 NIV

> *Frightened to the core of their being, frightened into giving honor to the God-of-Heaven.*
>
> REVELATION 11:13 MSG

Picture John, the beloved disciple, abandoned on the Isle of Patmos, spending the last days of his life alone with the "God-of-Heaven." There he received and recorded everything he heard and saw. He called his writings the Revelation of Jesus Christ—not a revelation *about* Jesus Christ but the revelation *of* Jesus Christ. If you long to see Jesus, if you want to receive His greatest blessings, I challenge you to read it, and I promise you, as John did, "Blessed is he who reads and those who hear the words of the prophecy" (Revelation 1:3).

Do you know why so few actually read the Revelation? Because our enemy does not want us to know "the things which must soon take place" (Revelation 1:1). He prefers confusion, unconcern, neglect, and fear. So he tells us there is too much symbolism, too many interpretations, that it's too hard for simple people like you and me to understand. He does not want you to read about the devil and his demons being thrown into the lake of fire. He does not want you to see myriads of myriads and thousands of thousands pouring honor and praise upon Jesus. Let's defy him and let us see Jesus revealed in all His glory, let us hear the shouts of praise that are written in the Revelation.

> *Worthy is the Lamb that was slain to receive power and riches and wisdom and might and honor and glory and blessing.*
>
> REVELATION 5:11–12

*[Do] not . . . be quickly shaken in mind or alarmed, either by a
spirit or a spoken word, or a letter seeming to be from us, to the
effect that the day of the Lord has come.*

2 THESSALONIANS 2:2 ESV

Jesus is coming again—maybe soon! Does that thought shake you,
or cause fear? Or does the thought of His coming lift your spirit,
give you grace to persevere? When you think of His coming do you
look up, look inward, or look around? For each reaction tells you
something about yourself. Thankfully the Lord has not left us in
the dark about what will happen. And above all, He doesn't want
you to be afraid.

After the resurrection, Jesus remained on earth for forty days,
teaching the apostles from the Scriptures and instructing them
about the kingdom of God. In particular they were told to expect
the Holy Spirit to come and that Jesus would return unexpectedly
in the last days. Paul describes the scene: Jesus will descend from
heaven with a shout. Those on earth will hear the voice of the archangel and the sound of a trumpet. Christians who have died will
arise first, then all those who are alive upon earth will join the
throng and ascend into the clouds. After that, we will always be
with the Lord (see 1 Thessalonians 4:16–17). Look up, for your
redemption draws nigh!

———————

*Oh clap your hands, all ye peoples; shout unto God with the
voice of triumph.*

PSALM 47:1 ASV

*Then they cried out to the LORD in their trouble; He delivered
them out of their distresses.*   PSALM 107:6

Psalm 107 is written in celebration of God's deliverance from all
kinds of trouble. These are some of the victories He has secured for
His own—including you and me:

- He redeems us from the hand of the adversary. (2)
- He delivers us out of distresses and leads us in a straight way. (7)
- He brings us out of the wilderness into an inhabited city. (7)
- He satisfies the thirsty soul and fills the hungry with what is
  good. (9)
- He humbles our hearts. (12)
- He saves us from distress. (13, 19)
- He brings us out of darkness and from the shadow of death. (14)
- He broke the bands apart. (14)
- He shattered the gates and cut the bars of iron. (16)
- He delivered us from destruction. (20)
- He brings us out of trouble, stills the storms, and guides us to
  our desired haven. (28–30)
- He changes our desert into a pool of water and turns dry land
  into springs of water. (35)
- He establishes us in an inhabited city. (36)
- He provides a fruitful harvest, blesses and multiplies us
  greatly. (37–38)
- He sets us securely on high away from affliction. (41)
- He makes His families like a flock and makes the upright glad.
  (41–42)
- He treats us with lovingkindness. (1, 8, 15, 21, 31, 43)

*Do not fear. You have committed all this evil, yet do not turn
aside from following the Lord, but serve the Lord with all
your heart.*

1 SAMUEL 12:20

The only son of a Christian couple married with his parents'
approval. But after five years he and his wife divorced. The church
prayed. A year later they married each other again. The son said,
"We tried divorce but it just didn't work out." A woman had married and divorced six times, but her seventh husband became a
Christian. Because of his new way of life, she became a believer in
Christ too. Now they tell everybody that Jesus saves. A wife prayed
for her husband's alcoholism for forty-two years before he trusted
Christ and stopped drinking. They spent their final years celebrating victory.

If your child marries the wrong person, even though you tried
to dissuade her, there is redemption. If there's been divorce, even
five divorces like the woman Jesus met at the well in Samaria, even
after six, there is still grace. If your family members don't speak to
each other, restoration can happen. If your loved one is lost, confused, or has no spiritual interest, there is hope. If your husband,
wife, child, or friend is addicted and has relapsed several times,
there is still hope. How do I know? Because of Jesus!

*In him we have redemption through his blood, the forgiveness
of sins, in accordance with the riches of God's grace that he
lavished on us with all wisdom and understanding.*

EPHESIANS 1:7–8 NIV84

I am leaving you with a gift—peace of mind and heart. And the
peace I give is a gift the world cannot give. So don't be troubled
or afraid.

JOHN 14:27 NLT

Author C. S. Lewis wrote, "To be a Christian means to forgive the inexcusable, because God has forgiven the inexcusable in you."[39] A good question to ask ourselves is: How can we *not forgive* other people when God has forgiven so much in us? The verse above speaks of some of God's greatest gifts to us—things "the world cannot give"—peace of mind, a heart at rest, a spirit untroubled, and a soul that is not afraid. Gifts that we do not deserve and could never earn!

Since we are glad recipients of his grace, do we respond in grace? Have we become hardened by a world of ungrace? Do we ever think someone else doesn't deserve forgiveness, another hasn't earned our respect, while another didn't appreciate us enough? God help us to live by amazing grace.

No more setting goals, writing mission statements, and trying to master the habits of highly successful people. We are free to love God, follow the Holy Spirit, and drink deeply from springs of Living Water, celebrating what Jesus has done for us.

Each one should use whatever gift he has received to serve
others, faithfully administering God's grace in its various forms.

1 PETER 4:10 NIV84

*Even if you should suffer for righteousness' sake, you will be
blessed. Have no fear...*

1 PETER 3:14 ESV

What does it mean to suffer for righteousness' sake? It *does not
mean* suffering for *un*righteousness! Peter, the Lord's disciple who
suffered for both reasons, said that we get no credit when we sin
and are harshly treated, even though we endure it with patience;
but "if when you do what is right and suffer for it you patiently
endure it, this finds favor with God" (1 Peter 2:20).

In simpler terms, if you suffer because you refused to trust God
or acted in the flesh, a bit of Fatherly discipline is on its way, and
you deserve it; but if you obey faithfully and still get in trouble, that
is suffering for the sake of righteousness. The suffering is not your
fault, God will use it for good in some way, and He is pleased that
you endured it patiently.

Those in the family of believers will bear the image of our Father
and His Son. We will also be like our Heavenly Father in reactions,
attitudes, and character. Have you ever been told that you look or
perhaps *act like* your daddy? Oh, dear! But to look like our Heavenly Daddy, well, that would be glory for me! In the meantime,
beware, lest you fall.

---

*Lest you also fall from your own steadfastness... grow in the
grace and knowledge of our Lord and Savior Jesus Christ.*

2 PETER 3:17–18 NKJV

Peace be to you. Do not fear, you shall not die.

JUDGES 6:23 ESV

Gideon's fear was legitimate because he had gazed upon the Sovereign LORD and because of that one careless act, he probably would die. He needed reassurance. So the One who doesn't mince words addressed his fear directly by reassuring Gideon that He would not die. One of the most important factors revealed in this story is Gideon's willingness to confess. If only the rest of us could open up about our fears as easily as he did! Healing from fear comes when you articulate it. Confess it as the sin of faithlessness and use the experience to encourage others in their faith.

The fear of death is one of life's universal fears. Even those of us who long to see Jesus still are hesitant to exchange the known for the unknown. We dread the dying, not death itself because we believe the promise of eternal life. The benefits of having a new body while dwelling in our celestial home compel us to keep on trusting. We have been taught that death is an enemy; it is the last enemy each of us will need grace to conquer. If you, or someone you love, fears death, talk to God about it. Call Him by name. He loves for you to address Him as Father, your Abba. He loves with intensity, guides with infinite wisdom, protects with everlasting arms, and when life ends, He carries us to our eternal home.

The name of the LORD is a strong tower; the righteous runs into it and is safe.

PROVERBS 18:10

There was a trembling in the camp, in the field, and among all
the people. Even the garrison and the raiders trembled, and the
earth quaked so that it became a great trembling.

1 SAMUEL 14:15

I heard once that Maya Angelou became so depressed that she sent
her son away: *"Get out of here before I hurt you."* She was actually
thinking about suicide—perhaps a double homicide. After her son
walked out the door she called a cab and went to see a doctor. She
said she wasn't in his office five minutes before she realized he
couldn't help her. She went to see a mentor and friend who told her
to write a list of things she was thankful for. He handed her a pencil and paper and said, "Write! Write first, 'that I can hold a pencil.'
Then, 'that I can write,' 'that I can hear,' 'that I can see,' 'that I can
walk,' and keep on writing." She wrote a full page of things she was
thankful for and even before she finished her list, the black cloud
lifted and she was full of joy.

How do you process your emotions? Why not try writing? Try
to list forty things (God's number for change!). Write until your
feelings change, until the fear goes away, until the depression lifts,
until the answer comes. This is how many of the psalms of David
were born.

My God, my rock, in whom I take refuge; my shield, the horn of
my salvation, my stronghold.

PSALM 18:1–2

From the depths of despair, O Lord, I call for your help. Hear my cry, O Lord. Pay attention to my prayer.

PSALM 130:1–2, NLT

Have you ever been in a situation when you didn't know how to pray? Maybe you were able to utter only one phrase, like "Father have mercy." When this happens it is usually when we feel uncertain, deeply troubled for something we have neglected, or have made a downright sinful choice that we would rather not think about. We play games with El Roi, thinking we might just hide or at least try not to draw the Lord's attention our direction. How silly we are.

This Psalm is not identified by its author, but by its purpose. It is written out of concern for the nation of Israel—a prayer that the Almighty would deliver them out of insurmountable problems that may have threatened their very existence. The writer had already admitted that if Yahweh had marked every iniquity among His people, if He had kept records of sin, they could not stand. So he asks that He not hold them accountable.

In words that we would use today, the Psalmist was interceding for the people he loved as well as for himself, begging for forgiveness, asking for pardon. He prayed in faith looking forward to a day of redemption. These are the prayers that our Lord delights to answer for those who are redeemed today.

I am counting on the Lord, yes, I am counting on him. I have put my hope in his word.

PSALM 130:5 NLT

An evil spirit from God is terrorizing you . . . seek a man who is a
skillful player on the harp; and it shall come about when the evil
spirit from God is on you, that he shall play the harp *with his*
hand, and you will be well.

1 SAMUEL 16:15–16

In the days of Saul and David, the ministry of the Holy Spirit was different. Instead of an abiding Presence in God's redeemed, the Spirit came upon a person for a special purpose and moved away when His work was done. He was God's power for God's work. David knew the Spirit's presence when he became king, and simultaneously the Spirit left Saul. Moving into his emptiness of soul, an evil spirit began to torture Saul, causing him to be deeply troubled.

Even though this spirit was demonic, God allowed him to torment the former king. Satan is a tool in the hands of God. Even though Saul knew the Spirit had left him, he still called upon the LORD who in turn sent David with his harp. When he played, Saul would be refreshed, and the evil spirit would depart.

When you are sick, troubled, depressed, or filled with fear, turn on the praise music, hymns, or classical piano and let music fill the room. It soothes the soul, welcomes the Holy Spirit, and defeats the devil.

———————

He sent His word and healed them, and delivered them
from their destructions . . . Let them also offer sacrifices of
thanksgiving, and tell of His works with joyful singing.

PSALM 107:20, 22

When Saul and all Israel heard these words of the Philistine,
they were dismayed and greatly afraid.

1 SAMUEL 17:11

What exactly were the words that caused them such fear? Goliath's voice boomed words such as these: "Why bother using your whole army? Am I not Philistine enough for you? Pick your best fighter and pit him against me." He dared them: "If he kills me, the Philistines will become your slaves; but if I get the upper hand and kill him, you will all become our slaves and serve us" (see 1 Samuel 17:9). He belched out the final challenge: "Give me a man that we might fight together" (1 Samuel 17:10).

The Israelites must have feared Goliath's appearance, too. When he stepped forward he stood nearly ten feel tall, wearing a bronze helmet and 126 pounds of armor. His sword and shin guards were bronze, and his rail-like spear had a tip that weighed fifteen pounds. Not one word, one shuffle, one groan or sigh issued forth from Saul's petrified army.

Then came David—the smallest, youngest, most inexperienced, but the Israelite who knew God best. He spoke, "Who is this uncircumcised Philistine that he should taunt the armies of the living God?" (1 Samuel 17:26). The scales tipped in David's direction. For faith outweighs the heaviest weapon, the largest giant, the fiercest enemy, the greatest fear. And God Alive is greater than any force on earth. David killed Goliath with one stone and a slingshot. Is there a giant taunting you?

*Now it happened afterward that David's heart troubled him
because he had cut Saul's robe.*

1 SAMUEL 24:5 NKJV

In the last days of Saul's life, his heart was full of insane jealousy
and rampant fear. He pursued David relentlessly and tried to kill
him several times. David did not retaliate. One day he and a few
of his men entered a cave to rest. In the darkness they watched as
Saul entered and reclined upon the cool clay near the front of the
cave, making it impossible for David to leave. David waited until
the king was sleeping soundly, then cut a piece of fabric from the
hem of Saul's robe and put it in his pocket.

He waited nearby until Saul awoke and left the cave. David
shouted, "My lord the king!" When Saul turned to look, David
bowed before him, showed the piece of his robe, and asked, "Why
do you listen to the people who say I am trying to harm you?" He
showed him the piece of his robe and continued, "The LORD placed
you at my mercy back there in the cave. Some of my men told me to
kill you, but I spared you . . . 'I will never harm the king for he is the
LORD's anointed one' " (1 Samuel 24:8–10 NLT).

---

*Everyone must submit to governing authorities. For all
authority comes from God, and those in positions of authority
have been placed there by God.*

ROMANS 13:1 NLT

This will not cause grief or a troubled heart to my lord, both by having shed blood without cause and by my lord having avenged himself.

1 SAMUEL 25:31

It was Abigail who spoke these words to David. With God-given insight she calmed his troubled heart, reminding him that he was the chosen leader of Israel. God would not hold him accountable for the bloodshed of many wars. There would be no blemish on his record. He would not have to bear the weight of his many acts of war or even of any needless bloodshed and acts of vengeance. After her words of encouragement, she paused, then added, "When the LORD has done these great things for you, please remember me, your servant!" (1 Samuel 25:31 NLT).

David did remember Abigail. When her husband died of a stroke, David took her as his wife. Abigail has gone down in history as a woman of discernment and a loyal servant of Jehovah Elohim. The love between David and Abigail is one of passion and drama. But, as in all Bible stories, there is another story within the story. It is the account of a woman who loved God but was originally married to an evil man with strongly held beliefs contrary to her own. It's a story with a moral for every man or woman living with an unbeliever. There is always hope for redeeming love.

For your husband is your Maker, whose name is the LORD of hosts; and your Redeemer is the Holy One of Israel, who is called the God of all the earth.

ISAIAH 54:5

I am greatly distressed... and God has departed from me and
no longer answers me, either through prophets or by dreams;
therefore I have called you.

1 SAMUEL 28:15

Sin separates us from the love of God. He doesn't stop loving His own, but He cannot look with approval upon sin. Saul had sinned, and in the most hypocritical way. In obedience to God, he had purged the nation of all mediums and spiritists, but later when he didn't hear from God, he conjured up the dearly departed Samuel.

How can such duplicity abide in the hearts of God's servants? A preacher speaks against the local "Gentlemen's Club" until a picture surfaces of him slipping out the back door one night. A woman speaks against drugs until her family organizes an intervention to challenge her own addiction. An evangelist buys himself a private jet with the tithes and offerings of the church.

There's a famous unattributed quote that says, "There is so much good in the worst of us, and so much bad in the best of us that it ill behooves any of us to find fault with the rest of us." It's a bit of a tongue-twister, but it reminds us of an important truth: It is always best to leave such matters in the hands of God through the church. "Your sins will find you out!" (Numbers 32:23). The exposure is not to shame us but to lead us to repentance.

If we confess our sins, He is faithful and righteous to forgive us
our sins and to cleanse us from all unrighteousness.

1 JOHN 1:9

Rulers are not a cause of fear for good behavior, but for evil. Do you want to have no fear of authority? Do what is good and you will have praise from the same.

ROMANS 13:3

If your conscience is clear you will not fear authority, even when surrounded by local policemen, the Royal Canadian Mounted Police, or the Texas Rangers. But when you are guilty of some offense, your heart races and your palms sweat at the mere sight of a patrol car.

One morning, I rounded a corner and picked up speed after carefully observing the school zone speed limit. Then I spotted a rack of red lights flashing behind me. My stomach tightened into a hard knot. I pulled over and began jabbering nonsensically to the officer, interjecting that the car up front was going much faster than I. He muttered, "I can't catch them all!" Flipping open his book of citations, he began scribbling my name, accusing me of driving 38 in a 30-mph zone. Yes, there is genuine fear of authority for those behaving badly!

Perhaps you have ignored laws or taken lightly the limits set for our good. Maybe you have disobeyed God's laws. Seems we all need somebody to watch over us. And we should be thankful for those who do.

Obey your leaders and submit to them, for they keep watch over your souls as those who will give an account. Let them do this with joy and not with grief.

HEBREWS 13:17

Since ... we know what it is to fear the Lord, we try to persuade others.

2 CORINTHIANS 5:11 NIV

We must all appear before the judgment seat of Christ. It will be an awards ceremony on the highest level. It is not a judgment for sin for it concerns those who are redeemed. Still, the idea of standing before Jesus to have our work evaluated is enough to rattle most of us. From the moment of our new birth, we have a desire to please Him. We want to hear Him say, "Well done."

At the Judgment Seat of Christ, we will actually be evaluated for our response to God's grace, and it is not an occasion to fear. In his first letter to the Corinthians, Paul said that our works will be appraised and divided into two groups. To appraise actually means "to receive, care for, or preserve" or searching for something worth keeping and truly valuable. Some of our works will be found valuable like gold, silver, and precious jewels; others will be laid aside, like wood, hay, or stubble being prepared for burning. Do you wonder how the decision is made? The Righteous Judge will discern between our deeds done to glorify God and those that were self-promoting (see 1 Corinthians 3:13).

Be careful of your motives. When we receive a crown, it will be our supreme joy to lay it as an offering at the feet of King Jesus.

Worthy are You, our Lord and our God, to receive glory and honor and power.

REVELATION 4:11

Listen to Me, you who know righteousness, a people in whose heart is My law; do not fear the reproach of man.

ISAIAH 51:7

God is speaking to those who know righteousness, people familiar with the written law. It is *not* written to the unrighteous, untaught, preoccupied, or to those with no knowledge of the truth. Through the mouth of Isaiah, the LORD is leaving this directive with the upright. The first verse of the chapter singles out "those who seek the Lord and pursue righteousness."

After reminding them of their roots and of the blessings they had received through Abraham and Sarah, He begins to comfort them with words they would need for the future. Even though calamity comes upon the earth and people of the earth will die, His salvation lasts forever and His righteous rule will never end. In a more modern translation, "Do not fear the reproach of man" is written "Do not be afraid of people's scorn, nor fear their insults" (Isaiah 51: 7 NLT).

Adonay Jehovah will come to rule with might and reward His own. He will shepherd His lambs and care for the sheep of His pastures. We too will be there to feel His embrace. Fear of man's reproach cannot tamp down the joy of that day.

Like a shepherd He will tend His flock, in His arm He will gather the lambs and carry them in His bosom; He will gently lead the nursing ewes.

ISAIAH 40:11

Like one who takes off a garment on a cold day, or like vinegar on soda, is he who sings songs to a troubled heart.

PROVERBS 25:20

With the wisdom of Solomon, we are informed how to love and comfort someone with a troubled heart. The verse reminds us not to laugh off any emotion that causes distress. When someone is concerned enough to talk about a problem, it is too serious to be treated in a trivial manner. Have you ever tried the sing-songs-to-a-troubled-heart approach? *Cheer up, things could be worse. Put a smile on your face.* Have you ever been ministered unto in that manner? *You know, everything works out for good, right?* Even a verse that we all hold dear is not uplifting when everything else is going south. It's like a burst of cold air from a Texas norther.

Whether trying to comfort with a text from the Bible or singing hymns to a depressed soul, remember that timing is all important. As is careful listening to our Helper, the Holy Spirit. He will nudge you when to speak, what to say, or when to sing. Listen well, even if you have to listen seven days, as did Job's friends, before a single word is appropriate. Remember, "A word fitly spoken is like apples of gold in a setting of silver" (Proverbs 25:11 ESV). Do not set out on our own to do the work of God, instead, "keep in step with the Spirit."

If we live by the Spirit, let us also keep in step with the Spirit.

GALATIANS 5:25 ESV

Do not be afraid of sudden terror . . . when it comes, for the
Lord will be your confidence and will keep your foot from being
caught.

PROVERBS 3:25–26 ESV

What would our lives be like if the Lord became our full confidence? We find the answer from the poetic lines above penned by Solomon: "Do not be afraid of sudden terror." The Lord is the source of wisdom. He exhibited wisdom and He gives wisdom to those who ask for it. In fact, wisdom is called a "tree of life to those who embrace her," for "happy are those who hold her tightly" (Proverbs 3:18 NLT).

There were two trees in the Garden of Eden that proved to be a test of character for Adam and Eve—the tree of life and the tree of the knowledge of good and evil. Both bore fruit luscious and delightful to behold. Like the basket of citrus that sits in my kitchen. It presents a simple, pleasing choice that my husband and I make every day.

Imagine Eve making a choice—fruit from the tree of life, which Elohim invited her to eat, or fruit from the tree of knowledge, the one God said *not to* eat. Seems we all make that choice every day of our lives. May we choose well!

How blessed is the man who finds wisdom and the man who
gains understanding. For her profit is better than the profit of
silver and her gain better than fine gold.

PROVERBS 3:13–14

Enter the rock and hide in the dust from the terror of the LORD
and from the splendor of His majesty.

ISAIAH 2:10

The excellence of the LORD is so overwhelming that anyone who perceives it feels like hiding. Instead of joy, they're filled with terror. It's contrary to our expectations. Those who usually run toward light will flee holy light, the splendor of His majesty. His presence is too much to handle. Isaiah continues with vivid description—"the proud look of man will be abased and the loftiness of man will be humbled, and the LORD alone will be exalted in that day" (2:11).

His exaltation and man's humility reveals how far above and beyond our comprehension He is. We don't even know when to approach Him and when to fall on our faces. We are too shallow to comprehend the depths of God, too naïve to take hold of His excellencies. In the midst of this confusion, I find myself longing for the day when He will be approachable Light, a welcoming Presence, when His Majesty and Holiness will be celebrated and embraced instead of feared. In that day, there will be peace, no more antagonism or war, and His people will say, "Come, let us go up to the mountain of the LORD, to the house of the God of Jacob; that He may teach us concerning His ways and that we may walk in His paths. For the law will go forth from Zion and the word of the LORD from Jerusalem" (Isaiah 2:3).

We were afflicted on every side: conflicts without, fears within.
But God, who comforts the depressed, comforted us by the
coming of Titus.

2 CORINTHIANS 7:5–6

Which hurts the most: conflicts from outside ourselves, from another person or unforeseen circumstance, or fear that grips our heart from within, untamed thoughts, a nagging conscience, unresolved issues with someone you love? What if you had both at the same time? What if you had four overwhelming problems at once? This was the situation of the Apostle Paul.

On one occasion, he had conflicts without and fears within. On another he was "afflicted in every way, but not crushed; perplexed, but not despairing; persecuted, but not forsaken; struck down, but not destroyed" (2 Corinthians 4:8–9). One day he experienced fear on the inside and conflicts outside, and the next day he was boxed in on all sides. On the right, he was afflicted with continual trouble. On the left, he was perplexed, uncertain, confused, and doubting. Up front, he was persecuted, and behind, he was being "struck down" by his own failures.

Maybe you have family issues on the right and confusion to the left; relationship problems in front and trailing behind is disappointment. Paul found grace to persevere and so can you. For there is always the "But God Factor." You can be afflicted *but not crushed*, perplexed *but not despairing*, persecuted *but not forsaken*, struck down *but not destroyed*. But whether you are boxed in, or fearful, and desperate, the Comforter comes offering grace. His grace is wide enough to cover all sides at one time.

*This poor man cried, and the L*ORD *heard him and saved him out of all his troubles. The angel of the L*ORD *encamps around those who fear him, and delivers them.*

PSALM 34:6–7 ESV

Early one morning I read the preceding verse—actually I *misread* it. What I thought I'd read was "*the* poor man cried and the LORD heard him." What I understood was that a poor man had prayed, God heard, and "saved him out of all his troubles." On that particular day I was also in trouble and afraid. Two decades later, I don't remember why, but truth from that verse lingers. Encounters with God are not easily forgotten.

After reading, I prayed, quoting the verse. My prayer began something like this: "Father, the poor man cried, you heard." I waited, and in the stillness I knew that God was listening; in the awe-filled moment, I kept still and quiet, thinking a blink or a word might break the connection. When I said amen and opened my eyes, my gaze fell upon the first word of the verse. The word "this" caught my attention, captivating my thoughts. "*This*" man; not "*the*" man! And in that moment, *this* meant me, the person now reading the verse—me in my room, me whose fear was being replaced with joy. The verse was written about a man thousands of years before I existed, and it was also written about me. It is also a verse for you. Do not be afraid. The LORD hears you and will save you.

You will call upon Me and come and pray to Me, and I will listen to you.

JEREMIAH 29:12

> *Do not let your heart be troubled; believe in God, believe*
> *also in Me.*

JOHN 14:1

"Troubled" is an interesting word with a broad range of meaning. It means to be agitated, to have inward commotion, to lose calmness of mind, disturb equanimity, to be disquieted, made restless, experience doubt, to be rendered anxious or distressed, or, and most importantly, to be stricken with fear and dread. "Troubled" is the word that described the fear in the heart of King Nebuchadnezzar when he saw handwriting on the wall. It explains the feelings of Jesus' disciples when their Master spoke of going away. It can identify pinprick problems or major catastrophes, nagging doubt or serious betrayals, unmet needs and major illness. Job was troubled, as was David, and Solomon, Isaiah, and Jeremiah, along with you and me.

There is enough trouble to go around, enough heart-pain to touch us all, but there is one thing that should never trouble any of us. Do not let your heart be troubled that God might be disconnected from our need or our fears. He is still on His throne; still Sovereign, Omnipotent, Faithful, and full of grace. And He loves you with everlasting love.

> *God can take your trouble and change it into treasure. Your*
> *sorrow can be exchanged for joy, not just a momentary smile,*
> *but a deep new joy. It will be a bubbling experience of new hope*
> *that brings brightness to your eyes and a song to your heart. In*
> *the midst of the darkness, you will learn lessons you might never*
> *have learned in the day.*   BARBARA JOHNSON[40]

He became frightened, and beginning to sink, he cried out,
"Lord, save me!"

MATTHEW 14:30

"Are you saved?" It was the pertinent question asked in the Christian circles I orbited as a child. Having believed in Christ when I was nine, I didn't understand what being *saved* was all about. I only knew that I believed in Jesus and that something remarkable happened the day I yielded myself to Him. Since then, I have been learning more about what it means to be "saved."

Salvation is much more than a singular event but one that began at a point in time, continues day after day, and will be completed on the day that we step into eternity. If you have been saved, you are also being saved, and you will be saved. The first day of my salvation is one I will never forget, even though I don't remember the actual date on the calendar. Jesus singled me out, drew me to Himself, and became a very present, ever-abiding reality. Today I am living in salvation part two, where I am "(daily delivered from sin's dominion) through His [resurrection] life" (Romans 5:10 AMP). Pressing on, living by faith and growing spiritually, means that someday I will know salvation part three. I will be completely redeemed and eternally saved. God always finishes what He begins.

Although you were formerly alienated and hostile in mind,
engaged in evil deeds, yet He has now reconciled you in His
fleshly body through death, in order to present you before Him
holy and blameless and beyond reproach.

COLOSSIANS 1:21–22

> *For if we go on sinning willfully after receiving the knowledge*
> *of the truth, there no longer remains a sacrifice for sins, but a*
> *terrifying expectation of judgment.*
>
> HEBREWS 10:26–27

Every day that we live as one of God's children, He bears our burdens, delights in us, and actively protects and keeps us. He is always with us, showing us the path to take, revealing the stumbling blocks, and working from inside out to keep us from sin. And if you love Him, you must be especially happy about that last truth!

The writer of Hebrews is talking about sins committed "willingly" after receiving the knowledge of truth. A Christian, being delivered from sin, will not go on sinning, nor does he want to. If a person were to continue a sinful lifestyle, he or she would need to be re-redeemed, and that would demand another sacrifice for sins—which is not possible, since Jesus died for sin once and for all.

If a person has only heard, has a limited knowledge of the truth, and does not believe it, but walks away from it, then there is nothing left but a terrifying expectation of judgment. But for those of us who do believe, there will be no judgment at all. The redeemed will live with God eternally in perfect peace and joy.

> *And they sang a new song, saying, "Worthy are You to take the*
> *book and to break its seals; for You were slain, and purchased*
> *for God with Your blood men from every tribe and tongue and*
> *people and nation."*
>
> REVELATION 5:9

*Do not fear; have not I myself commanded you? Be courageous
and be valiant.*

2 SAMUEL 13:28

In the most frightening of circumstances, we can exhibit the character of Christ, for we know that adversity, confusion, and pain are part and parcel of life. Nothing happens by accident to a child of God. Whatever comes has the permission of a good and loving God and is used for our ultimate good. The injuries of man, acts of revenge, plans that go awry, fears that obsess, and difficult missions in life are used by our Lord to develop certain qualities in us or move us to obey. Christ-like character is being produced in our hearts by the Holy Spirit who abides there (see Galatians 5:22–25).

The fruit of the Spirit is not something we can attain through discipline and hard work—even work for the Lord. It grows when we respond to events without arguing or complaining, believing all the time that Jesus loves us and that God is in control. It's the kind of reaction Paul exhibited when members of the church were disloyal, the same action displayed by Peter when he had to rebuke a brother in Christ, and most important, the characteristic that replicates the attitude of Jesus when He stood before His accusers and did not speak one word of self-defense.

---

*But the fruit of the Spirit is love, joy, peace, patience, kindness,
goodness, faithfulness, gentleness, self-control; against such
things there is no law.*

GALATIANS 5:22–23

Whoso is despising the Word is destroyed for it, and whoso is fearing the Command is repayed.

PROVERBS 13:13 YLT

What is your attitude about the Word of God? Do you believe the Bible? Do you honor the Book? Do you reverence the truth contained in its pages? How important is it in your daily life?

"Oh, the depth of the riches both of the wisdom and knowledge of God!" wrote Paul in the book of Romans. "How unsearchable are His judgments and unfathomable His ways!" (Romans 11:33). These words of praise pour from his pen after a conversation of God's righteousness and sovereignty in salvation. The unsearchable or unfathomable riches of Christ are "past finding out"! They are beyond comprehension, inexhaustible in their depth of meaning, limitless in their revelation. We cannot plumb the depths or trace the footprints of His riches. No one "has known the mind of the LORD, or... become His counselor" (Romans 11:34).

Because of Who God is and what He has done, Paul exalts Him with these words: "For from Him and through Him and to Him are all things. To Him *be* the glory forever. Amen" (Romans 11:36). As you worship Him today, repeat those words to the Only Wise God Who is worthy of all glory forever.

Faith comes *from hearing, and hearing by the word of Christ.*

ROMANS 10:17

Haven't I commanded you? Strength! Courage! Don't be timid;
don't get discouraged. GOD, your God, is with you every step
you take.

JOSHUA 1:9 MSG

Every step that you take? Really? A step into ICU to visit a comatose child? A step toward the bed where a heavily medicated husband rests? That step from the auditorium to the microphone up front? The countless going-nowhere-quickly steps as you vacuum the carpet? Running steps, shuffling steps, hesitant steps, uphill steps, jumping-up-and-down-with-joy steps? Yes, all of those and more. God is with you every single step you take.

"If we're following the course God has placed before us, we will have thorns and thistles wherever we go," International speaker Joni Eareckson Tada wrote. "Oh sure, there will be plenty of beautiful green vistas and sunlit fields along the way to make our journey pleasant. But...we can also count on our fair share of problems and pain. God will make certain of that, so that we'll make certain we stick close to Him every step of the way."[41]

Hoping to increase my fitness level, I wear a tiny device on my wrist at night and slip it in my pocket before my first step from bed to breakfast. Yesterday I took 5,829 steps—and God accompanied me 5,829 times.

The LORD directs the steps of the godly. He delights in every
detail of their lives. Though they stumble, they will never fall, for
the LORD holds them by the hand.

PSALM 37:23–24 NLT

Saul... was very afraid... also there was no strength in him, for
he had eaten no food all day and all night.

1 SAMUEL 28:20

When you are weak physically, you are vulnerable to temptation, sin, and fear. All of us—body, soul, and spirit—function as one entity. No single part operates independently but each is vitally connected to every other part. So we cannot truthfully claim "I feel good" when a toe is broken or "I am just fine" spiritually when we are wounded emotionally. Life just doesn't work that way, for before our birth we were "intricately and curiously wrought (as if embroidered with various colors)" (Psalms 139:15 AMP). Pull one thread and the work begins to unravel.

God is compassionate about the physical, mental, and spiritual aspects of our lives. He "crowns our lives with lovingkindness and compassion, heals all our diseases, and satisfies our years with good things" (from Psalm 103:1–5).

The psalmist begins with "soul music"—*Bless the Lord O my soul.* "Soul music is the very soul of music," wrote Charles Spurgeon. "Jehovah is worthy to be praised by us in that highest style of adoration which is intended by the term bless."[42] When we praise the Lord, we reach down into our very soul and from the depths of who we are, bring up the highest praise.

Bless the LORD, O my soul, and all that is within me, bless His
holy name.

PSALM 103:5

I sought the LORD, and He answered me, and delivered me from all my fears.

PSALM 34:4

God had been working behind the scenes when my parents named me Gracie. My name would be a constant reminder of God's grace. If only I could live up to my name, I would find everything I needed to live successfully and find peace and rest.

Regardless of your name, all of us live a grace story. God does not accept us or love us because we're special, because we deserve to be loved, or because we are attractive or brilliant (or unattractive and a bit dense). He loves us because of grace. Before we even believe in Him, He draws us to Himself by grace. We chose to believe because His grace enables us to see the truth and accept it. We experience a lifetime of graceful interventions as we follow His plan for us. And the best part? Grace helps us today, right where we are, enabling us and giving us the power to do what we cannot do ourselves.

Some of us need a bit of life-tweaking; others could use a complete life-over. Change happens inside out through the Holy Spirit. Unworthy recipients with wandering hearts, we can ask for the grace to accept His grace. Then you will radiate grace as your story moves forward one scene at a time.

God is able to make all grace abound to you, so that always having all sufficiency in everything, you may have an abundance for every good deed.

2 CORINTHIANS 9:8

You will be hearing of wars and rumors of wars. See that you are not frightened, for those things must take place, but that is not yet the end.

MATTHEW 24:6

For as long as I have been alive I've heard this message: "Don't let the news upset you, there will always be wars and rumors of wars." With that assurance, mothers console their children, youth ministers teach teens, pastors comfort churches, and prophets warn Christians. Even today, I hear of wars and rumors of wars in stores and businesses, churches, in Bible study groups, and at kitchen tables. This is a promise we may wish were not in the Bible. But God is faithful to reveal what we need to know.

God doesn't want us to respond in fear. These things must take place. Your heart can be lifted by a simple change of focus. God is still in charge of His universe. Encouragement based upon truth is enough to lighten a troubled heart, stop shaking knees, and settle stomachs.

Today wars are being waged in the same place, among the same people, for the same reasons as those hundreds and thousands of years before. What some tend to forget is that God is in the midst of it all. He is the Lord of Hosts, Jesus is Captain of the King's Army in control of multitudes of Angels, and the Holy Spirit leads—not from in front, or from behind, but from inside out.

In all these things we overwhelmingly conquer through Him who loved us.

ROMANS 8:37

The LORD made a covenant and commanded them, saying, "You
shall not fear other gods, nor bow down yourselves to them nor
serve them nor sacrifice to them."

2 KINGS 17:35

I doubt that you would bow down to an idol or worship a stone god, but perhaps you would stand in front of a new car or an antique car, a bigger house, a larger annuity, a long-awaited child, or some other treasure and begin to worship it. The blessing of God slips into an empty place in our soul, curls in, settles down, and we begin to adore it. What God has given for our good or our edification can easily become an item of worship if we lose sight of His glory and grace. Instead of being full of His Spirit, we may have allowed spaces and holes in our hearts that can be filled with idolatry.

Anything that takes your heart away from the LORD, anything that steals your love, any person who comes between you and your allegiance to the Most High God is an idol.

"His dominion is an everlasting dominion, and His kingdom *endures* from generation to generation. All the inhabitants of the earth are accounted as nothing, but He does according to His will in the host of heaven and *among* the inhabitants of earth; And no one can ward off His hand or say to Him, 'What have You done?'" (Daniel 4:34–35).

With these words King Nebuchadnezzar praised and worshipped El Elyon the Most High God.

Little children, guard yourselves from idols.

1 JOHN 5:21

I am the Lord your God; you shall not fear the gods of the
Amorites in whose land you live.

JUDGES 6:10

How do these words apply to Christ-ones in our day? Today, when we are surrounded by false gods and false religions? This day, when Christians are being killed in the most gruesome ways? Today, as hundreds are imprisoned for their faith, thousands are denied basic human rights, and some are publicly massacred? Yes, the words still apply! For in the midst of all persecution, our God still reigns.

He who formed us and loves us will never leave or forsake His beloved. When we are afraid of other gods, we're telling our All-Powerful, Omnipotent God that He is not big enough to take care of His own. We may begin to think that the Omniscient God, the All-Seeing One whose name is El Roi, has blinked or closed His eyes completely. To fear other gods reveals a lack of faith. What more does He need to say other than "I am the Lord your God—I Am Jehovah, the Self-Existent One, God Almighty, Elohim, the True God, the Three-in-One God, Father, Son, and Holy Spirit"? If He is for us, who can be against us? Do not fear any other god!

Who is among you that fears the Lord, that obeys the voice of
His servant, that walks in darkness and has no light? Let him
trust in the name of the Lord and rely on his God.

ISAIAH 50:10

If you should suffer for the sake of righteousness, you are blessed.
Do not fear ... and do not be troubled.

1 PETER 3:14

There is a theme in the Bible that we tend to ignore—suffering for the sake of righteousness. Yet suffering is an important part of the Christian life simply because we are believers in Jesus, the Suffering Savior. Because Paul wanted to know Jesus better, he prayed "that I may know him and the power of his resurrection, and the fellowship of his sufferings, being made conformable unto his death" (Philippians 3:10 AV). He also told other believers that suffering for Jesus' sake was as much a gift as the ability to believe in Him (see Philippians 1:29). Our sufferings, in some mysterious way, are "filling up what is lacking in Christ's afflictions for the sake of ... the church" (Colossians 1:24 ESV).

This does not mean that His sufferings were insufficient. He paid the full price for our redemption. But as we follow in His steps, faithfully representing Him as the Savior of the world, we will suffer as He did. When we present His message and our representation of Him results in suffering, we are "filling up" or "finishing" His sufferings for the gospel. In addition, because we are a part of His body He suffers when we suffer.

Thank Him that He allows you to know Him better through your suffering and do not be afraid.

For I consider that the sufferings of this present time are not
worthy to be compared with the glory that is to be revealed to us.

ROMANS 8:18

Hear my voice, O God, in my prayer: preserve my life from fear of the enemy.

PSALM 64:1 AV

Prayer is our best resource and our greatest weapon when we are afraid. The word "fear," which can also be translated as "dread" or "terror," is written as a warning to us not to live in constant fear or dread. The verses following tell us that the enemy shoots "in secret at the perfect" (Psalm 64:4 AV). What are the silent enemies? The counsel of evildoers, words sharp like swords, bitter speech that penetrates like arrows, comments shot from places of concealment, injustices devised, well-conceived plots coming from the depths of an evil heart (see Psalm 64).

Into this silence, David comes pleading, "Hear my voice, O Elohim." And He hears! For prayer, whether shouted from mountaintops or uttered in total silence, always reaches the intended ear of God. The words we speak to God do not need to travel far. Prayer is more communion than communication. Silent prayer, heart cries, and communion of soul are more powerful, conquer more often, and save more effectively than any other weapon or tool.

Elohim not only hears but acts on behalf of His own. It is He who will shoot the arrow. Through His power, our silent enemies will stumble. He will turn their own words against them and they will fear the Lord. Then the righteous will be glad in the LORD and take refuge in Him, and the upright in heart will feel His glory.

Through God we shall do valiantly, and it is He who will tread down our adversaries.   PSALM 60:12

When you lie down, you will not be afraid; when you lie down,
your sleep will be sweet.

PROVERBS 3:24

This promise is set amidst a discussion about wisdom, understanding, and knowledge—contrasting these life-giving principles with fear and making them synonymous with the gift of sleep. Blessed is the man or woman whose sleep is sweet. Wisdom also promises you will enjoy length of days, many years of life, and peace (Proverbs 3:2). Following the pathway of kindness and truth, you will find favor with God and a good reputation among man (Proverbs 3:4). Because of your trust and your choice to seek God, He will make your pathway straight (Proverbs 3:6).

Experts say that lifestyle factors in daytime affect the quality and quantity of sleep at night. Once again professionals find themselves in the good company of biblical truth. The three aspirations above, pursued daily, ensure restful nights. They are not only imperatives from God but they are traits of His own character. He founded the earth by His wisdom, established the heavens by His understanding, and by His knowledge "the deeps were broken up and the skies drip with dew" (Proverbs 3:19–20).

When you find your mind churning during sleepless nights, try to identify the fear that is stifling your faith. Confess it to God. Turn on the lights and read the book of Proverbs. Pray for understanding and knowledge. Ask God for His gift of sleep.

———————

Then you will walk in your way securely and your foot will
not stumble.   PROVERBS 3:23

> *Do not be anxious about anything, but in everything by prayer*
> *and supplication with thanksgiving let your requests be made*
> *known to God.*

PHILIPPIANS 4:6 ESV

Be anxious about what? No thing! Be thankful for? Every thing! In fact, we are instructed to be thankful *in* everything (Philippians 4:6) and *for* everything (Ephesians 5:20 ESV)! Do the two different prepositions make a difference in the verses' meanings? Only if you believe in the inspiration of every jot and tittle of Scripture! According to the dictionary, "in" means "position, in place, in time, or in state"; "for" means "in behalf of, or for the sake of something."

In everything—in whatever state, whatever time, whatever place, in that be thankful. In sickness, in health, in loneliness, in ecstasy, in doubt, in fear, in love, in depression, in wealth, in poverty, and in every other condition that you find yourself in, be thankful.

For everything—for life, for protection and provision, for family, for meaningful work, for the church, spiritual gifts, friends and relationships, for the children, and for every gift from His hand be thankful. Thank God for salvation, for eternal security, and for your present blessing in Him. For every single thing that you now have or will have in the future, give thanks.

> *Gratitude unlocks the fullness of life. It turns what we have*
> *into enough, and more. It turns denial into acceptance, chaos*
> *to order, confusion to clarity. It can turn a meal into a feast, a*
> *house into a home, a stranger into a friend.*

MELODY BEATTIE[43]

*They cried out to the LORD in their trouble; He saved them out
of their distresses. He sent His word and healed them, and
delivered them from their destructions.*

PSALM 107:19–20

This psalm is a call to praise for the redeemed. "Give thanks to
the LORD" was written five times by the author. He reminds us six
times to be thankful for God's lovingkindness. He is faithful to
guide, to provide food and water, shelter and protection. He satisfies the hungry soul with what is good. He gives freedom, counsel,
protection, forgiveness, and peace.

The writer addresses fear, trouble, and distresses four times
with identical words: "Then they cried to the LORD in their trouble,
and He brought them out of their distresses" (see Psalm 107:6, 13,
19, 28). It is truth worthy of repetition, for we are prone to forget
the trouble and fear from which we've been delivered, and we fall
short of our purpose—to glorify God and enjoy Him forever. When
we are thankful, we honor Him most.

This is the month when most of us celebrate the Thanksgiving
holiday. It is a day set apart by the Founding Fathers of our nation
to offer thanks to God for His blessings. Psalm 107 would be a
good prayer list to use with your family. Always be careful to honor
God by both thanks and giving.

------

*Let them also offer sacrifices of thanksgiving, and tell of His
works with joyful singing.*

PSALM 107:22

But He said to them, "It is I; do not be afraid."

JOHN 6:20

The truth of Isaiah 26:3 in the Living New Testament reads like this: "You will keep in perfect peace all who trust in You, all whose thoughts are fixed on You!" The Amplified Bible expands the meaning: "You will guard him and keep him in perfect and constant peace whose mind (both its inclination and its character) is stayed on You, because he commits himself to You, leans on You, and hopes confidently in You."

In *What Women Should Know About Facing Fear*, Christin Ditchfield brings into focus our need for obedience and faith-building.

> One of the most important things you can do is to overcome fear: Bring your needs to God, thanking Him that He is already at work, answering your prayers. And let His peace protect you.
>
> Keeping our thoughts fixed on Him is key. Ask Peter! He discovered he could walk on water when he focused on Jesus. But then he looked at the wind blowing and the waves crashing all around him, and fear and doubt started to sink him. That's why we've got to stay focused on Jesus, and fix our eyes on Him. [44]

Whatever fear you face today, you will find peace in the simple realization that Jesus said, "It is I." He is always with us.

In peace I will both lie down and sleep, for You alone, O LORD, make me to dwell in safety.   PSALM 4:8

Moses himself was so frightened at the sight that he said, "I am terrified and trembling."

HEBREWS 12:21 NLT

There is a contrast between the two mountains—Sinai and Zion—and they symbolize our lives. For we will either linger "terrified and trembling" upon Mount Sinai striving to please God, or we will dwell on beautiful Mount Zion where God is pleased with us and grace and freedom prevail.

On Mount Sinai, God appears in blazing fire with whirlwinds in darkness and gloom. On Sinai, we live under the law—trying to please God by our goodness or appease His wrath by careful obedience. The law written on tables of stone and delivered by Moses had already been broken before he stood on the foothills and threw them to the ground. On that day, the people could not bear to hear God's words; they were gripped with a fear so fierce that "those who heard begged that no further word be spoken to them" (Hebrews 12:19). On Sinai we will live in fear.

Or we may dwell on Mount Zion as a part of the general assembly and the church of the firstborn, where our lives will be regulated by the New Covenant, our hearts sprinkled by the blood of Jesus. On Zion we will know forgiveness, mercy, and freedom. We will fellowship with God, through His son. Instead of judgment, we will find redemption and grace.

———————

How blessed is the man whose strength is in You, in whose heart are the highways to Zion!   PSALM 84:5

Peter wouldn't eat with the Gentiles . . . He was afraid of
criticism from these people who insisted on the necessity of
circumcision.

GALATIANS 2:12 NLT

You haven't really trusted God until you have attempted something that can't be done on your own power. For some, including Peter, accepting open criticism is that thing—the one thing that requires more strength, control, and patience than any other issue. It may be the one thing that causes fear.

Why is criticism so harmful and hurtful? Because it strikes at the very core of our being. Criticism is much more than disagreeing about the value of your work—the project that took months to complete, the report that required six weeks of research, the paper that challenged your writing skills, the meal that took hours to prepare. Criticism goes beneath and beyond all painstaking planning and meticulous detail to the very heart of the person who accomplished it. It tells the builder the foundation cracked, the author his book is nonsense, or the disciple that he is a hypocrite.

This was Peter's problem. He played to the crowd and was criticized and rebuked for his duplicity. Some of the harshest words from the lips of Jesus were directed toward inauthentic Pharisees: "You are like whitewashed tombs which on the outside appear beautiful, but inside they are full of dead men's bones" (Matthew 23:27).

But You, O LORD, are a shield about me, my glory, and the One
who lifts my head.   PSALM 3:3

Don't be afraid, Paul, for you will surely stand trial before
Caesar! What's more, God in his goodness has granted safety to
everyone sailing with you.

ACTS 27:24 NLT

God had already given Paul the good news first—"there will be
no loss of life among you" (Acts 27:22). He would not die on this
storm-tossed ship. But before he could utter one word of joy, God
gave the bad news. He would stand trial before Caesar. Have you
ever been at the receiving end of such a conversation? "Nobody
died in the fire, but the house was a total loss." "We no longer need
you at this job, but we do offer two weeks of severance pay." "We
can save your leg, but you will need three surgeries and ten months
of rehabilitation."

We call that a conundrum! You don't know whether to laugh or
cry, feel happy or sad, relieved or worried, thankful or appalled.
But then faith kicks in and common sense takes over. *It could have*
been much worse! That's when God's grace comes into play. He
makes grace *abound* so that you will *abound* in every good work
(see 2 Corinthians 9:8).

If the event is designed for your good, then His grace is sufficient for you. If it causes you pain, His grace will sustain you. If
it is something outside the realm of your understanding, He will
supply grace enough to calm your fears and grace to understand by
faith alone.

———————

My grace is sufficient for you, for power is perfected in
weakness.   2 CORINTHIANS 12:9

Do not let your heart be troubled... In My Father's house are
many dwelling places.

JOHN 14:1–2

Jesus ascended into heaven forty days after His resurrection. He sat down at the right hand of God the Father and He remains there interceding for the saints. He is preparing a place for us to dwell with Him forever. On days filled with stress and a deep-seated longing to be at home with Him, I picture Jesus as the carpenter of Jerusalem in the wood shop with Joseph, perfecting his skills for future work in another place, in another realm. Blueprints dancing in His mind of future homes in heaven for folks like me and you.

I don't dream of a *mansion just over the hilltop* but a cabin beside the river with trees and flowers that I won't need to tend. I want to see Jesus, read books, visit people I love, meet the saints, drink pure water, and take a few intergalactic trips. I want to thank the people who prayed for me during earth time and see some for whom I prayed. I want to sit by my mother and hold my baby girl. Have you ever thanked God for what He has prepared for us?

In times of worry and fear, pause to remember these words attributed to Corrie ten Boom: "Look back on the prayers you have prayed for that person you are worrying about. Not one of those prayers is lost. They are kept in heaven. What a comfort. What an encouragement."

*Joseph of Arimathea, being a disciple of Jesus, but a secret one
for fear of the Jews, asked Pilate that he might take away the
body of Jesus; and Pilate granted permission.*

JOHN 19:38

This man was not one of the twelve disciples (noun), instead he
was "discipled" (verb), taught and trained by Jesus Himself. How
fortunate to be a close friend, a willing student, a committed follower of Christ Jesus. Matthew described the relationship: "There
came a rich man from Arimathea, named Joseph, who himself had
also become a disciple of Jesus" (27:57). He *became* a disciple—a
confident, strong-hearted, fearless follower of Christ! Disciple—in
the verb form—means "to follow his precepts and instructions; to
make a disciple; to teach, instruct."

Do you wish you could have been in the shoes of Joseph, having personal access to the Living Word, sitting at His feet, being
taught by Him? Before you get lost in longing for what might have
been, take notice of what you now have—an even closer relationship with Jesus who lives in you; a resident Teacher, the Holy Spirit
abiding, leading you into all truth. And even while He is teaching
you from within, He is seated in heaven interceding for you.

Follow the footsteps of Joseph. Stay close to Jesus, and become
a true disciple.

---

*As evening approached, Joseph . . . who had become a follower
of Jesus . . . took the body and wrapped it in a long sheet of clean
linen cloth. He placed it in his own new tomb.*

MATTHEW 27:57–60 NLT

I believed in you, so I said, "I am deeply troubled, LORD."

PSALM 116:10 NLT

The psalm begins with an outburst of love to the One Who hears and answers prayer. How blessed we are that the Sovereign Ruler of all mankind, Designer of the universe, lends a listening ear to us. Since He dwells closer than a heartbeat, it is easy for us to express our need. "I am deeply troubled, LORD." Prayer is the love language between us. Or as Charles Spurgeon wrote, "the silken bonds which bind poor hearts to God."[45]

We are told to pray about everything with prayer and supplication. And there is a difference! In prayer we praise Him for who He is, we call Him Father. We wait and listen to the Holy Spirit, consider the day ahead, thank Him for our good and perfect gifts, and express our love for Him. We confess our sins and find grace. Prayer is a not a discipline that we practice but a soul-sustaining communion.

In supplication we cry out, we bow to the Almighty, to El Shaddai, the great I AM. As supplicants to the King, we bend low and look up. We are the hungry begging bread, the wounded seeking solace, the bewildered asking help, strugglers seeking counsel, the broken chasing wholeness, the sick calling the Great Physician. And when we seek, we shall find.

Pray at all times in the Spirit, with all prayer and supplication.
To that end keep alert with all perseverance, making
supplication for all the saints.

EPHESIANS 6:18 ESV

Since fear is crippling—a fearful life, fear of death, fear of judgment—is one not yet fully formed in love.

1 JOHN 4:18 MSG

Eugene Peterson, translator of *The Message*, addresses the fear that cripples us—"a fearful life, fear of death, fear of judgment." He is not writing of three distinct fears but three categories of fear that encompass our total self—living, being, and dying. They concern things unknown, uncertain, indefinable, and incomprehensible. In these we live by faith. Here we plea for grace. It is at this point we realize that we are not yet fully formed in love. Because "well-formed love banishes fear" (1 John 4:18 MSG).

Most of us would have to agree that our fear has not been completely banished. We are people in process, facing uncertainty while learning to fear less, growing in faith, loving more consistently, but sometimes completely misunderstanding God and His plan. Fear is the basis of all sin, the underpinnings, the substructure upon which selfhood and ego thrives. If we would have victory over fear, it must be pulled out by its roots and replaced with love.

Before we are crippled by fear, let us pray as the disciples: "Lord, increase our faith" (Luke 17:5). Lead us to dive deeply into the healing waters of Scripture, find peace in the arms of God, hope in fellowship with others in Christ, and healing in the love of Jesus.

"My steadfast love shall not depart from you, and my covenant of peace shall not be removed," says the LORD, who has compassion on you.

ISAIAH 54:10 ESV

They cried out to the LORD in their trouble; He saved them out of their distresses.

PSALM 107:19

When you are in trouble, do you cry out? To whom? Do you grab your phone and call a friend? Text a message? Make an appointment with the psychiatrist? Pray? In any trouble or fear, from disturbing to devastating, in limitations physical or spiritual, even in problems of our own making, the LORD delights in us when we call on Him first. In the words of the psalmist, He is the One, the only One, who can save us out of life's distresses, whether large or small.

One morning I headed to the bedroom to retrieve my cell phone from the nightstand when I spotted the twist-pins that I'd planned to use to attach a dust ruffle to our bed. Easily distracted woman that I am, I plopped onto a stool about ten inches high and began to work my way around the bed. By the time I finished, my legs were frozen into a permanent knees-to-the-chest Z. I tried to stand up. But from that position, it could not be done! I tried several methods to rise up and walk, but failed.

I called for help. I yelled! I turned on the TV, loud, certain that a news commentator shouting from the bedroom would awaken somebody! I was wrong. Amazingly, a thought came when I prayed. I rolled forward until my knees hit the floor, then I was able to stand. Praise the Lord! I would live to see another day.

He who dwells in the shelter of the Most High will abide in the
shadow of the Almighty . . . You will not be afraid.

PSALM 91:1, 5

I found the following story years ago on a torn-out page from a magazine. I would love to give the author credit, but there was no byline. The story, which I adapted, helped me understand what it means to "abide in the shelter of God's wings."

After a forest fire in Yellowstone National Park, park rangers trekked up a mountain to assess the damage. At the base of a large tree one ranger found a chicken, obviously dead, barely recognizable, swaddled in ashes, looking like a statue on the ground. Curious about the eerie sight, he bent to take a closer look, then poked at the chicken with a stick. The charred body of the mother hen toppled over, and three tiny yellow chicks scurried from under her wings.

The hen, being keenly aware of impending disaster, had coaxed her offspring to shelter and gathered them under her wings, instinctively knowing the toxic smoke would rise. She could have flown to a low branch to find safety, but she had refused to abandon her babies. When the blaze overtook them, the heat had literally burned her small body to a crisp. The mother had remained steadfast. Because she had been willing to die, those under the cover of her wings would live. That is what our gracious God has done for us in Jesus Christ.

He will cover you with His pinions, and under His wings you
may seek refuge.   PSALM 91:4

> *I wrote that letter in great anguish, with a troubled heart and*
> *many tears. I didn't want to grieve you, but I wanted to let you*
> *know how much love I have for you.*
>
> 2 CORINTHIANS 2:4 NLT

How difficult confrontation can be! Especially with someone you love, even with words of truth. Before they are spoken, we must deal with our own heart. Have you suffered, as Paul did, *great anguish, a troubled heart, and many tears*, because you knew that God was sending you to speak words that would not be well received? How is it possible for a Christian to handle a sensitive matter with someone we love and not damage the relationship? Only by handling it biblically.

The purpose should always be to restore relationships "*in a spirit of gentleness*" (Galatians 6:1), not to accuse, affix blame, or convince anyone that you are right. The wrong kind of confrontation invalidates gentleness. Kindness in these situations is only possible by God's grace.

Paul's first letter to Corinth provided correction and advice. His desire was to restore sound doctrine and encourage the church to serve and love each other. His second letter majored on comfort, grace, and gratitude. We too may suffer pain, persecution, trouble, and fear as we serve others, but our hearts will also be full of love, grace, and hope.

> *If we endure, we will also reign with Him; if we deny Him, He*
> *also will deny us; if we are faithless, He remains faithful, for He*
> *cannot deny Himself.*   2 TIMOTHY 2:12–13

We do not want you to be unaware, brethren, of our affliction
which came to us in Asia, that we were burdened excessively,
beyond our strength, so that we despaired.

2 CORINTHIANS 1:8

One morning I was troubled by my judgmental attitude toward a
friend. Had I judged her harshly because I struggled with the same
sin? Isn't that the way we are? The log in our own eye blocks out
the splinter in another's. In other words, when we struggle with a
certain temptation or become familiar with a particular sin, we easily spot it in another person. We deflect. We can actually name it
for them as we ignore it in our own lives! How inherently evil is our
flesh! The solution comes not in becoming "burdened excessively
so that we despair" but confessing our own sin quickly that we may
be healed.

After I confessed my wrong attitude, I opened my Bible study
program, and there on the screen in screaming red and black was
the word "Comfort" centered in the middle of a verse that gave me
peace. The need for comfort is astonishingly relevant today. God
not only gives comfort but He is our comfort—today, in every circumstance, for a precious purpose. He *comforts* us so that we may
comfort others with the *comfort* with which we have been *comforted*
by God (2 Corinthians 1:3–4). Paul knew by experience that God
is the God of all comfort and he wanted the point made clear to the
church.

———————

If we are comforted, it is for your comfort.

2 CORINTHIANS 1:6

Do not be afraid any longer, *but go on speaking and do not be silent.*

ACTS 18:9

The verse above shows Jesus speaking to Paul in the night by a vision, but it could also be said to you and me right now, wide awake. For when it comes to speaking the truth about Him, we should be just as committed to spreading the gospel as the Apostle Paul. Do not allow fear to keep you from using your spiritual gifts, your unique personality, your own vital connection to the Lord Jesus to communicate truth to those who may have never heard. We have within our soul the grace needed to stop fear in its tracks and keep it from stifling our witness. We are called for this purpose.

You may be wondering, how can I, untrained in theology, awkward in public speaking, talk about such critical issues to a person with real needs? Being a faithful witness is much simpler than that. It means being yourself, totally and completely, not hiding your love for God, but not trying to be God. You cannot call, convict, or convince anybody, but you can represent Him well and pray. Be sincere in your love for others. And speak truthfully in ways that honor Christ and glorify God.

Who is adequate for these things? For we are not like many, peddling the word of God, but as from sincerity, but as from God, we speak in Christ in the sight of God.

2 CORINTHIANS 2:16–17

*While Paul was waiting for them in Athens, he was deeply
troubled by all the idols he saw everywhere in the city.*

ACTS 17:16 NLT

Paul was deeply troubled by idolatry. He feared it because it was
everywhere in the city. Isaiah was troubled by idolatry too. His pen
drips with sarcasm as he described the state of Israel—You plant
a tree, the rain makes it grow, then it becomes something to burn.
You cut it down to make a fire. You roast meat and eat beside the
fire. Half of the tree becomes firewood and from the other half you
make a god. You bow down to the image and worship it, praying
"Deliver me, for you are my god." How futile! How senseless! Their
eyes were blinded, their hearts hardened and rebellious (see Isaiah
44:14–17).

God has revealed Himself to every man so that they are without
excuse. Still some refuse to acknowledge and glorify Him or give
Him thanks. Flawed in their thinking, their hearts darkened, they
become foolish in their understanding and practice idol worship.
People are hard-wired to worship—if not the One True God, they
will worship a false god and embrace a false religion. It is part of the
darkened soul's DNA. But God is greater than natural impulses,
innate desires, or any preprogramming.

---

*There is no other God besides Me, a righteous God and a
Savior; there is none except Me. Turn to Me and be saved, all
the ends of the earth.*

ISAIAH 45:21–22

We have heard that some persons have gone out from us and troubled you with words, unsettling your minds, although we gave them no instructions.

ACTS 15:24 ESV

Troubled by words, unsettled minds, and needless fear! Because those troubling words came from impure mouths, unlearned minds, or false prophets. How much of what we hear today comes from such sources? How much of it is hearsay? What part of it is gossip? Let us test the spirits to see if they are of God, search the Scriptures to see if it is so, take the words we hear to our Father in prayer before we dare speak them to another.

The words being talked about in this passage are from the mouths of some who once were thought to be Christian. Maybe they considered themselves part of the family of God. But the very fact that they "have gone out from us" proved that they never were one of us. These are the most dangerous enemies of our Lord, for they learned the language of believers and convincing arguments against the truths they once considered gospel.

Like Daniel, you can intercede for them!

I prayed to the Lord my God and made confession, saying, "O Lord, the great and awesome God, who keeps covenant and steadfast love with those who love him and keep his commandments, we have sinned and done wrong and acted wickedly and rebelled, turning aside from your commandments and rules."

DANIEL 9:4–5 ESV

*My circumstances have turned out for the greater progress of
the gospel...most of the brethren, trusting in the Lord because
of my imprisonment, have far more courage to speak the word of
God without fear.*

PHILIPPIANS 1:12, 14

It is important for us to know that our own circumstances, whatever they are right now, will turn out for the greater progress of
the gospel just as they did for Paul. God in His amazing creativ-
ity turns irrational into reasonable, harmful into helpful, bad into
good, and backward steps into forward progress. Give God time
and He will make all things beautiful.

What were Paul's circumstances? As he wrote he was being held
in a small house chained by the wrist to a Roman guard. He could
receive visitors, speak to them, teach, and write with his one free
hand. Having no privacy must have been difficult for Paul, but with
great tenacity he persevered. Does his courage motivate you to continue the work God has called you to do?

We can, by following Paul's example of faith. He was sure that
everything that occurred in Philippi, both his sufferings and his
joyful relationship with the believers, would promote the gospel
and eradicate fear.

---

*Indeed, we had the sentence of death within ourselves so that
we would not trust in ourselves, but in God who raises the
dead; who delivered us from so great a peril of death, and will
deliver us, He on whom we have set our hope. And He will yet
deliver us.*   2 CORINTHIANS 1:9–10

> *Have no fear of them, nor be troubled, but in your hearts honor*
> *Christ the Lord as holy, always being prepared to make a*
> *defense to anyone who asks you for a reason for the hope that is*
> *in you; yet do it with gentleness and respect.*
>
> 1 PETER 3:14–15 ESV

Whether you are afraid or fearless does not depend upon another's behavior—not their rudeness, offensiveness, unkind questions, or dogged determination to trip you up. It depends entirely on your own preparedness of heart and passion for God's glory. It is also governed by your attitude about the needs of others. We should be ready to defend the gospel, ready to give a reason for our hope. Readiness is not about memorizing certain Scripture verses, handing out gospel tracts, or practicing rhetorical questions.

Readiness hinges upon the hope that resides in you. You are well prepared when your soul overflows with joy, when hope springs forth from a heart of gentleness and respect toward all people. According to the words of Peter, fear and trouble flee the one who "honors Christ the Lord as holy." It is a matter of focus rather than of studious preparation.

When we tap into the depths of God's grace, plug into the flowing current of love, our fear of others is pushed aside and hope flows freely.

> *Now may the God of hope fill you with all joy and peace in*
> *believing, so that you will abound in hope by the power of the*
> *Holy Spirit.*
>
> ROMANS 15:13

He became troubled in spirit, and testified and said, "Truly, truly, I say to you, that one of you will betray Me."

JOHN 13:21

Is it hard to think of Jesus being "troubled in spirit"? But He was a man tempted in all points, just as we are. In Hebrews the writer says that He had to be "made like his brothers in every respect, so that he might become a merciful and faithful high priest in the service of God, to make propitiation for the sins of the people" (Hebrews 2:17). It is good to remember that our Lord lived life as we do—tempted, tested, exhausted, and at times "troubled in spirit." If you have ever been betrayed by someone you trusted, you know the feelings He had when facing the disciples.

He was never less than God, but He was also the man, Jesus— feeling pain, knowing rejection, hating betrayal, fearing death. The One completely undeserving of any ill handling was being treated as if He were one of us—weak, easily tempted, prone to wander, deserving punishment. We can only imagine the thoughts and feelings of The Christ, betrayed by someone He had chosen and loved, who walked with Him in intimate fellowship and worked by His side. Considering that, being "troubled in spirit" is putting it mildly, even for the God-Man.

All the great prevailing grace of God is ours for the drawing on, and it scarcely needs any drawing on, take out the "stopper" and it comes out in torrents.

OSWALD CHAMBERS[46]

> *Do not fear them, for the LORD your God is the one fighting for you.*
>
> DEUTERONOMY 3:22

Can we take this verse literally? Is God fighting for you? How does He do this? Sometimes He does it without even engaging the one who is fighting against you. Remember His Sovereignty. It is the most comforting of His virtues. He is Almighty, and that means having the power to do anything and everything "to carry out the will of a Divine nature."[47] He cannot be Almighty without being able to complete His own purposes, His own will to the nth degree. He fights for us by being true to Himself, never allowing one thing to contradict His character or His plans for us.

He also fights for you by using Spiritual forces, angels, praying friends, or Spirit-led individuals to stand with us and provide help. He fights for you by providing words of truth through the study, the preaching and teaching of Scripture. These are powerful, life-sustaining, life-transforming words.

During one of the most difficult seasons of parenthood—those vital years when children leave home and make most decisions for themselves—my prayers changed completely. I relied heavily upon the fact that God was fighting for me, for my children. As I depended upon the nature and character of Him, He granted the desires of my heart in His time, according to His will.

> *The name of the LORD is a strong tower; the righteous runs to it and are safe.*
>
> PROVERBS 18:10

> *I heard a loud voice from the throne, saying, "Behold, the*
> *tabernacle of God is among men, and He will dwell among*
> *them ... and He will wipe away every tear from their eyes; and*
> *there will no longer be any death."*
>
> REVELATION 21:3–4

John the Apostle had seen Jesus and could not control his reaction. He fell at His feet like a dead man. Why? Didn't he recognize Him? He was the beloved disciple. But this was not the Jesus he had seen before. He was not the One whose breast he had leaned upon at the Last Supper. This Jesus was not his fishing buddy, not even the man who had called down fire from heaven at his request. He didn't look anything like the tortured crucified Jesus, nor like the one he'd met in Galilee afterward. This Jesus looked different from the Jesus he had seen in a vision earlier on Patmos.

This was Jesus, the King of Kings and Lord of Lords in all His glory. On second glance John knew He was the Son of God, but He was also the Ancient of Days. He recognized Him now, but he could not come near Him. John was completely stricken until he heard Jesus speak. "Do not be afraid." It was Jesus, all right, and He held the keys to death and the resurrection.

Does that put your needling fear in its place? He is before every human fear, and after every fear is conquered. He is First and Last, and those of us who live in the meantime can live fearlessly because He is.

When the doors were shut where the disciples were, for fear of
the Jews, Jesus came and stood in their midst and said to them,
"Peace be with you."

JOHN 20:19

The disciples feared the Jews more than any other opponent so they
met secretly, with fear, under cover of darkness, in locked houses.
It was there that Jesus came, stepping through the bolted door. He
stood before them and displayed His resurrection body. It still bore
the scars of piercing sword and thorn-embellished crown. But He
was healthy and strong. His first words were "Peace be with you."

Of course they were frightened, but this emotion was nothing like the distraught, mind-numbing fear that had seized them
before. Jesus breathed on them and said, "Receive the Holy Spirit"
(John 20:22). And that was enough to radically change His disciples from cowards huddled in fear into a powerful, life-giving force.
Seven weeks later at Pentecost, the crowd would notice the remarkable difference.

As Elohim had breathed life into Adam, Jesus breathed into
them the breath of life—New Life where they would know and
preach the forgiveness of sin. When we encounter Jesus today, we
receive Him in the Person of the Holy Spirit, and when He comes
in, we have power, grace, and peace—all that we need to know
Him and make Him known.

By grace you have been saved through faith; and that not of
yourselves, it is the gift of God; not as a result of works, so
that no one may boast.   EPHESIANS 2:8–9

But for you who fear My name, the sun of righteousness will rise with healing in its wings; and you will go forth and skip about like calves.

MALACHI 4:2

"Whenever I fear my usefulness in God's work is ending due to age or circumstance, I remember a pear tree that once stood on the east corner of our church building." Thus began the story from LaWanda Bailey, a grandmother, author, musician, retired teacher, and my friend.

"Out of nowhere, a Texas storm blew up and almost ripped off one of the tree's big branches. One end of the branch leaned into the ground, and the torn end clung to the trunk. A mere shred of split wood and bark kept the branch attached. We all said it was a real pity about the tree and that somebody ought to saw the limb off, but we were too busy with meetings and such. While we dilly-dallied, the branch did its best to hold on.

"As spring progressed, snowy blossoms crowned the top of the tree. Then one Sunday morning we arrived to find that broken branch covered in blooms. It was a sight to behold—clusters of lush, white flowers resting on a broken limb. The pastor told us to remember that tree when we think we're too broken to carry on.

"When storms hit, don't fear that you're losing your usefulness. Tighten your grip on the Lord with whatever loose ends you have left. God will make you blossom in marvelous ways. Hang on."

I am the vine; you are the branches. If you remain in me and I in you, you will bear much fruit; apart from me you can do nothing.
JOHN 15:5 NIV

I am afraid . . . that perhaps there will be *strife, jealousy, angry
tempers, disputes, slanders, gossip, arrogance, disturbances.*

2 CORINTHIANS 12:20

Strife happens! Even in the church. As hard as it is to admit, much
of it comes from well-meaning people with overactive mouths. It
happened in Corinth. Such conflict had occurred that Paul feared
it might not be resolved. He also addressed a dispute in the church
at Philippi. His letter emphasizes joy, but in one area he was not
one bit pleased. He had to address a problem in the congregation—
two of the women, helpers of Paul himself, could not get along.
Apparently the disagreement was a serious one that went much
deeper than the color of the carpet or the use of hymnals. Deep
enough that it had to be addressed publicly, probably by the elders.

Recorded here in Scripture for the world to see are the names of
two women who would go down in history as ones causing strife.
"I urge Euodia and I urge Syntyche to live in harmony in the Lord"
(Philippians 4:2). Fearing their attitudes might affect the work of
the ministry, Paul asked some of those closest to his heart to help
the women work it out. We don't know the end of the story, but we
know enough to cause all of us to consider our own legacy.

———————

*While we have opportunity, let us do good to all people, and
especially to those who are of the household of the faith.*

GALATIANS 6:10

*I am afraid that when I come again my God may humiliate
me before you, and I may mourn over many of those who have
sinned in the past and not repented.*

2 CORINTHIANS 12:21

We live in a shameless society. Some never even notice, nor
acknowledge sin, much less worry about it. Others minimize the
offense or make excuses. Few practice self-examination and confession. Paul was an exception. He felt humiliated by sin and mourned
over those who would not repent. Do you know the blessed relief
of forgiveness? When we confess, several amazing things happen.
Here are some of them:

- Your sin is cast behind God's back: see Isaiah 38:17.
- He is merciful and remembers sins no more: see Hebrews 8:12.
- Our transgressions are removed as far as the east is from west:
  see Psalm 103:12.
- He treads our iniquities under foot and casts all sins into the
  depths of the sea: see Micah 7:19.
- He does not keep a list of forgiven sins: see Psalm 130:3.
- He forgives and cleanses us from unrighteousness: see 1 John 1:9.

---

*Summing it all up, friends, I'd say you'll do best by filling
your minds and meditating on things true, noble, reputable,
authentic, compelling, gracious—the best, not the worst; the
beautiful, not the ugly; things to praise, not things to curse. . . .
Do that, and God, who makes everything work together, will
work you into his most excellent harmonies.*

PHILIPPIANS 4:8–9 MSG

> *Come to me, all of you who are weary and carry heavy*
> *burdens . . . Take my yoke upon you. Let me teach you . . . and you*
> *will find rest for your souls.*
>
> MATTHEW 11:28–29 NLT

"Come to me." It is an invitation often issued by Jesus. Come to the Bread: "I am the bread of life; he who comes to Me will not hunger" (John 6:35). Come to the Living Water: "If anyone is thirsty, let him come to Me and drink" (John 7:37). Come to have Life: "You are unwilling to come to Me so that you may have life" (John 5:39–40).

Three loaves of bread were offered by Samuel to Saul, the King of Israel, picturing Father, Son, and Holy Spirit—the Three in One LORD meeting the total needs of those who belong to Him (see 1 Samuel 10:3), Jesus is water—clear, pure, and absolutely necessary for life. And He is Himself life. Come to Him, not to some representative of Him, not to some substitute god, not to the church board or committee, not even to what He has said! Come to Jesus! The Father went to great lengths, including the sacrifice of His Son, so that we may "come boldly to the throne of grace, that we may obtain mercy and find grace to help in time of need" (Hebrews 4:16 NKJV).

> *At the most unexpected moments in your life there is this*
> *whisper of the Lord—"Come to Me" and you are immediately*
> *drawn to Him. Personal contact with Jesus changes everything.*
> *Jesus promises to relieve our burdens of stress and fear but only*
> *if we will Come to Him.*
>
> OSWALD CHAMBERS[48]

Fear not, Daughter of Zion; behold, your King is coming, seated on a donkey's colt.

JOHN 12:15

Do not be afraid of anything, for "your king is coming." Most kings in that day rode into town on an impressive horse, maybe even a white horse or in a chariot embellished with gold. Someday Jesus, the Messiah, will come in Kingly glory. But first He came through the gates of Jerusalem riding on a donkey. The unique manner of Jesus' entrance symbolizes at least two things: His humility—the willingness to submit to the authorities even unto death, and His ultimate purpose—to bring peace on earth.

At that second coming, He will be the King, and there will be peace on earth. All fear, anxiety, worry will disappear. Along with every trouble, sickness, despair, and pain! The negative feelings you have had about yourself, all your insecurity, and all accompanying fear will be gone. And we will reign with Him. The one who has this hope fixed on Jesus "purifies himself, just as He is pure" (1 John 3:3).

Lord Jesus! Come quickly.

You, O LORD, will not withhold Your compassion from me; Your lovingkindness and Your truth will continually preserve me . . . Be pleased, O LORD, to deliver me; Make haste, O LORD, to help me . . . Let all who seek You rejoice and be glad in You; Let those who love Your salvation say continually, "The LORD be magnified!"

PSALM 40:11, 13, 16

The fear of the LORD leads to life; then one rests content,
untouched by trouble.

PROVERBS 19:23 NIV84

There is no need to be afraid of anything in this life when you fear the LORD. Most Proverbs are written in a pattern of contrasting parallel lines. The first line makes a statement, the second shows the contrast. It offers two different ways of saying the same thing. Others present a mental and spiritual tug-of-war that shows the difference between two perspectives such as righteousness and perverseness. "The fear of the LORD leads to life" may literally mean that it increases or lengthens life or makes for a better quality of life. Whoever takes God seriously by having a healthy fear of Him increases the value and longevity of his life. The fear of Yahweh is able to supplant all other fears. You may rest content, untouched by trouble, enjoying extra years and added days.

His grace is great enough to meet the great things,
The crashing waves that overwhelm the soul,
The roaring winds that leave us stunned and breathless,
The sudden storms beyond our life's control.
His grace is great enough to meet the small things,
The little pin-prick troubles that annoy,
The insect worries, buzzing and persistent,
The squeaking wheels that grate upon our joy.
(Annie Johnson Flint)[49]

I have been young and now I am old, yet I have not seen the
righteous forsaken or his descendants begging bread.

PSALM 37:25

In God I praise His word, in God I have trusted, I fear not what flesh doth to me.

PSALM 56:4 YLT

If your love for God is real, you will love His Word. And, I might add, if you love His Word, you will not fear what humankind might do to you. One of my favorite verses of Scripture connects love of truth with love for Him and His love for us. "He who has My commandments and keeps them is the one who loves Me; and he who loves Me will be loved by My Father, and I will love him and will disclose Myself to him" (John 14:21).

Having His Word does not mean owning a facsimile of the Ten Commandments or a copy of the Bible. But do you *have* them? Does the truth abide in your heart? If so, the Holy Spirit can remind you of His words, and they are with you wherever you go. Jesus added that you must also keep them. When your conscience is guided by His Word and you respond in obedience, your love for Him is verified and your relationship grows. But there is more.

"He who loves me will be loved by My Father, and I will love him" (John 14:21). The words promise a unique and intimate fellowship, between the eternal God and those who love Him and His Word. Do you want to know Him better?

Jesus answered and said to him, "If anyone loves Me, he will keep My word; and My Father will love him, and We will come to him and make Our abode with him."

JOHN 14:23

Behold, God is my salvation, I will trust and not be afraid; for
the LORD GOD is my strength and song, and He has become my
salvation.

ISAIAH 12:2

We enjoy salvation every day as we are delivered from the power
and dominion of sin. So, it is possible to be delivered from *fear* day
after day as we bring our weakness before the Lord and ask Him
to become our salvation. Do you struggle with worry and anxiety?

The dictionary defines worry by its effects upon the worrier—"to
divide, part, rip, or tear apart." But the actual meaning of the term
is "concern over the future." How irrational such a focus becomes,
since we cannot see what is not yet here. In other words, we are
being ripped apart by something that has not yet happened. Only
God knows what will occur the next day or even the next hour, but
we, in a desire to control our own lives, *imagine* what *might* happen.
Then we *believe* what we have *imagined*. And that tears us apart.

As Corrie ten Boom says: "When we worry we are carrying
tomorrow's load with today's strength, carrying two days in one.
We are moving into tomorrow ahead of time. There is just one day
in the calendar of action—today."[50]

I bless the LORD who gives me counsel; in the night also my heart
instructs me. I have set the LORD always before me; because he is
at my right hand, I shall not be shaken.

PSALM 16:7–8 ESV

Do not be afraid; for behold, I bring you good news of great joy which will be for all the people.

LUKE 2:10–11

As His tiny shoulders slipped into time and space, the baby's breath filled the heart of His mother with great joy. To Mary, the young woman chosen to be the God-child's mother, pondering things of the heart came naturally. She, along with Joseph and her cousin Elizabeth, may have been the only people on earth who knew that this baby would bring great joy *for all* the people. She knew He was the Son of God, but did she know that He would be the Savior? Did she have any idea what being Savior would require?

The truth is, those little shoulders would grow, develop strength, ripple with manly muscles, and someday bear the weight of a heavy wooden cross and carry a massive load of sin—the sin debt of all those who would believe on Him. He would die to redeem you and me. But on this day, Mary wrapped Him in a blanket, being careful to swaddle His shoulders and cup His head and tiny ears with washed wool. Christ the Lord slept peacefully, the King of Kings nestled contentedly in a straw-filled manger.

Who can add to Christmas? The perfect motive is that God so loved the world. The perfect gift is that He gave His only Son. The only requirement is to believe in Him. The reward of faith is that you shall have everlasting life.

ATTRIBUTED TO CORRIE TEN BOOM

Let all who are around Him bring gifts to Him who is to be feared.

PSALM 76:11

The mention of bringing gifts to God reminds me of the Magi who came to the crib of Jesus bearing gifts of gold, frankincense, and myrrh. They were not astrologers or mediums but scholars specializing in astronomy and natural science. Men of character, students of prophecy, full of wisdom, and devoted to God. They knew the prophecies of Micah and followed the star toward Bethlehem (see Micah 5:2). They came for a specific purpose—to worship and honor the future King, for they knew that this child was Messiah.

When they finally saw the star, they "rejoiced exceedingly with great joy" (Matthew 2:10). And when they saw the Child and Mary His mother, they did what they had come to do. They fell to the ground and worshipped. They opened their hearts and their treasures to Him. The gifts they brought were fit for a king and had significant meaning. Gold to symbolize His purity and deity, frankincense to recognize the fragrance of His life, and myrrh to picture His sacrifice and death.

Have you recognized Jesus as King in your own life? Have you ever fallen on your face in worship and yielded your life to Him? He is worthy of your gifts, your worship, and your praise.

———————

For a child will be born to us, a son will be given to us . . . and His name will be called Wonderful Counselor, Mighty God, Eternal Father, Prince of Peace.

ISAIAH 9:6

Do not fear what you are about to suffer . . . Be faithful until
death, and I will give you the crown of life.

REVELATION 2:10

The Lord's request is enough for me, sans the crown. Gifts are not
my love language. It would, however, be good to have some offering
to place at the feet of Jesus when we gather around the throne to
worship Him.

But the major importance of the verse above is the first part: "Do
not fear what you are about to suffer." The warning comes to Smyrna,
one of seven churches mentioned in the Revelation. It was located in
a prosperous, seaport city north of Ephesus. Jesus called Himself the
one "who was dead, and has come to life" as well as one who knew
their tribulation and the opposition they faced (see Revelation 2:8,
9). Unfortunately, some who claimed to be Jews were hypocrites. He
branded them members of the Synagogue of Satan. Jesus identified
with the church's suffering and encouraged them to be faithful even
though some would be imprisoned, tested, and would have great
tribulation.

God has never promised that life would be free-flowing with
prosperity or expensive gifts. But He promised spiritual blessings,
closeness with Himself, and sufficient grace to be faithful to the
very end.

But we are not of those who shrink back to destruction, but of
those who have faith to the preserving of the soul.

HEBREWS 10:39

O Zion, that bringest good tidings, get thee up into the high
mountain; O Jerusalem, that bringest good tidings, lift up thy
voice with strength; lift it up, be not afraid; say unto the cities of
Judah, Behold your God!

ISAIAH 40:9 AV

This is a turning point in Isaiah's prophecy, where he moves from
messages of judgment to deliverance and restoration, and it was
something to shout about. All warfare had ceased, Israel's iniquity
had been removed, and her sins paid double. "Clear the way for the
LORD in the wilderness; make smooth in the desert a highway for
our God," he writes, "then the glory of the LORD will be revealed,"
(Isaiah 40:3, 5). If the announcement were being made today, it
might be "Roll out the red carpet, sprinkle flower petals, for the
time of God's blessing has come!"

But is the Old Testament message recorded in Isaiah's fortieth
chapter still relevant to us? Of course it is. The words are empha-
sized again in the New Testament by Matthew (3:1–4), Mark
(1:1–4), Luke (1:76–78), and John (1:23). And John the Baptist, a
prophet in the desert, prepared the way for Jesus Christ. Part of
this prophecy is fulfilled at the cross, and the final fulfillment will
happen in the Millennium.

Meanwhile, we too need to prepare for the coming of our Lord
into our own lives by sweeping away the rubble and clearing the
way so that He may come in and abide.

The grass withers, the flower fades, but the word of our God
stands forever.   ISAIAH 40:8

He said to them, "Where is your faith?" They were fearful and
amazed, saying to one another, "Who then is this, that He
commands even the winds and the water, and they obey Him?"

LUKE 8:25

How weak some of us are as we trod the earth yoked with Jesus,
the Commander of both wind and water! How afraid we are over
our problems when we are told to be filled with the Holy Spirit,
the One who moved upon the face of the waters at creation. How
weak the faith of some who know Almighty God, El Shaddai, our
provider and sustainer. No wonder that Jesus, seeing their reaction
to the storm, asked the disciples, "Where is your faith?"

It is a question we should ask ourselves. Where is the faith we
had in the first place, when we climbed into the boat with Jesus?
Where is the faith we had to say yes to His call? If only we could
forget our troubles and fears as easily as we forget our blessings!

God has a word for us when we get to this place. I love these
words from the New Testament in Modern English translated by
J. B. Phillips.

———————

Delight yourselves in the Lord, yes, find your joy in him at all
times. Have a reputation for gentleness and never forget the
nearness of your Lord. Don't worry over anything whatever; tell
God every detail of your needs in earnest and thankful prayer.
And the peace of God, which transcends human understanding,
will keep constant guard over your hearts and minds as they rest
in Christ Jesus.

PHILIPPIANS 4:4–7 PHILLIPS

> *But the fearful, and unbelieving, and the abominable, and*
> *murderers, and whoremongers, and sorcerers, and idolaters,*
> *and all liars, shall have their part in the lake which burneth with*
> *fire and brimstone: which is the second death.*
>
> REVELATION 21:8 AV

In the list of those destined for the lake of fire, the fearful are mentioned first. It's as if fear, the fear that even believers sometimes allow, is unthinkable, intolerable, or unmentionable in a heart that's redeemed. You will not find fear—except for the fear of God—in any list of Christian virtues, nor included in personal goals and mission statements. Nobody has to work at becoming a better fearer. Just forget to guard your heart, lighten up on Bible study, neglect prayer, skip church, and fear will invade your soul like kudzu in an untended vineyard.

Being "fearful" partners in the verse above with seven other destructive traits. "Fear" is preceded by "the"—"the fearful." Some people become so fear-ridden that the emotion describes them completely—they become identified as merely one of "the fearful"! What a sad state of affairs! God's people, living in union with the All-Powerful, All-Sufficient, Life-Sustaining LORD but still unable to conquer fear. Faith and love cures fear, but it may take repeated applications before the person becomes known as unafraid.

> *Now may our Lord Jesus Christ Himself and God our Father,*
> *who has loved us and given us eternal comfort and good hope by*
> *grace, comfort and strengthen your hearts in every good work*
> *and word.*   2 THESSALONIANS 2:16–17

Do not be afraid; I am the first and the last.

REVELATION 1:17

The Apostle John had been abandoned on an island—a situation that was supposed to be punishment. But what his enemies failed to recognize is that they had placed this aging writer in the perfect place to produce a book. Yes, he was in exile, but he was not alone. Before he took his pen in hand, he heard the voice and saw a vision of the risen Lord saying, "Write in a book what you see" (Revelation 1:11).

I can only imagine the scene—parchment spread, graying head bent low, steady hands gripping the quill as words spilled across the page. I'm thinking he was in a zone, as we writers describe it. He says he was "in the Spirit on the Lord's Day" (Revelation 1:10)! Receiving and recording, hearing and writing, line upon line, precept upon precept, until the seven messages to the churches were finished. I see him standing, walking about, singing praises, worshipping, massaging his fingers, and sitting again. "Write the things which you have seen, and the things which are, and the things which will take place after these things" (Revelation 1:19). With that simple outline in place, he continued until the masterpiece was finished.

The Revelation—the Unveiling of Jesus, the King of Kings and Lord of Lords. For you and me, that knowledge of Him makes it possible to live fearlessly, in holiness and commitment and joy as we wait for the final fulfillment of the revelation.

> *This is the one to whom I will look: he who is humble and*
> *contrite in spirit and trembles at my word.*
>
> ISAIAH 66:2 ESV

Three short statements from the pen of Isaiah reveal much about God and His purpose for mankind. The LORD Himself is quoted: "Heaven is My throne and the earth is My footstool" (Isaiah 66:1). With these words he declares His Majesty, His power and supreme position. He is also the Creator of all, the One who breathed life into every living creature. "My hand made all these things, thus all these things came into being" (Isaiah 66:2). His love—the trait that describes Him best and most often—is evident as Isaiah conveys the LORD's desire for those He created. He is the very essence of love and loves all people, but He looks attentively and highly esteems one "who is humble and contrite of spirit, and who trembles at My word" (Isaiah 66:2).

How can we become Unafraid when we live in a fallen, sinful world? We can begin by praying for a contrite spirit, seeking a life of humility, and asking ourselves: Do I tremble at God's Word? It is our source of life, the light for our journey. My prayer is that you will allow the inspired Word of God to fill you, make worship part of your daily experience, and develop a faith so strong that worry, anxiety, and all fear become mere memories. Walk in the Word until Jesus comes.

> *May Your unfailing love rest upon us, O LORD, even as we put*
> *our hope in you.*
>
> PSALM 33:22 NIV84

Acknowledgments

Thank you, Joey Paul, of Hachette Book Group, FaithWords, for your grace, kindness, and practical help in creating the best book possible with an ever-evolving, always challenging manuscript. You are the best! Thanks also for the editorial genius of Becky Hughes.

To Wendy Lawton, my more-than-wonderful agent, friend, advisor, and fan. You have helped me become a better writer, a better friend, and much better at balancing the writing life with an occasional rocking chair and porch rail. Thanks to you and to Books and Such Literary Agency for representing me well.

A special thanks to Pastor Tom Pennington at Countryside Bible Church, of Southlake, Texas, for your ministry of shepherding and teaching the church. Your sermons, encouragement, and grace keep me grounded and growing.

Thanks also to spiritual leaders and friends who have helped me live Unafraid in complicated and sometimes critical times—the late Dr. Bob E. Hamilton, Kay Arthur of Precept Ministries, LaRue and Major Speights, Dr. Kelly Carr, and a supportive group of writing friends.

Thank you to two friends who read the manuscript in its earliest form and offered encouragement, Dr. Marie Saunders and Bruce Page. Thanks to the circle of friends who have encouraged me and served brownies and soup at appropriate times.

Thanks to my husband, Joe, our three sons, daughters-in-law, and six amazing grandchildren who have loved me well.

Last, but most important, thank you to the Good Shepherd Who always leads me to green pastures and still waters. Because You are with me, I will fear no evil.

Notes

1. A. W. Tozer, *Keys to the Deeper Life* (Grand Rapids, MI: Zondervan, 1988), 72.
2. Louie Giglio, "How Great Is Our God" (YouTube video, published March 17, 2011). https://www.youtube.com/watch?v=PtpTk2ENq7o.
3. Peter Scazzero, *Emotionally Healthy Spirituality Day by Day* (Grand Rapids, MI: Zondervan, 2014), 142–143.
4. Mike Mason, *The Gospel According to Job: An Honest Look at Pain and Doubt from the Life of One Who Lost Everything* (Wheaton, IL: Crossway Books, 1994), 49.
5. Kay Arthur, *LORD, I Want to Know You* (Old Tappan, NJ: Revell, 1984), 63.
6. Ken Sutterfield, *The Power of an Encouraging Word* (Green Forest, AR: New Leaf, 1997), 15.
7. Stephen Charnock, *The Existence and Attributes of God* (Grand Rapids, MI: Baker, 1980), Vol. 2, 219–220.
8. See Zechariah 14.
9. D. Martyn Lloyd-Jones, *Spiritual Depression: Its Causes and Cure* (Grand Rapids, MI: Eerdmans, 1965), 143.
10. Franklin D. Roosevelt, Inaugural Address of the President (Washington DC, March 4, 1933).
11. Phillip Yancey, *Disappointment with God: Three Questions No One Asks Aloud* (Grand Rapids, MI: Zondervan, 1988).
12. Kay Arthur, *LORD, I Want to Know You* (Colorado Springs, CO: WaterBrook Press, 1992), 40.
13. Amy Carmichael, *If: What Do I Know of Calvary Love?* (Fort Washington, PA: Christian Literature Crusade, 1938).
14. Martin Luther King, Jr., "I Have a Dream" (speech, Lincoln Memorial, Washington D.C., August 28, 1963). http://www.americanrhetoric.com/speeches/mlkihaveadream.htm
15. Mike Mason, *The Gospel According to Job*, 292.
16. Ibid., 291–292.
17. *The Christian Treasury* (Edinburgh: Johnstone, Hunter, & Co., 1869).
18. International Inductive Study Bible, *Ecclesiastes* (Eugene, OR: Harvest House, 1992), 1063.
19. Andrew Murray, *Humility: The Beauty of Holiness* (Old Tappan, NJ: Revell, 1972), 13.

20. Philip Yancey, *Prayer: Does It Make Any Difference?* (Grand Rapids, MI: Zondervan, 2006), 42.
21. Jack Canfield, *The Power of Focus* (Deerfield Beach, FL: Health Communications, Inc., 2000), 168.
22. Eugene Peterson, *The Message: The New Testament Psalm and Proverbs* (Colorado Springs, CO: Navpress, 1993), 590.
23. Edith Shaeffer, *What Is a Family?* (New York: Thomas Nelson, 1975), 6.
24. Harry Verploegh, *Oswald Chambers, The Best From All the Books* (Nashville, TN: Oliver Nelson Books, 1987), 112.
25. Erwin Lutzer, *Failure: The Back Door to Success* (Chicago: Moody Press, 1975), 128.
26. Adapted from Gracie Malone, *LifeOvers* (Grand Rapids, MI: Reville, 2007), 31–32.
27. Linda Dillow, "A Friend," Shulamite Ministries Blog, 1 February 2001.
28. Henrietta C. Mears, *What the Bible Is All About* (Minneapolis: Gospel Light, 1966), 226.
29. Arthur, *LORD, I Want to Know You*, 26.
30. Beth Rudy, *A Prayer Pal, 30 Day Devotional* (East Petersburg, PA: Author Rudy, 2013), Day 16.
31. Jeannette Clift George, message notes from Women's Retreat, Irving, TX, 2005.
32. Dr. J. Sidlow Baxter, *Going Deeper* (Grand Rapids, MI: Zondervan, 1959), 44.
33. Stuart Briscoe, *What Works When Life Doesn't* (West Monroe, LA: Howard, 2004), 60.
34. Oswald Chambers, *My Utmost for His Highest* (New York: Dodd, Mead, 1935), December 14.
35. Thomas Merton, *Thoughts in Solitude* (New York: Farrar Straus Giroux, 1958), 83.
36. Matthew Henry, *The Matthew Henry Commentary of the Whole Bible* (Grand Rapids, MI: Zondervan, 1961), 1794.
37. Chambers, *My Utmost for His Highest*.
38. Saint Augustine, *The Confessions* (San Francisco, CA: Ignatius Press, 2012) I, 3.
39. Michael Johnson, "C. S. Lewis on the Problem of Forgiveness," *Desiring God*, May 26, 2011, http://www.desiringgod.org/articles/c-s-lewis-on-the-problem-of-forgiveness.
40. Barbara Johnson, *I Am So Glad You Told Me What I Didn't Wanna Hear* (New York: Thomas Nelson, 1996), 30.
41. Joni Eareckson Tada, *God's Presence in Life's Chaos* (Colorado Springs, CO: Multnomah, 1989), 29.
42. Charles H. Spurgeon, *The Treasury of David* (McLean, VA: MacDonald, 1975), 275.